WHY YOU'RE RICHER
THAN YOU THINK

Why You're Richer Than You Think

EMYL JENKINS

With an introduction by
GRAY D. BOONE

RAWSON, WADE PUBLISHERS, INC.
New York

Library of Congress Cataloging in Publication Data
Jenkins, Emyl.
Why you're richer than you think.
Bibliography: p.
Includes index.
1. Antiques—Valuation. I. Title.
NK1125.J45   745.1′075′0973   81-40266
ISBN 0-89256-186-6   AACR2

Published simultaneously in Canada by
McClelland and Stewart, Ltd.
Composition by American-Stratford
Graphic Services, Inc.
Brattleboro, Vermont
Printed and bound by Fairfield Graphics,
Fairfield, Pennsylvania

Illustrated by Sue Hall Waldron
Designed by Jacques Chazaud
First Edition

For Clauston, Langdon, and Joslin,
whom I can never repay for the time,
patience, and love they contributed
to the writing of this book.
And for Elizabeth Daniel, friend and mentor.

Many people contributed to the writing of this book. Because one of the pleasures of being an appraiser is every day seeing or learning something new, I wish to thank the thousands of clients who have allowed me to come into their homes and share their treasures with them. Special thanks and acknowledgment go to the many people who specifically contributed information or suggestions for this book: Dexter MacBride, Robert Guthrie, Elizabeth Shaw, Tom Norris, Tom Hartnett, Ralph and Terry Kovel, Robert Volpe, Dale Evans, J. Lyle Beauchamp, Hank Harris, David Robertson, and the Insurance Information Institute. Also, without the diligence and loyalty of Susan Harris and Janella Smyth the manuscript would never have been completed. Thank you, Mabel Bason and John and Anne Sanders, who started it all, and Elyse Sommer, who encouraged me to do the inevitable. But most of all, thank you, Mother, Daddy, and Aunt Mary, for the years, now past, which have led to today's accomplishments.

The prices and values stated in *Why You're Richer Than You Think,* both in the value guides in Chapters 10, 11, and 12, and in the text, were compiled from actual prices quoted by retail merchants, antique dealers, manufacturers' price lists, precious metal quotations, and auction house sales results. Because prices change at an alarming rate of speed, many price lists are outdated before they are distributed. There are also variations in the retail marketplace in both new and antique goods based on geographical location, regional tastes, and supply and demand. The prices stated in *Why You're Richer Than You Think* have been carefully researched but are to be used as guidelines rather than as exact values. The author disclaims any and all responsibility for any transactions based on prices or values quoted herein.

CONTENTS

INTRODUCTION

We were on a film location in the wilderness of Washington's Cascade Mountains. Sitting on the porch of a weathered dude ranch after a long day of shooting, the young actor began to rub the thick arms of an old oak chair, its patina bronzed by decades of mountain wear. "This is the stuff I want to live with—furniture with substance, solid and beautiful."

That's the single most important reason why people are collecting antiques—buying them from dealers and auctioneers or ferreting them out of attics. In fourteen years of publishing I've watched this "hobby" become a national preoccupation, a strong trend destined to grow with each generation. In Washington or Wilmington, and from Princess Anne, Maryland, to New Harmony, Indiana, people are turning to antiques as important keys to their lives that give a feeling of belonging, roots, evidence of our heritage and loving care. They want to fill an old reed basket with fresh-dried herbs and hang it above the kitchen sink. They want to eat breakfast at an antique gateleg table that shines with the care of many generations. They want to look at a painting and see the artist's brush strokes, not a shiny cardboard imitation.

But as owners of these old items, we are actually their *custodians*—saving and preserving them for future generations to study and admire. At the same time, we have the chance to live with these wonderful old things, which actually become mirrors of our ancestors' lives, bringing history off textbook pages and into our daily routine. For instance, take a moment to admire that antique quilt hanging on your wall or covering the bed. As you trace your finger over the tiny, even stitches, you're propelled back for a moment—back to the day many decades ago when a group of neighborhood women sat around the quilting frame and shared news about their families and friends. No radio blasted, no electric fans circulated the air— today and tomorrow that quilt stands as a reminder of past golden moments, and the care afforded it now makes for magic moments your children will enjoy in decades to come.

That old mantel clock you inherited from your great-aunt, those farm tools in the shed, and a stack of dusty old Indian prints you found in the attic—these are typical of family treasures to be enjoyed, preserved, and protected as their value increases year after year. And as you begin to acquire and identify antiques, you will watch your personal investment portfolio increase. Total the value of your net worth, then compare what it will be on the basis of escalated values of your antiques *alone* in just five years. The growth is amazing. And, as new collectors learn every day, your antiques will work for you—while new furniture diminishes in resale value the moment the delivery truck rolls up to your front door. That makes good economic sense.

Whether you're the lucky possessor of a $20,000 chest or the recipient of a few beloved family heirlooms, the chance to live with the beauty of our past is both a reward and a challenge. Regardless, you're richer than you think.

GRAY D. BOONE

WHY YOU'RE RICHER
THAN YOU THINK

1

Warning! I Know More About What's in Your House Than You Do!

I spend more time in other people's homes than I do in my own.
I know where wealthy collectors hide their silver.

I have appraised priceless antiques that even museum curators have never seen.

And I have seen fakes that the owners bought as rare antiques supposedly worth thousands of dollars.

I save insurance companies hundreds of thousands of dollars every year by helping them uncover false and fraudulent claims.

And I work for individuals, people like you, helping them, after burglaries, fires and moving disasters, to recover insurance money that they had given up hopes of ever collecting.

I have checked out mansions and cottages, dusty attics and cluttered basements, all over the U.S.A., and according to at least one man, broken hearts when I have told people that their silver was plated, not sterling. And I have discovered unidentified treasures ready to be discarded as worthless.

In short, I know more about your personal property and what it is worth than you do. And, let me warn you, so do most thieves!

How I Know More About Your Possessions Than You Do and Why You Should Read My Book

Let me help you learn about your property so you can help yourself. As a senior member of the American Society of Appraisers, America's most prestigious multi-disciplinary appraisal society, and a member of their International Board of Examiners, I can both show you how to inventory your household property and help you learn the age and value of your antiques, silver, and china. I will share with you the same information I tell my clients before they file an insurance claim or an estate tax form or buy an antique for investment purposes.

For years I have written articles on personal property and appraising that have appeared in insurance journals, antiques publications, the American Bar Association *Journal,* and other national magazines. My monthly column in *The Antiques Dealer* is the only professional appraisal column of its kind. I speak at state and national conventions on the value of personal property and antiques. My appraisal clients include major museums, historic restorations, corporations, institutions, banks, insurance companies, CPAs, and attorneys. National magazines call me, asking my opinion of personal property and appraising. Every year I travel thousands of miles lecturing, teaching, and appraising.

But now I want to come into your home and show you why you should be more aware of your silver, china, furniture, antiques, collections, even those treasures hidden away or packed in storage. Based on my experience as an appraiser, I can honestly tell you why you're richer than you think.

The Time Has Come for You to Know What I Know

The crime rate is rising incredibly today. This, combined with the continually increasing value of all personal property—antique and new, means the time has come when you *must* know what you own. No longer can you sit back and think, "The robbers won't hit my house," or "I'm safe from fire." I know from firsthand experience that disasters can happen to anyone.

This book is a direct outgrowth of my day-to-day work. I have learned that not only do most people not know the value of their personal property, they do not even know what they own.

Would you buy a $30,000 car without knowing its make or getting insurance for it? Would you leave that car unattended on a dark street with its motor running and the keys in the ignition?

Of course not.

Yet you leave your house, apartment, or condominium filled with thousands of dollars of silver, jewelry, antiques, expensive furniture—literally all your worldly goods—without knowing what you have, and often, grossly underinsured.

What *Why You're Richer Than You Think* Can Do for You

You have taken what you live with for granted long enough. This book is written for you. It is designed to help you get your house in order. If you will follow the guidelines provided for you here, you may protect yourself from losing thousands of dollars when it comes to buying antiques or paying estate taxes.

In the chapters that follow you will learn:

• How to systematically list what you own.
  I describe a simple step-by-step procedure which you can follow in making your own inventory or appraisal. This is the same method professional appraisers use.

• Whether what you own truly is an antique or a collectible.
  By learning how to recognize distinguishing characteristics of copies and legitimate makers' marks you will learn about what you already own while you also become a more astute shopper.

• How rapidly personal property is increasing in value today.
  The phenomenal rise in values has led to heavy investing in antiques. Is this wise? If you are going to invest, what should you buy? What is overpriced? What about the quality of today's manufactured furniture? How do you protect what you already own? What kind and how much insurance do you need? These and other urgent questions are answered throughout the book.

• When and how to seek professional appraisal help if you need it.
  You will learn what an appraiser can and cannot do for you. Learn who and what a "certified" appraiser is. Learn how to keep down appraisal fees and what to expect to pay for appraisal services.

You live with your belongings. You love them and cherish the memories they hold for you. You anticipate passing on these treasured possessions to the next generation—and the next—as a token of your taste and appreciation of beauty. I have written this book because I, too, share your love and concern for silver, good furniture, fine china, and for its safety. Take my book and use it in your own home to protect your treasures, your investments, and your peace of mind.

2

Do You Know
What You Own?

Today, on every hand you're being told how to go out and *invest* in gold, silver, antiques, and collectibles. Flea markets, antiques shops, and auction galleries are springing up as fast as investment advisors. Price lists and guides cover every conceivable subject from barbed wire and pocket knives to American Chippendale highboys.

But wait! Before you become an expert in carnival glass or Mission furniture, before you invest in gold stocks or a bombé secretary—look around you. What are you overlooking?

Do you know the value of what you already own? When was the last time you counted your silver forks? Did your neighbor ever return the tablecloth she borrowed? How much would it cost to replace your living room rug today?

Consider your wedding presents, those souvenirs you bought on trips, the gifts you've received over the years, the furniture you bought five, ten, or even thirty years ago, the pieces you inherited and have always cherished.

Do you know what you've got? Take my word for it. You're richer than you think!

The Chest Test

Start right now. Pick up paper and pencil and take the chest test.

Choose any place in your home where you store or hide an assortment of household items—linen, china or crystal accessories, pieces of silver you seldom use, jewelry, candlesticks, trivets, etc. Usually the place is a chest in your dining room, living room, or foyer. But you may use the bottom of a corner cupboard, a sideboard, or credenza, or even a trunk or blanket chest. If you're an impeccably organized person, or if you wish to be really hard on yourself, choose the attic or basement. Do not select a chest or closet where you store only clothes.

Now that you have the specific place in mind, begin listing, *from memory,* the items you have stored there. In other words, make an inventory of everything in the chest, cupboard, or trunk.

"I can't do that!" or "That's ridiculous, I can't remember *everything,*" you complain.

But what if, instead of beginning to read this book, you had just opened your front door to discover that your house or apartment had been burglarized? Or what if you had just received a call that your house had burned?

The first thing you have to do after a loss of personal property is to list what you have lost. Otherwise you cannot (1) help the police look for your property, (2) file a claim with your insurance company, or (3) claim your property if it is recovered. Knowing that sooner or later you are going to *have* to know what you own, bite the bullet, plunge in and take the chest test.

Simply start making a list of the items stored in the place you have selected. Once you have finished making your list, go to the chest and check your accuracy.

What You Did and Did Not Find

If you are like the majority of people who have taken this chest test, you found that you left off many items stored in your chest. And what about the items on your list that you *thought* were in the chest but weren't there?

If you are like most people, you have put your belongings away carelessly, often cramming extras into a drawer or cupboard at the last minute before guests arrived, or in an attempt to "straighten up" a little. "I'll go back and see about that later," you said to yourself, but "later" may be weeks, months, even years away, and meanwhile you forget where you put your things or that they even exist.

For a firsthand comment on how easy it is to forget even those pieces you store right at your fingertips, ask any painter what he hears when people unload their storage cabinets.

"There's Grandmother's plate, the one with flowers. I looked all over for it last Christmas and it was right under my nose all along!"

Or, "Look at these candlesticks! I forgot I even had them. They're black!" Then, turning the tarnished candlesticks over, the owner exclaims, "Sterling! I didn't know that."

That last comment tells you that not only do you forget what you have and where you last put your things, but you also don't really know *what* you have. Sterling or plated candlesticks? What if they had been stolen? Worth $25 or $250?

And that plate you were looking for ... it had flowers on it, but were they daisies or forget-me-nots? Knowing something like that can make a difference between getting it back or giving it up.

Don't Think You Can Rely on Your Memory

When you took the chest test, if like most people, you found that you did not remember even half your valuables hidden or stored away, don't despair. You are not alone. In fact, you are only normal.

Time magazine recently reported on memory studies made by psychologist Elizabeth Loftus. The article explained that most people cannot even make the correct identification of articles they see and handle every day. *Time* featured fifteen slightly different sketches from which the reader was to select the correct face of a penny. Nobody at our house got it right.

Ms. Loftus commented that people have poor recall because they haven't observed objects carefully in the first place. That observation comes as no surprise to the appraiser. I wish I could receive a bonus every time I point out a feature about a desk or tray that the owners never have noticed.

Once, while looking at a silver service, I made a casual comment that the two pots did not match. One had a flower design and the other a grapevine design. The amazed owner said, "I've never seen that and I've polished this set for thirty-five years!"

One insurance executive told me that his favorite trick is to blindfold a client in the client's own living room and ask the person to name everything in it.

"They always miss at least twenty percent," he said, "and that's the living room, where everything is out and visible!" (If the property in the house were worth $80,000 and it was destroyed, you'd be out at least $16,000 without an inventory!)

In my work I am often called in after a disaster to try to help the victims and the insurance company reach a decision about the value of the property for a monetary settlement. Many times the dialogue goes something like this:

> *Appraiser:* What furniture was in the dining room prior to the fire?
>
> *Wife:* Let's see now. There was a table and chairs ...
>
> *Appraiser:* How many chairs?
>
> *Wife:* Eight. No, wait ... there were ten. I stored two extra side chairs up in the attic. The room only holds eight chairs.
>
> *Husband:* No, dear, you're wrong. There weren't ten chairs, there were twelve. Remember, you used the other arm chair in the guest bedroom. I distinctly remember putting three chairs up in the attic.
>
> (At this point I write down, eight, ten, or twelve dining room chairs.)
>
> *Appraiser:* Can you tell me what you paid for the chairs?
>
> *Wife:* Well, we didn't really buy them. Joe's sister had inherited them

from her husband's aunt, but she couldn't use them . . . so, when Joe's mother died, we traded them bedroom furniture for the chairs. I guess you'd have to say that we sort of inherited them.

Appraiser: What style were they?

Wife: Well, they went up in the back like this . . . (lots of hand gestures).

Appraiser: What about the legs? Were they straight or were they curved?

Wife: Yes.

Appraiser: Which? Straight or curved?

Wife: They were . . . What were they, Joe?

An exaggeration? Hardly. And this is furniture, big, bulky wooden furniture about which I'm trying to get a description. You should hear the descriptions of crystal and china patterns! If you can't describe it, how can you put a value on it?

When You Do Remember . . . Five Years Later

Insurance companies are plagued with calls from clients who, two, five, or even ten years after they have settled a personal property loss claim, remember items they forgot to report at the time of a robbery or disaster. What can they do?

The law varies from state to state as to when the statute of limitations on such an insurance claim expires. Presently, the standard policy states that the owner has one year in which to change and add to his initial claim. However, there are some states that allow up to six years for reopening or adjusting a claim. So, if you have suffered a recent loss of personal property and, while reading this book, discover additional losses, check with your state insurance commissioner's office to find out your rights for adjusting your claim if the need arises.

Cheating Yourself

It is never easy to lose personal property. But I can assure you from my experience of working with people who have suffered such losses that those who knew what they had and who had adequate insurance took the loss much better than those who felt they were cheated because they couldn't remember what they had.

Sometimes they blame the insurance company. "My agent should have *made* me compile a list."

Without a list, you can't remember what you owned. Ask anyone in a police crime prevention unit.

"The best cure is an ounce of prevention," one officer told me. Without a list, people don't know what they're missing, especially items they don't use every day.

"You know the cut glass pitcher sitting out on the buffet?" the officer asked parenthetically. "You didn't remember it when you made out the list. Then, four weeks after the robbery, you want to use the pitcher. You go to the buffet to get it and it's gone. Too late."

The Room Test

The room test is a particularly good one to give to a family member whom you're trying to persuade to update his or her insurance or appraisal. Give it to your parents, for example. (A lot of my calls come from young couples who want me to force their parents or aunts or grandparents to have an appraisal made.)

Or, if you have been trying to convince your husband that all the bric-a-brac around the house was a good investment and not just a dust-gathering collection, give him this test.

If you find your husband seated in a comfortable chair in the den where there are bookcases or shelves decorated with candlesticks, porcelain, or pewter figurines, wooden carvings, books and other items, ask him to tell you what is on the shelf behind him. Or ask him to name all the pieces of furniture in the living room or dining room and then to tell you what accessories are placed around on the tables—lamps, ashtrays, vases, etc.—and what pictures are hanging on the wall.

(If he, or your parents, or aunt, or child, whoever is taking this test, gets a perfect score, then give him the job of making out the inventory that *you* need!)

Women Die, Too

In all the talk about husbands dying, the fact that women die too is often overlooked! But who is it who usually has taken a primary interest in the furnishings and personal property in a home? A woman. And if she dies first, her husband often is totally unaware of the value of the property in his house.

I remember doing an appraisal for a man in his mid-fifties who was suddenly widowed. His concern was that the house, now empty during the day, might be broken into.

"I haven't any idea what is in this house," he explained to me. "I don't know what's in the drawers, or how valuable anything is. But I do know that my children would kill me if something happened to these things. They loved their mother and treasure her belongings."

As it turned out, there were many fine pieces and valuable paintings. When my client received his appraisal he was amazed at the total value.

"As far as the artwork goes," he said, "if someone had offered me $50 for the lot, I would have sold it to them and then thrown in a piece of silver to make sure they weren't getting cheated! I never really looked at it."

The Next Step

Just for fun, list all the furniture and accessories that are in one room—obviously not the room you are in—*from memory*. (Most people's jaws drop when they hear the "memory" part.) To really test yourself, while you're making this list try adding some description to the items. Does the Victorian table in your basement that you've been meaning to refinish have a rectangular top or a square top? What shape are its legs? How many drawers are there in that pine chest in your son's or daughter's room? Describe the scene of a painting or picture in your living room. If you can't describe it in words, you might try drawing it.

Now go one step further. What is the table worth today? What would it cost to replace the pine chest or picture in your living room? And, incidentally, do you know how much insurance you have on all of your personal property?

3

Why Your Possessions
Are Valuable

If you are like the majority of people I work with, you have no idea how much your personal property has risen in value. But the police are certainly aware. One officer told me that one of the biggest surprises victims of jewelry robberies get is when they learn the current value of an old high school ring. A ring bought for only $15 or $20 years ago, today easily costs from $75 to $125.

Are You a Victim of Time?

If you are over fifty years old, you set up housekeeping in an era when a silver spoon was $3 to $5 and a chair cost $10 to $20. That silver spoon today would cost you $30 to $60 and the chair would be $250 to $350!

Often I find that people in this age group simply do not believe me. Or, if you have tried to convince your parents that they need better insurance coverage, perhaps you have shared this experience with me. I can't even get my own mother to face the reality of how much personal property bought in the late 1930s costs now.

"How can you say that it would cost $1,000 to replace my fourposter bed when the entire bedroom suite only cost $180 when we bought it?" she asks.

In reality, this same bedroom suite—bed, dressing table, stool, mirror, chest of drawers, and bedside table—would cost at least $3,500 to buy today.

The Price Is Right, or
Why Personal Property Is So Valuable Today

Inflation affects everything, and personal property is no exception—antiques, silver, furniture, china, carpeting, draperies, lighting, linens, books.

The reason so many householders are not aware of the value of their property is that they haven't bought any major pieces of furniture or added to their silver or china in the last five or ten years. It has been during this decade that inflation has become so rampant. Most china, crystal, silver, and furniture companies now "update" (a polite word for increase) their price lists at least twice a year.

When people are totally unaware of the *new value* for personal property and they have an appraisal made, the appraiser's word is often doubted. I had such an experience a few years ago when I appraised a rather modest lady's desk dating from the 1920s. The piece certainly was not an antique, but it was attractive and could be used in any room in a house or small apartment. However, it was also a manufactured piece identical to literally hundreds of other desks made during that time. You could only classify it as a good reproduction—nice used furniture. When I appraised the piece at $350 the owner was visibly stunned. "This is surely *too high,*" she insisted.

Once clients question the value an appraiser puts on a piece, you know that they are thinking, "If she is that far off on *that* piece, what about the other prices?"

There were two possibilities for my client. She could call in another appraiser. Or she could shop around and check the cost of another desk, similar to or exactly like hers. At my suggestion, this is what she decided to do. A couple of weeks later she called.

"Remember my desk?" she asked. "Well, I shopped around—and frankly I didn't find a single desk that was as nice as mine, and they were all $300 or $400! Don't you want to raise the value a little?"

The truth is that if you're not in the marketplace you just don't know the prices. That incident took place about four or five years ago. Today I would appraise the desk at around $600.

And what would the situation have been if the desk were the real thing, a true antique—an eighteenth-century American maple desk? Four or five years ago it was possible to buy such a desk for $1,500 to $2,000. Today, it would bring $5,000 or more.

Ah, Yesterday

If, in 1966, you had bought a new walnut corner cupboard made by a reputable furniture company, you would have paid around $250 for the piece. Today, that same corner cupboard would cost you $1,350. That's an increase of $1,100 or 440 percent. If you had bought a tester bed at the same time, you would have paid $200 for it. Today that bed carries a price tag of $1,380. And a simple two-drawer bedside table to go beside it has increased from $50 to $300 during the same time span.

But Don't Get Carried Away—
Things Are Seldom as They Seem

Personal property is often overvalued when the owner *thinks* his item is something which it is not—particularly an antique. Such mistakes are fanned by today's glamorous media stories. How often do you see a photograph in the newspaper with a caption which reads something like this:

*Rare Newport Blockfront Desk
Sold at Auction for $300,000*

or, *Old Master Painting Discovered
in Attic Brings Over $1,000,000
at International Art Auction*

The headlines are as spectacular as possible—and as scant on information as possible. They do not tell you that the desk had descended in Benjamin Franklin's family or that the Old Master painting was found in the attic of a Polish church where it was hidden during World War II. Meanwhile, the possibility of finding such a hidden treasure leads the unknowing public to dream that any object can or might be a rare and valuable one. Yet discoveries *do* happen.

A friend of mine passing a mall antiques show spied a delightful hooked rug. She hadn't expected to spot anything she would be interested in (after all, antiques displayed in front of a Baskin-Robbins ice cream parlor tend to lose their charm). But the rug had kittens on it, was colorful and "cute," and well priced. Still she hesitated—until she got home that afternoon and began thumbing through the *Antiques* magazine that had arrived in the day's mail. There she saw the same hooked rug illustrated as part of the Henry Ford Museum collection, in Dearborn, Michigan. Needless to say, she returned immediately and bought the rug. Quite a discovery for an afternoon's shopping.

The Truth About $1,000,000 Art Objects

Hugh Hildesley, vice-president of the Sotheby Parke Bernet Auction Gallery, stated in an interview that 84 percent of all the items sold in their New York gallery in 1980 brought *under* $1,000. In contrast, only 200 items brought over $50,000, although some of those 200 items did sell for $2,000,-000 or $3,000,000 or more.

At Christie's, the equally glamorous auction house on Park Avenue, the *average* price per item ranged between $4,000 and $5,000. So you may indeed uncover a hidden treasure—but don't count on making $1,000,000.

Silver—Additional Problems

Silver prices have jumped, fallen back, increased, and leveled off. The increase in silver prices is perhaps no more startling than those for furniture or china. But there is one factor that has made everyone more aware of silver prices: *silver theft.* Thefts of all types of precious metals have increased dramatically, encouraged greatly by the storefront and street corner dealers who buy these precious metals from *anyone,* no questions asked. (By the way, burglars are now using metal detectors to discover the hidden silver in your house.)

If you own sterling silver, learn its current value. Most states have a limitation on the amount of insurance you can recover for your lost silver *if you do not have additional insurance specifically on your silver.* The amount varies, but the usual limit is $1,000. Do you have more than $1,000 worth of silver? Even if you bought your silver as recently as 1977 you may be shocked to learn how quickly you can pass $1,000 on today's market.

Just as an example, here are the prices of two of the most popular silver patterns, "Repoussé" by Kirk, and "Prelude" by International. (Other patterns will be discussed in detail in Chapter 10).

Kirk "Repoussé"

	1977	1981
Teaspoon	$31.00	$ 54.60
Knife	38.00	48.00
Fork	44.00	86.40
Tablespoon	72.00	157.20

International "Prelude"

	1977	1981
Teaspoon	$26.25	$ 52.80
Knife	33.25	55.20
Fork	37.25	73.20
Tablespoon	63.50	116.40

If you have nineteen pieces of "Repoussé" or "Prelude"—six teaspoons, knives, and forks, and one tablespoon—you have over $1,000 worth of silver.

Let's say that you're one of those people who claims, "I can't afford the insurance." Poppycock! Fifty cents for $100 worth of insurance? Fifteen dollars for $1,000 worth of silver? It's one of the best bargains around, and cheaper than most life insurance.

The "Buy Now" Mentality

There's another side to the inflation factor of personal property values, this one with an ironic twist. As everything is affected by inflation—food, travel, entertainment, clothes, etc.—some people are looking around and saying, "It costs $100 for four people to have a fine dinner. A simple shirtwaist dress costs $75. Why should I spend all my money on goods that are *consumable* and *disposable?* I want to buy something that lasts, from which I can receive continued enjoyment and that will escalate in value."

This line of thinking has led people with some disposable income into buying antiques and furniture *now.* This means more demand for a limited number of available items. And so the price for the chest, plate, bowl, or picture increases.

Antiques dealers are selling more to the twenty-five to thirty-five-year-old age group, whose attitude seems to be "buy now." Combine with that train of thought the reasoning that "if I don't buy it now, it's going to cost more next year, or the next, or the next," and you understand the many different facets of inflation affecting personal property and antiques values.

Quality

Quality is reflected in price. To maintain high quality in manufacturing today, prices have to rise. This rise is passed on to you, the customer; thus the very high-quality reproduction secretary that cost $2,500 in 1973 costs you $6,500 today.

But there is another side to quality. Because many people can't or won't pay $6,500 for a secretary, manufacturers are substituting cheaper materials in currently manufactured pieces. There are some obvious changes almost anyone who looks at a piece of new furniture today can see.

Inside, Outside

Look at the interior of a drawer. How is it joined to the front? Are those nails? Previously, they used to use dovetails—mortises and tenons that locked the pieces together.

No, wait—those aren't nails, those are staples!

And what about the drawer bottoms?

Wood? No.

Plywood? No.

Chipboard or composition board? Yes.

If you've looked at moderately priced new furniture lately you've probably already observed these concessions to cost. But, after all, who sees the inside of a drawer?

What's going on on the outside? I spoke to a furniture dealer whose lines include Henredon, Baker, and Heritage, as well as Thomasville, Drexel, and other well-known manufacturers. "There's been plastic introduced even in some of the fine lines," he explained. Moldings around the edges of tables and decorative touches, such as brackets connecting table tops and the legs, are two examples he showed me.

"What does this do to repairing a piece of furniture once it breaks?" I asked, thinking about my children's shattered plastic toys—particularly my daughter's plastic doll house furniture.

"In the case of a corner bracket, there's no problem. You just get another one and stick it on. But when the plastic edge molding gets chipped or damaged, you've got a real problem."

He then went on to explain other cost-cutting procedures, one of which will be particularly offensive to the lovers of good woods and beautiful grains. Some companies are engraving grains onto blond boards. The result is a particle board with a nice-looking oak grain printed on it.

And what happens to it when it gets damaged? Well, he told me about the time one of his workers was putting a bedroom suite together and his hammer slipped. A huge hunk was knocked out of the nightstand and they were left with a gaping hole in the piece. This would not have happened had the piece been made out of good, hard, solid oak.

Let this be a warning to you in buying new furniture today. Ask if the piece is wood or "wood grained." Take notice of furniture ads that use such descriptions as "mahogany veneer on hardwood" or "cherry solids."

If you look at a piece of furniture made even as recently as the 1950s or 1960s and compare it to those made today, you will notice some real differences.

One antiques dealer I know keeps a brand-new Chippendale-style desk in stock, just to use to show the difference in finish, materials, and overall "look." "That one desk sells more antiques than all the salesmanship in the world," he told me.

Why Early Attic Looks So Good

This then is why so many antiques dealers today are buying the fine old reproductions and selling them in their shops—not as antiques, but as good quality reproduction pieces and with high prices. The dealers are recognizing the quality of the old reproductions, pieces like those you have in your homes. These old "early attic" reproductions are gaining new respectability and higher price tags. There will be more about this whole movement throughout the book and particularly in Chapter 12.

Scarcity

Another reason why dealers are upscaling the value of these old reproductions is scarcity. When you can't get the eighteenth-century lowboy but your customers want a lowboy, what are you going to do? Sell them a nineteenth-century or even early twentieth-century lowboy. Whether or not the antiques dealer sells the nineteenth-century lowboy for what it is—a nineteenth-century piece, or tries to pass it off as an eighteenth-century piece, is something I'll deal with later.

Supply and Demand

More people want antiques or antique look-alikes than ever before. It's the old supply-and-demand story. Our country has not been wracked by war for over one hundred years. Generally, over the last one hundred years, the quality of life has greatly improved. The middle class has grown substantially. How do you show your prosperity? By the house you live in and the furnishings you choose to have around you. If you already had these in your family, you have held on to them. If you are self-made, you seek what others have—symbols of the past. Add to this the investment quality value of antiques today, and the result is—everyone wants them.

This unprecedented demand has antiques dealers all singing the same sad song. "I can't replace my stock when I sell it," they moan. "If I am lucky enough even to find a ... Tiffany lamp ... lowboy ... Ming vase ... Georgian tea service, or Windsor chair [whatever he or she is looking for] ... I'll probably have to pay as much for it *wholesale* as what I got for my last one."

What does this mean to you, the owner of these pieces the antiques dealers want? Your possessions are worth more than you think, and if you ever need to replace them, you might be in for a long and expensive search.

Sorry, Discontinued

"While this may be true of antiques," you think, "I don't need to worry. None of my things are old. They're only ten, twenty years old." Well, you've just read how both inflation and quality affect value. But there's more news, and it's not good—even items that you expect to be able to replace are no longer available, especially in silver.

A clear example of the cutback in production can be seen by comparing one silver company's price list of February, 1975, with their price list of 1981. The lists give prices for sterling silver hollowware—teapots, goblets, children's cups, letter openers, etc. The 1975 list had 228 items. In 1981, prices were given for 95 of these items. Next to the 133 other items was one word—DISCONTINUED. (Of course, the prices that were there were staggering—the set of six decanter labels that cost $73.50 in 1975 cost $150 in 1981, and the baby cup that cost $47 in 1975 cost $170 in 1981.) But cost aside, the companies just aren't making what they used to.

Also, when considering replacement of silver items, remember the tremendous meltdown that occurred in the early months of 1980, when silver prices reached $30, $40, and $50 an ounce. The result of that unparalleled meltdown is that there just is not as much silver for sale in antiques shops as there was. And, when you find the piece you're looking for, you're going to have to pay more for it because of its new scarcity.

To replace just one sterling fork today costs between $50 and $100. If your fork costs $75 and you have twelve forks, you have an investment of $900. And if you've got twelve forks, you're also going to have twelve knives ($550) and twelve spoons ($660), twelve ice tea spoons ($540), twelve salad forks ($750) . . . or, up to this point, a value of roughly $3,400.

Nostalgia and Sentiment

America's love affair with our colonial past shows no signs of letting up. It started most recently with the 1965 celebration of the Civil War Centennial and caught accelerated momentum with the 1976 Bicentennial, and it still goes on.

The First Time . . . 1876

There have been other times when Americans glorified their country's past. After the 1876 Centennial celebration, Pennsylvania (especially Philadelphia) furniture became the rage—as was all eighteenth-century formal Chippendale furniture. As a result, late nineteenth-century cabinetmakers turned out Chippendale chairs, Chippendale lowboys, Chippendale secretaries, all copied from the original eighteenth-century pieces. The trained eye can distinguish these nineteenth-century pieces from the eighteenth-century original pieces (more about that later).

The Second Time Around . . . 1926

Some fifty years later, coinciding with the 150th anniversary of the Revolution in 1926, there was another rebirth of interest in American antiques. (The first American Wing of the Metropolitan Museum of Art opened two years before.) During the 1920s, however, the public also wanted "Colonial" or "Pilgrim" furniture. This demand was met by reproductions of Windsor chairs, gateleg tables, Welsh dressers, and joint stools, as well as pieces representing the Queen Anne, Chippendale, and Federal periods. There were numerous fine companies making reproductions at that time—Margolis, Charack, even names still familiar to us today like Baker and Kittinger. But perhaps best known was Wallace Nutting the famous collector, writer, and artist, who also made reproductions. In 1930, in the *Supreme Edition* of the *Wallace Nutting General Catalog* (reprinted by Schiffer Limited), Wallace Nutting wrote, "A broker whose office was furnished by me said he believed the prestige derived from the equipment of his office would pay for it [the furniture] in three months. Anyhow, he died rich."

"Shrewd businessmen have told me that pieces bearing my name will soon be coveted by collectors. The thought did not originate with me. Think it over."

If you had parents or grandparents who followed Nutting's advice, you may well be sitting on what is now a valuable collector's item. The Windsor bow-back side chair, which Nutting sold in 1932 for $30, can now fetch $750, and the Windsor fan-back arm chair, which sold between $50 and $60, can now bring $1,250!

Today's Nostalgia ... 1976

The astounding price rise in these pieces is due to the quality of the pieces and to our yearning for such styles of furniture. "We've moved out of Spanish Provincial and stark modern back into a traditional look," one furniture dealer told me.

"Do you know that my salesmen are even selling traditional 'Colonial' furniture in California?" another manufacturer said, slightly amazed himself. And why not? It is hard to know which came first, the renewed interest in crafts—quilting, crewel, needlework; accessories—straw baskets, tin candlemolds, blue and white china; or the return of traditional furnishings—wing-back chairs, china hutches, even roll-top desks. But they are all back and at prices never before equaled.

The current demand is now centered around two types of earlier furniture, the country or primitive look—corner cupboards, trestle tables, Windsor chairs, etc., and the formal look—imposing Chippendale secretaries, Queen Anne highboys, Sheraton banquet tables, etc. Both styles are available in antiques and reproductions, and both are expensive.

When the public wants an item badly enough to *compete* for it, especially when the supply is limited, as in the case of antiques, the price goes up.

Why Your Grandmother Threw Away Her Grandmother's Antiques

Not everyone, however, has always loved "old things." In fact, many of our grandmothers threw away *their* grandmothers' furniture and accessories. I have found this particularly true in the South around the turn of the century.

In the southern states the 1860s brought great loss of personal property. After the Civil War, hard times followed for many years.

But economic conditions improved around the turn of the century and for the next twenty-five years, people had the money to buy new furniture. So they often discarded those pieces from the 1830s, 40s, and 50s, the "old things" they had used out of necessity and, to demonstrate their new economic security, replaced them with new items.

And why not throw the old away? In 1910 a piece of furniture that had been made in 1850 was only sixty years old and not considered an antique but rather just old, used furniture.

In the 1980s the piece from the 1850s looks good to us. After all, it's 130 years old by now—an antique. Furthermore, now that we are more economically secure we like to point with pride to furniture our great, great-grandparents had. It would be quite different if we had our great, great-grandparents' pieces because we couldn't afford anything new. Instead, today we have a new generation eager to buy *with pride* those exact same pieces that Grandmother threw away.

The New Antiques—Collectibles, and Their Rapid Rise

What Grandmother did not realize when she threw away all of those "old things" was that she was making the remaining items from the nineteenth-century rare or hard to get for later generations. At the same time, our population has increased. Thus, there are more people wanting the remaining pieces. What happens when the demand forces the price beyond reasonable reach, or when the supply dries up?

When the first situation occurs, the buyer looks around to see what she can afford. When it is difficult to buy an eighteenth-century Queen Anne chair for under $2,000, but you can buy a Victorian chair for $500, the Victorian chair is quickly snatched up as a substitute.

When the supply of pieces from a particular time or in a particular style dries up, the collector looks for something else to collect. If you have collected antiques yourself, you have had the experience of watching whatever you collect continually become harder to find.

This is one reason why the demand for pieces from the 1920s to even the 1950s has become so great. Items from these years, while hardly antiques, have become "hot." In this category are such items as the art glass made by Tiffany, Lalique, and Quezal, furniture of the Art Deco and Mission periods, and even such kitchen or store items as Saltine cracker boxes and Coca-Cola trays. The value of these pieces ranges so widely that they are found in country flea markets and international auction house salesrooms alike.

The collecting public realizes that there will never be any more Mission furniture or any more nineteenth-century Haviland Limoges china or any more brilliant cut glass that equals the old in quality and styling. The public buys, the items become harder to obtain, and the prices soar upward. Once the market for the items is established, scholars come out of the woodwork. Books are written, price guides appear, magazine articles glamorize the pieces, and soon everyone wants to collect the "new antiques."

Furthermore, production cutbacks by manufacturers are leaving empty shelves in gift shops and department stores and the public is returning to antiques shops and auction houses to buy what it can no longer find in retail stores.

A Fresh Look at Your Hodge-Podge

So, if you look around you, what do you find in your home? Most people have a hodge-podge of personal property. There are the new items you have bought, mixed in with gifts and pieces you have inherited from one side of the family or the other, and more bric-a-brac than you can possibly display at one time—much less remember. Clearly, they are worth a great deal more than you realized.

4

Beginning the Inventory, or the Emyl Method

(Easy Method for Your List)

The Right Tools

To make your inventory you will need (1) paper and pen (or tape recorder), (2) a tape measure or yardstick (a ruler will be too short in many instances), (3) magnifying glass, (4) flashlight—as strong as possible, and (5) optional equipment—scales, a black light, and calipers.

The most obvious way to make your inventory is to list and describe each piece in a notebook. However, if you own or have access to a tape recorder you may wish to consider taping your account of your property. Certainly this is the quickest way to make your inventory, and once you have the tapes you can then either put them away for safe-keeping or have them transcribed. (I'll tell you later where to keep your appraisal and why.)

For years I have used a tape recorder in my appraisal work and find that it saves me hours on each job. Not only can you talk faster than you can write, but your descriptions will tend to be better when you do not suffer from writer's cramp and can avoid your own poor spelling. After I finish each job, my secretary then transcribes the tapes into permanent typed form for my clients. I suggest that you, too, may want to have a written list to refer to at some time. Thus, it may be worth the time (if you do it yourself) or expense (if you hire someone) to transcribe the tapes.

In my work I use a micro-cassette recorder, which is small, lightweight, and reliable. Since I move around so much and like to have my hands free to handle the objects I am appraising, I simply attach a lariat to the hook at the side of the machine and slip the recorder around my neck, much like a microphone, thus giving me maximum freedom of movement.

In order to make distinctions between pieces, especially those which are very similar, you will need a tape measure or yardstick for making measurements.

Because marks can be hard to see if they are rubbed, faint, or small, you will also need a strong flashlight and a magnifying glass. (Incidentally, if your silver hasn't been polished for years and you need to see the marks on it, you might invest in some silver polish, but remember—don't get carried away and polish the whole piece now. Save that for later.) You will also need the flashlight and magnifying glass when looking under pieces of furniture you do not wish to move.

Optional Equipment

If you plan to do a thorough job of analyzing your silver you will need an accurate scale. Postal scales, baby scales, bathroom scales, even fish scales have been used to weigh silver. The professional appraiser uses troy ounce scales, the official measurement for silver. Troy ounce scales are available from chemical and jewelry supply houses. But if you wish to make a conversion yourself, multiply each regular ounce by .9114583 on your hand-held calculator.

Another tool that the professional appraiser often uses in his work is an ultraviolet or black light. There are several models of portable black lights available but you may not wish to invest in this equipment for a one-time use. However, if you are interested in porcelain or paintings as investments, you will find a black light essential. You can make your own black light for only the cost of a black light bulb, available at hardware stores and novelty shops. Just screw the bulb temporarily into any lamp fixture that it will fit.

Black lights are used for finding damage and identifying fakes. They are generally used in analyzing glass, finding damage in porcelain, discerning repairs to furniture and sculpture, and revealing over-painting of pictures. To use a black light properly the room must be thoroughly darkened. A closet is best. The black light, which is actually violet or purple, then "sees" through the surface, revealing cracks, changes in texture, glue, blotches of paint, and other irregularities which the naked eye would miss. When there is an irregularity the change in color or composition shows up "black" or "purple."

The black light is most useful for your purposes in examining china. Mended sections, cracks, and, even more importantly, erasures or additions of factory marks show up under this light. If you examine the bottom of any porcelain piece with a black light and see an area that fluoresces a different color you can be sure that either a mark has been removed and the bottom glazed over to hide the erasure or that a mark has been added to the surface.

Just such a bogus piece of china surfaced while I was writing this book. A call came from a local TV reporter.

"I understand you're an expert on china," he began.

"I specialize in silver and furniture," I explained, "but I know a lot about china. What's the problem?"

"An antiques dealer just getting started in the business has bought several antiques from another dealer. There's some R. S. Prussia in the group that may be fake. Will you look at it? We need someone to help the dealer get her money back if it is fake."

Since I am familiar with R. S. Prussia china I told the reporter to come by. When he and his camera crew arrived, we unwrapped the "antiques"—some dented nineteenth-century silverplate, a couple of recent prints, and a pair of left-and-right-handed mustache cups.

Somewhere in the back of my mind I remembered reading about fake mustache cups and saucers—but where?

Meanwhile, even a quick glance at the cups and saucers convinced me these were not R. S. Prussia. I didn't even need to look at the mark. (But where had I read about them, I wondered?)

"These definitely are *not* R. S. Prussia pieces," I stated.

The usual question followed. "How do you know?"

At this point I turned one cup and saucer over. R. S. Prussia was plainly visible.

"Let's compare this mark with another R. S. Prussia mark. There's *no* question this is the real R. S. Prussia mark," I insisted, taking a celery dish out of the corner cupboard.

"My husband inherited this celery dish from his grandmother's home, a South Carolina plantation," I explained.

I turned the celery dish over.

"See!" I proclaimed.

"See what? It looks the same to me," the reporter said.

I had to agree. They did look just about the same.

"Let's use the black light," I suggested.

We took my light and the china and ducked into the coat closet.

The light showed a distinctly different color surrounding the R. S. Prussia mark on the cup and saucer bottoms. There was no such distinction around the R. S. Prussia mark on the celery dish.

Next I began scraping at the center of the cup bottom around the spurious mark. A thin, flaky white substance began peeling off. We looked at the surface under the black light again.

My scraping revealed two changes—the same color surface as the outer part of the cup bottom showed up and there was a faint impressed mark which appeared to be J . . . . oo.

I wanted to scrape the entire mark off, but the reporter was hesitant. After all, the cups belonged to someone else and there was a lot of money invested in them—$600, in fact.

"Six hundred dollars?" I gasped. "Let's make a phone call."

I called Terry Kovel, the antiques pricing expert, and began explaining.

"Terry, there's a TV reporter here and we're looking at a couple of R. S. Prussia mustache cups and saucers."

"With violets on them?" she asked.

"Yes."

"I'm looking at the same cups," she laughed. "Got a pair right here in front of me. We just taped a TV segment on fake R. S. Prussia."

"What is that mark showing up underneath the R. S. Prussia 'seal' . . . J?" I asked.

"JP 1200. We scraped the mark off to read it."

The mystery was solved. As I hung up I remembered what I had been struggling to recall.

I hurried to my library and returned with Dorothy Hammond's *Confusing Collectibles*. There, on page 82, was the story of the R. S. Prussia "seals," and on page 80 the identical "left"- and "right"-handed mustache cups were illustrated. Interestingly, those cups had been marked "Brandenburg" and with a blue anchor, and not with the bogus R. S. Prussia mark.

Eventually I probably would have remembered where I had read about the R. S. Prussia "seals," but it was the black light that provided the real evidence.

And yes, the antiques dealer got her money back.

Finally, if you wish to examine furniture carefully in order to correctly identify its age, you will find a pair of calipers handy. With the current rage for ladder-back and Windsor chairs, there are many deceptive pieces in the marketplace.

Because early furniture was most often made from green or unseasoned wood, the parts of the furniture later dried out and shrank. It is this shrinking that causes the side boards of a secretary or chest to split, drawer bottoms to split or separate, and the round turnings on chair members or bedposts to slightly change shape. The expert hopes and expects to find irregular shapes of finials, legs, and spindles.

A trained eye or sensitive hand can usually detect these irregularities once you know what you are looking for. But the beginner will find calipers helpful. Take calipers bought at any hardware store and simply place them around the round part of the piece of furniture you wish to check. Tighten the calipers until they barely touch the wood and rotate them around the wood. (If you tighten them firmly, you can mar the wood when you turn them.) If the calipers become tight and drag, or if you see a space appearing between the instrument and the wood, then you have an irregular shape. In other words, the once round part has now shrunk and become elliptical or oval.

If, on the other hand, the calipers measure a perfectly round turning, beware. Modern kiln-dried wood shows very little shrinkage and remains perfectly round.

If the piece is genuinely old, the round parts will not be perfectly round.

The Right Format

Before beginning to make your inventory, decide what form you want the listing to be in. The ultimate purpose of your list is to have a document which can be used to:

1. Help you adequately insure your personal property by knowing what you own.
2. Serve as a record of what you owned if your personal property is stolen, damaged, or destroyed.
3. Provide sufficient descriptions to aid in the recovery of your property in the event it is stolen and later found.
4. Provide sufficient descriptions and value guides of your property so you can receive adequate compensation for your property if the need arises.

Whether you verbally describe into a tape recorder or write out the descriptions of your pieces, the format will be the same. The following is the one I use in making appraisals and is a simple form which you can follow.

First, you *name* the item you are appraising. Next, you *describe* the item. Finally, you decide whether or not you wish to declare a monetary *value* on the item.

Some of you will use this book as a guide to make a simple list or inventory of your personal property but will omit any values for these pieces. Others of you will wish to go a step beyond the inventory and make your own appraisal by assigning actual monetary values to your pieces. These values will be based on (1) prices you already know and (2) price guides provided in my value charts.

To see how this simple format is actually going to work, study the two examples that follow. I divide my paper into three columns. The first column is for two entries—what the object is and where it is located. You will decide how specific you wish to be about the location of each piece. The easiest way to make your inventory is to proceed in a logical room-by-room sequence. If you follow this plan, make a room heading at the beginning of each new room or area, as I do in the first example. Often this is the only location identification needed.

You will also notice in this first example that only furniture is listed. This is because I recommend arranging your personal property in categories—furniture, silver, china, and crystal, etc. I have found this type of organization makes it easier for you to make the inventory in the first place, and then to locate a specific item on your inventory after it is completed.

When you begin some of the other categories, such as silver or accessories, you may wish to be more specific in stating a location. Then the left-hand column may look more like this second example.

EXAMPLE ONE:

Article	Description	Appraised Value (optional)
FOYER:		
Chest of drawers	Chippendale style. 4 Drawers. Made by the Baker Furniture Company.	$950
Side chair	Antique. Carved rose at the top. Needlepoint seat. Victorian. Inherited from Rogers family.	$275
Fern stand	Reproduction. Round top, long pedestal, Queen Anne feet. Mahogany.	$150
LIVING ROOM:		
Camel-back sofa	Hickory Chair Co. Gold upholstery.	$1,750
Lounge chair	Round back, loose cushion. Green and gold upholstery—legs hidden by skirt.	500
Drop-leaf table	English antique. Mahogany with inlay. One drawer with brass pull. Straight legs.	$650 in 1975 ? 1982

EXAMPLE TWO:

Article	Description	Appraised Value (optional)
SILVER STORED IN DINING ROOM:		
12 goblets (Mother's. Kept in corner cupboard)	Sterling silver. Gorham. 272. Plain, with round base. No monogram.	$400 each
Silver service (stored in sideboard)	Sterling silver. Reed and Barton. No. 630. On raised feet with wooden handles and finials. 2 pots, sugar and creamer. Tallest pot approximately 8″ tall.	Not currently made
Silver service (on top of sideboard)	Silver plated. Derby Silver Co. Monogrammed "AMB." On round base. Plain. Coffee pot, sugar, and creamer. Grandparents' wedding present. Dates from 1890s or 1900. Very good condition.	$450

This format is simple to follow. In each chapter that deals with a specific category you will learn what information to include in the "description" column. An alternate appraisal method is to use index cards rather than typing paper or a spiral notebook. In this case your cards will look something like this:

SAMPLE FORM:

```
 _____    (Current date)
   (Name of item)            _____
                             Room left for
                             mark, if
                             present
   (Description)
 _____

 _____

 _____

 _____


   (Origin)
 _____
   (Date of item)              (Current value)
```

EXAMPLES OF COMPLETED INDEX CARDS:

```
                              2-17-81
   Tester Bed              _____

   Mahogany, straight canopy, with round, tapering posts. Shaped
   headboard and blanket rail.



   Custom-made. Cost $125 originally.
   1962                        $795
```

```
                              2-17-81
   Girandoles (pair)       _____

   Marble square base. Brass girl and boy figures, 3 lights. Crystal
   prisms with star design.



   Inherited from Aunt Martha Brown in 1952.
   1850s                       $495
```

Yet another alternative is to buy one of the "inventory" books available at bookstores. *Personal Antique and Collectible Record Book* published by Collector Books, and *The Kovels' Origanizer for Collectors* published by Crown are two such books. But whether you use a notebook, index cards, tape recorder or whatever, the basic format remains the same.

Name, Description, Value
First, *name* the item you are appraising. Next, *describe* the item. Finally, *value* the item if you wish.

The Right Organization—An Overview

To make the task go quicker, before you begin making your list, make a general survey of your personal property. I call this taking an overview of your items. Separate your property into two categories.

1. The items you know about.
2. The items you *do not* know about.

If this seems oversimplified, it is not. One reason why people don't get their lists made is because they make it hard for themselves. They begin in the middle, so to speak, starting with one piece that they know nothing about. They put it down something like, "Big mirror hanging in the hall." then they put down a large question mark. Next they move to an item they recently purchased. At this point they stop, sort through old bills looking for *that receipt alone,* and then they go back into the room where they began making the list and move on to the next piece.

The Known

Approach the job in a systematic way. First, look over your house or apartment. Then quickly jot down each piece you have bought or for which you know the specific value. This list will include new pieces and antiques alike.

Now look over this list and determine which items can be verified by canceled checks or bills of sale. Place an asterisk beside these items so that if you are planning to enter values on your list you will know which bills or canceled checks you wish to look for—*all at one time.*

Now look over this list again. Next to those pieces for which you remember the purchase price or *know* the current value, write down that figure. Most people eventually throw away bills, but you may well remember almost exactly how much you paid for an item that you bought last year, ten, thirty, or even fifty years ago.

My clients constantly tell me, "I remember that we couldn't afford these dining room chairs when we bought them, but we made the sacrifice. They cost $18 each and that was more than I was making a week teaching at that time!"

Obviously that $18 is going to be irrelevant in relationship to the present value of each chair. However, it will be interesting to see the contrast between yesterday's and today's values. And, if the item is a recent purchase but the bill of sale is discarded, the price you paid for the piece may still be relevant.

Even if you do not plan to list specific values on your inventory, make a note of those prices you know anyway. If you ever do need to establish a *current* value for these pieces, a knowledgeable appraiser can more easily provide an *updated* comparable value if she or he knows how much the piece cost originally.

Thus, your first list may look like this:

Living room sofa	1975 purchase*
Pair of side tables	$500 1978
Mirror over mantel	$450 1977
Corner cupboard	Antique purchase*
Dining room chairs	Drexel 1965? $600?
Dining room rug	$850 1972
Flower prints	1978 purchase*

(Remember, * means to look up the bill of sale or canceled check, assuming you keep good records.)

If you discover that you have included some items that, once you think about them, you really do not know about, underline these items in red or cross through them. These pieces will fall into the second category.

The Know Nots

This second category, the items you *do not* know about, is the group that will give you the most trouble. But if you think it is difficult to make the list with the pieces in front of you, just think what it would be like if they were stolen or destroyed.

These are the items you inherited, the bric-a-brac you picked up at yard sales or were given as gifts. To inventory these "unknowns" you should do one of the following:

1. Make a basic list to establish proof of ownership of what you possess, but omit or estimate values,.
2. Call in a professional appraiser to determine values.

Conclusion

Most people fall somewhere between the two extremes of those who know everything about what they own and those who know nothing about anything. Making an inventory can be an endlessly frustrating task or a rewarding one. Just remember to gather the right tools, take an overview of your property before you begin, and plan to consistently follow the simple formats I have shown you.

✿ 5 ✿

Getting Started—
What You Need to Know

The Pitfalls and How to Avoid Them

I've been meaning to call you for years," my client began. "But somehow, every time I thought about dragging out all that silver and china, I couldn't face it. Now my neighbors on both sides have been robbed. Can you come over this afternoon?"

Sound familiar? If so, don't despair. (Don't call either, if you expect to find an appraiser available "this afternoon." Today, most appraisers are booked for weeks, even months in advance.)

Most people just don't want to do the work involved in making a proper inventory. The majority of people start out without a scheme or plan, thinking that it will only take a short while to complete the list. Naturally, an hour later, when they realize they have more than they thought they did, or they have stopped to search for an item they suddenly remembered but can't find, they are frustrated and ready to quit. You can avoid all these frustrations by planning ahead.

The Time Pitfall

Before you start, face up to the fact that making an inventory is going to take time. Set aside an entire day—if you feel pushed to get the job done immediately. Or, plan to take several nights or a weekend to complete the job. Remember, you didn't buy everything you own in sixty minutes. How can you list it all so quickly? The advantage of spreading the job out over a few days' time is that it will not seem so tedious.

Mary was smart. She knew it was going to take a lot of time to make her own inventory. She began on a snowy Monday morning. After the children left for school, she put a sheet on the dining room table and opened her silver drawer. She hadn't used her silver for three months—since Christmas—and she was rushed when she put it away. Her silver was gold from tarnish, so instead of putting it out on the table, she took it straight to the kitchen and began polishing knives and forks. When the children got home she was polishing trays and goblets. She still hadn't begun her inventory.

To avoid this problem, which actually happens rather frequently, be *determined* to proceed with the job at hand. Save the polishing or cleaning or washing for later.

Another solution, if you're a compulsive cleaner, is to wait until you do your spring or fall cleaning. If you routinely rearrange linen closets or wash all your crystal, plan to make your inventory while you're doing that job anyway—if you think the burglars will wait for you.

The Pitfall of "Lost" Things

Before you start, be prepared for the fact that you may well find that you've lost or at least misplaced some items. In at least 50 percent of the appraisals that I make, I am told, "I used to have a dozen ice tea spoons, but now I can only find eleven," or, "I'll just have to send you a picture of my cut glass bowls when I find them."

Even more serious discoveries often are made when owners begin unpacking treasures from hiding or storage places. In one instance I remember, a trunk filled with wonderful nineteenth-century quilts had been severely water-damaged—unbeknownst to the owners—and the quilts had literally rotted to pieces. In another, an entire set of sterling silver had been packed in the same box with a dozen small salt and pepper shakers. The salt spilled all over the silver. By the time the box was opened, five years later, the silver had been eaten away by the salt, and many pieces were pitted beyond saving.

Even furniture that owners thought they had stored in the attic or basement after a move has not shown up when we began looking for it. If you can't find something, or if you discover broken or damaged pieces, don't let this divert you. Let it emphasize the reason why you need to finish the job at hand. Make a separate list of pieces you can't find as you go along, and if they show up later, mark them off. If they don't show up, then begin a concerted search for them *after* you finish the appraisal.

The "It's Not Worth It" Pitfall

"It is going to be too much trouble," you sigh.

"I don't want to mess with all that *stuff*," your husband complains.

"We don't have anything *worth* listing," you contend.

"I don't know enough to make my own inventory," you say, in one last attempt to avoid the job.

You may not know enough to begin making your list *right this minute*. But this book shows you how. In the following chapters I have divided personal property into four major categories. Within each of these categories I guide you step-by-step to learn about what you have and how to evaluate it. I identify makers' marks on silver and china, bric-a-brac, and accessories. I tell you what details to look for on furniture to help determine the age and quality of your pieces. And I warn you about fakes and copies that are in the marketplace today. I provide value charts to help you establish the worth of your property. And I help you know when you need to call in an expert.

After you have finished reading *Why You're Richer Than You Think,* not only will you know about what you own, you will also be better informed to make future purchases and even investments. And you will be better prepared should you become a victim of theft, fire, divorce, or estate problems for starters.

Familiarity Breeds Neglect—Another Type of Pitfall

Many of my clients undervalue the pieces they live with. Often this starts when a friend, interior decorator, or relative criticizes a piece. "I never have liked Victorian chairs," your decorator says, and that charming carved side chair instantly becomes a "give away." Sometimes undervaluing is the result of the previous origin of a piece.

My neighbor was debating about which of her things she should take to an art museum's appraisal day. Christie's had sent five experts to our museum to identify and appraise antiques, and she was going to be one of the first in line.

"Why don't you take this picture frame?" I asked. (I had not appraised her pieces, but this beautiful malachite Art Deco frame was undoubtedly valuable.)

"Oh not that!" she exclaimed. "Aunt Martha kept that in her back room and I only have it in the living room because it's the right size and color. It's no good."

"But have you ever really examined it? Is it marked? May I look at it?" I asked.

(You have to be very diplomatic when you're an appraiser and you're in a friend's home. If you say a piece is wonderful you're buttering her up—trying to get a job. If a piece is not good, and you say so, you're running the risk of losing a friend. This time I felt I was safe. Christie's, not Emyl, was going to put a final value on it.)

Turning the piece over, I saw exactly what I had anticipated: "Tiffany Studios/New York." It was indeed very valuable.

The lesson to be learned from this experience is, never overlook anything. In making your inventory, pick up every item. Look for every mark.

You may be surprised at what you find. Later chapters will tell you what to look for, and where, but now, as you formulate how you're going to work, plan to give every item some consideration.

The Price Pitfall

Don't undervalue the property around you by thinking it is worth only what you paid for it. I remember one woman who kept telling me how much everything was worth. Her value was the exact penny that she had paid for everything, whether she bought it last year or thirty years ago. Resist the temptation to dismiss a chair as "no good" because you only paid $25 for it twenty-five years ago. Use the value charts I provide and you will see how rapidly your values mount up.

Undervaluing your possessions is cheating yourself.

The Other End of the Price Pitfall—When You Overvalue

Sometimes you can overvalue. I've found those who do this usually err by not identifying an object properly, thereby thinking it something other than what it is, or by listening to others toss values around, rather than finding out what things *really* are worth—both pitfalls that I'll show you how to avoid. And most common of all is the error of believing family legends that inflate true value. That is a very polite way of introducing my next chapter, which might be titled *Granny—The Biggest Obstacle to an Accurate Appraisal.*

6

What You Need to Know About Grandmother

Grandmothers had a chance to accumulate possessions many years ago. And when they die, family legend tends to turn these possessions into instant antiques.

If your grandmothers like my grandmothers, were born in the 1880s, or approximately a hundred years ago, gifts they were given *at birth* are, or soon will be, antiques. (According to the United States Director of Customs, an item becomes an antique when it reaches one hundred years of age.) But when was your grandmother actually gathering her personal property?

First there were drawings, the dance cards, and memorabilia she saved as a schoolgirl—her mementos. Then there were her wedding presents, and they gave some *lavish* presents in those days—sets of sterling silver oyster forks and pearl-handled fruit knives. But lavish doesn't mean antique, and even if your grandmother who was born in 1880 was a child bride and married in 1896, her wedding presents, even the ones from Tiffany's, aren't *true* antiques.

After the wedding, the babies—your mother or father, aunts and uncles—began arriving. Families came sooner and were larger in those days. Thus, for the next few years your grandmother probably did not add too many precious possessions to her collection. (However, if she saved a Quaker Oats box, a Theodore Roosevelt campaign button, and the front page story of Lindberg's landing, you can cash in on her pack-rat habits.)

Actually, the time in her life when your grandmother was making her most expensive and tasteful purchases probably was between the 1920s and '50s. And, as my parents keep reminding me, in the middle of those years there was the Great Depression.

Yet the comment I hear so often when I'm making appraisals is, "I know you want to see my—— [lamp, silver, rocking chair, whatever]. It is a very old and valuable antique. It was my grandmother's."

Please don't misunderstand me. I share your love for your grandmother's treasures. In fact, I even expect to be a grandmother myself one day, and I hope my grandchildren will revere me *and* the treasures I am collecting— many made in the 1980s, incidentally. But it will be in the 2080s before my new Chinese panda bear rug is an antique!

Your Grandmother Did Not Live in the Eighteenth Century

Just as the 2080s are a long way into the future, so was the eighteenth century a long time in the past. The chances that you had a grandmother who lived in the eighteenth century are extremely slim.

Let's hypothesize that you were born in 1900 (which would make you almost an antique yourself). If your mother was forty years old when you were born, she would have been born in 1860. If her mother, your grandmother, was forty years old when your mother was born, your grandmother would have been born in 1820. This calculation is stretching each generation from its usual twenty-five-year span to forty years. Furthermore, most women in the nineteenth century had their children in their earlier years— their teens and twenties. Thus the chances of having a grandmother who was born over 180 years ago are extremely rare.

She Might Not Have Danced with Benjamin Franklin, But Don't Count Her Out Yet

Just because your grandmothers or even great-grandmothers lived much later, don't suddenly do a spring cleaning of all their possessions. A whole new field has emerged on the antique horizon: the "collectible."

The next chapter specifically defines the difference between antiques and collectibles. But at this point I want you to realize that some of the items you may have thought were true antiques because they did belong to your grandmother may not be as old as you thought. *However, this does not mean that they are not valuable.* In fact, it will cost you more to replace your grandmother's 1905 Chantilly teaspoon than to replace your great, great-grandmother's 1850 coin-silver teaspoon!

Tales of Long Ago

Another problem with grandmothers is that they pass on family legends. Now, family legends are grand. They bring history to life. They make heroes out of black sheep and silk purses out of sow's ears. Some family legends are accurate. But sadly, many are not. Often inaccuracies that occur in many family legends as they pass from one person to another result from the "number jumble." 1900 becomes 1800. 1876 becomes 1846, 1806, and eventually, 1776.

The truth is, antiques can be dated by the materials used, their style, the marks they bear, and even scientific evidence. But as long as there is sentimental attachment placed on any item, all the *facts* are dismissed as irrelevant, even by rational people.

Two comments I constantly hear from my clients exemplify this irrational thinking.

1. *"This vase* [or whatever] *can't be replaced.* It belonged to my Great-Aunt Maude and it is the *only one* I've ever seen like it."
2. *"This table* [or whatever] *is priceless.* You won't even be able to appraise it. President Fillmore visited our old homeplace and signed an important document on this table."

To these comments I say:

• Any piece can be replaced.
• Everything has its price.

Born Yesterday

Before you burn this book for its heretical content (you might save it—it will be an antique one day), let me confess that I have made statements like those about my own possessions. To me, what I have is more precious than what you have, just as your treasures are more precious to you than mine are. This is human nature and thank goodness for it.

It is family sentiment that preserves many of our antiques for the next generation. Antiques are not born old. They were all new at one time. But family pride and sentiment—*emotional attachment to material things*—have preserved the craftsmanship and styles of an earlier time. These heirlooms have now passed into your hands. You want to keep them and pass them on to the next generation, and so you should. This is commendable and gives each generation a knowledge of an earlier life-style and age. This is how we have learned about our civilization, our background, our roots.

The Truth About Replacement

As for antiques being irreplaceable, this simply is not true. A walk through any antiques mall or down New York's Second Avenue turns up literally thousands of duplicates. Granted, some items are one-of-a-kind. A sampler stitched by a schoolgirl, custom-made jewelry, an initialed dower chest—these were all individualized by the person who made them. But so is your home, once you live in it and give it your special touch. Yet, if you have to, you can and do find another home to take its place for shelter and protection.

The Table, President Fillmore, and Provenance

Often I am told that an item is priceless or at least extremely valuable because it has had some association with a famous person. The fancy word commonly used in the antiques world to describe this situation even *sounds* expensive—"provenance."

Provenance simply means the source or origin, or who owned the piece at one time. Provenance is also established when a piece is displayed in a museum or sold at auction. Provenance is a word that rolls off museum curators' tongues and is frequently used in describing pieces sold at Sotheby's and Christie's.

But provenance does not always mean profit. In fact, "provenance" can be compared to "George Washington Slept Here." You can hang the sign anywhere, but without documentation it doesn't mean much. Every piece you own has a provenance. Its provenance may begin with you, or it may go back in your family, or someone else's family, for several generations. The only time you can "cash in" on provenance, or prior ownership, is when the owner himself was of substantial note and when there is documentation.

Even when provenance is established, *the value of the piece ultimately lies in its own merit.* In other words, how good the piece itself is. Take as an example my client who owns a collection of German crinoline figurines. She is an international entertainer. Her name evokes memories of movies and television to three generations. But because her figurines are neither terribly old nor rare, their value is limited. Granted, if they were sold as her property, the figurines would find an eager buyer who would pay more money for them because they were hers. However, they would only sell for what they are . . . German crinoline figurines.

On the other hand, another of my clients has an extremely rare sterling silver cake basket made in London by Paul de Lamarie in 1742. The last such basket, which sold at Sotheby's, brought $85,000. My client is not famous. But if his cake basket were sold at auction right now, it would fetch upward of $90,000. *Quality* is the ultimate determinant in value.

So, before you dash out and declare your piece as one-of-a-kind, dating from the eighteenth century and touched by George Washington, look at the facts and the dates. See if they match. Remember that, in the end, it is not who touched or even owned a piece, but what the piece is and how well it was made that determine its value.

Daniel Webster's Pewter Goblet—Made in Sweden

The stories of mistaken family legends could be a book in itself. I remember in particular such impossible situations as Daniel Webster's pewter goblet, which was marked on the bottom, "Made in Sweden," which identified the piece as dating after 1914 (Daniel Webster died in 1852).

Then there was the wicker rocking chair, which the owner insisted was at least 350 years old since it had come over on the *Mayflower*. (Wicker rocking chairs like his were unknown in 1621—this one dated from the 1870s.)

My point is not to discourage you, but to educate you. The quality of a piece speaks for itself. Enjoy the family stories and pass them on. But unless there is documentation—specific dates of marriage, birth, or death, which coincide with the family story, or better yet, actual inventories or bills of sale, take the stories with a grain of salt. You must even be cautious about handwritten hearsay stories which could have been jumbled fifty, one hundred, or even more years before they actually were written down.

From my experience in other people's homes I have my own rule of thumb, which I pass on to my clients.

> Expect to find that the piece *you* consider most valuable may have only minimum monetary value. And be prepared to learn that a piece that you probably would give to the first friend who asked for it may be very valuable indeed.

7

The Language—Knowing What to Call What You're Looking At

The Antique

Before you begin tackling the second group of your property there is a matter of terminology or vocabulary that must be cleared up. First of all—what is an antique?

This elementary question is the most debated question in the antiques world today! It seems ironic that although everyone eagerly talks about "antiques," few people can agree on what an antique is. In fact, there are almost as many answers to this question as there are people giving answers.

The dictionary defines an antique as something old, not modern. But this over-simplistic definition does not tell us where modern stops and old begins. Basically, the question is, *When, in numerical years, does an item become an antique?* The two most widely accepted answers to this question are the "legal" definition and the "connoisseur's" definition.

Legally Speaking

As noted, an antique must have been made "prior to one hundred years before the date of entry," according to the U.S. Customs. Since antiques are international in origin, this legal definition is the one generally accepted by the public at large. The definition is a "sliding" rule which implies that an item made in 1875 became an antique in 1975 and that an item made in 1890 must wait until 1990 to become an antique. There is no consideration given to quality, style, craftsmanship, or any intrinsic characteristic the piece might have which would make it an exception to this one hundred-year rule.

Artistically Speaking

Quality plus age are considerations to the connoisseur. Museum curators, elite dealers, students, writers, and scholars on the subject of antiques generally agree that an antique is a piece made *prior* to 1820, or possibly at the latest, 1830. This first part of the nineteenth century, they reason, saw the end of fine handcrafted workmanship, which is synonymous with antiques.

By the 1820s and 1830s, America and other industrially developed countries of the world had power-driven tools, which meant consumer goods could be mass-produced. In addition, the steamboat, which Robert Fulton had invented in 1807, became the means to transport factory-made products along America's inland waterways. The Baltimore and Ohio opened its first railroad route in 1830, and the transcontinental railroad was completed in 1869. Now factory products—Hitchcock chairs, coin silver flatware, and Sandwich pattern glass could be sent from New England via train or boat to Kentucky, Florida, Canada, or California.

Eventually, the local craftsman began to fade from the scene. Once the individually crafted piece was replaced by the manufactured or mass-produced piece, the craftsman's art—hand-carved furniture, hand-beaten silver, hand-etched and blown glass—also faded away.

Now, this is not to say that all craftsmanship "died" on March 4, 1820, or April 19, 1830. Machine production is known to have existed in the metropolitan areas—New York and Boston for example—in the early 1800s, and many fine craftsmen continued creating wonderful handmade pieces in the 1880s, just as they still do today. However, by 1830, manufactured goods were plentiful and widely distributed.

Once the railroad was laid, commerce became profitable. Retail stores cropped up on main streets and crossroads alike. The people who could afford the new and fashionable *demanded* and *bought* the latest up-to-date mass-produced articles—furniture, and household decorations, as well as hats, boots, and dresses.

To the connoisseur, an antique is a piece distinguished by its hand-crafted uniqueness and fine quality, made before 1820 or 1830. Thus, at least forty or fifty years separate an "antique," as defined by the connoisseur, from an "antique" as defined by the law. Which definition you are going to accept and use is your choice.

The Right Age

Unfortunately, however, the confusion over antiques does not stop here. To further complicate matters there are other subheadings that you must understand if you are going to know what you already own and if you are to become a more knowledgeable buyer or investor in antiques.

To see what this confusion is and how it arose, let's look at one of the most popular of all antiques, the elegant and graceful Queen Anne chair.

The Real Thing

Queen Anne chairs became the fashion in England roughly between 1700 and 1730 and were named after the reigning monarch of the time. The Queen Anne chair is characterized by its slender vase-shaped back splat, gracefully curved cabriole leg, and dainty slipper foot. The style quickly crossed the ocean to America, and by 1720 Queen Anne chairs were made by American craftsmen, who continued to make them until the 1750s, when the Chippendale style became more fashionable.

It is appropriate here to note that during the eighteenth and early nineteenth centuries, styles that started in England eventually came to America, but there is generally about a twenty-year lapse in time between the first appearance of the styles in the two countries.

But back to the Queen Anne chair. Between 1700 and 1750, or roughly fifty years, these chairs were handmade by the eighteenth-century craftsmen in England and America. The Queen Anne chairs made at this time are known as *Period Queen Anne Chairs*. The word "period," when used in speaking of antiques, means *made at the original time of the fashion*. These chairs made between 1700 and 1750 are the true, undebatable Queen Anne chairs, which, by any definition, are antiques.

The Copy of the Real Thing Which Can Be a "Legal" Antique

Now, furniture fashions have cycles, just as the length of hemlines, the width of men's ties, and the height of women's heels have cycles. It is said that clothing styles go in seven-year cycles. Fashions in furniture styles are said to go in one hundred-year cycles. So, turn the calendar from 1750 to 1850, and you find Queen Anne chairs being made again. (Actually they were made this time in reaction to the elaborate and fussy Victorian style.) But this time there are certain changes.

To begin with, the chairs are now mass-produced with the help of power-driven tools in factories. Handmade nails are replaced by machine-cut nails. Hand-planed boards are replaced by circular sawn boards. Nineteenth-century liberties are taken with the original eighteenth-century designs. In other words, one hundred years after the original Queen Anne chairs were made, other chairs are made *in the Queen Anne Style,* but with differences which had evolved during the one-hundred-year time lapse.

But wait—1850? Why, if you agree with the legal definition of "antique" (an item over one hundred years old), these 1850 adaptations of the 1750 *Period* Queen Anne chairs are now also antiques. And so are those Queen

Anne style chairs made in 1860, 1870, and 1880. To make the distinction between antique *period chairs* and antique adaptations, the term *style* is used. Thus Queen Anne chairs made one hundred or more years after the Queen Anne period are properly called Queen Anne *style* chairs, as opposed to Queen Anne *period* chairs.

The Modern Copy of the Real Thing—The Reproduction

Now, jump yet another one hundred years ahead to 1950. Queen Anne chairs are still being made. Only this time they cannot possibly be called antique. The correct term for currently manufactured pieces that are copied from older period antiques is "reproduction." Generally, a distinction between a current or recent reproduction, one made in the 1950s up to the present, and an earlier reproduction, say one made in 1900 or even 1930, is indicated by the use of "old" before the word "reproduction."

These are the same "old reproductions" that I discussed in Chapter 3— the Wallace Nutting, Margolis, and Charack pieces, to name only a few, which are also showing up in antiques shops and auction houses and which are commanding very respectable prices today.

The Unreal Thing—The Fake

Up to this point I have not used the term "fake." Actually a fake is a piece made intentionally to deceive the public. The perfect example of a fake is the famous Brewster chair that was carefully and painstakingly created with the intent to deceive the public. This chair, which was typical of "Pilgrim" furniture, was proclaimed as a Massachusetts chair dating from Pilgrim times and bought by the Henry Ford Museum for $9,000. Later investigation revealed that, in reality, the chair was a fake made in 1969. There are not as many true *fakes* on the antiques market today (with the exception of art) as there are old reproductions and antique-style pieces (not period pieces, remember), which the dealers or auctioneers *misinterpret* or *misname* "period pieces." You will learn about periods, reproductions, and fakes in the chapters that deal with the specific categories of personal property. But for now, get your vocabulary down.

- *Period*—the term used to denote that a piece was made during the original time frame of the design.
- *Style*—the term used to denote that a piece is in the fashion or nature of an earlier period, but made at a later time.
- *Reproduction*—the term used to denote that a piece was made in recent years but copied from an earlier design.
- *Fake*—an item intentionally made to deceive the public into thinking it was made at an earlier time.

The Collectibles

But what about those pieces made in the 1890s or even 1930s, which are not copies of any earlier style and which are selling for thousands of dollars today? We have all read about Tiffany lamps selling for $150,000 and art glass from the 1920s bringing thousands of dollars at auction. These fine works of art, which meet the connoisseur's requirement of excellent craftsmanship, still fall short of even the legal definition of an antique.

There is a catch-all phrase that covers items made later than 1881 that are actively being bought and collected: "collectibles." Literally everything with any *historical* or *investment* interest these days is classified as a "collectible." Tiffany glass is collectible. So is barbed wire. Mickey Mouse watches are a collectible and so are Cartier gems. The two characteristics all collectibles have in common are: (1) there are no more being made (except for the new fakes, and there's plenty to say about that later), and (2) people are collecting them.

But why, many people ask, are collectors buying objects only twenty to seventy years old when they could be buying older antique pieces? The major reasons are design and nostalgia.

Design

Design is the distinguishing characteristic of those "collectible" items from the 1890s through the 1930s. Tiffany glass, Art Deco furniture, Louis Icart prints, Art Nouveau jewelry were all products of a distinct time in our civilization and culture. The tastes of this era were reflected in the designs of its "material culture"—from architecture to household furnishings.

It is impossible to mistake the characteristics of this time. When you see a piece of Art Nouveau jewelry—a brooch depicting a fully opened iris or lily with graceful, curved petals, you know immediately that the pin was made in the 1880s or 1900s. At no other time in history was a design that looks like that created.

Likewise, when you see an Art Deco chest of drawers you know it dates from the 1920s or 1930s. Nothing that looked like that was made in the 1860s or 1790s. Descriptions of these styles appear in Chapter 12.

By the time the vogue for these collectibles erupted, these pieces were becoming respectably old and actually fairly hard to find. Thus, the unique design of these pieces, plus their new, respectable age led to their appearance in the auction houses and antiques shops alongside other earlier pieces.

Nostalgia

But what about the Mickey Mouse watches and glass telephone insulators, the early Barbie Dolls and 1950 movie posters? These too are collectibles, and while they may not bring thousands of dollars, collectors are certainly willing to pay dearly for them. Why have they caught on?

I believe the major reason is nostalgia. In a world where permanence is becoming an obsolete word and a computer model is outdated a month after it is introduced, we yearn to hold onto the past.

The result? People are buying these collectibles. Buyers create a market. Once the market is established and a fad becomes popular, prices go up.

So whether you choose to keep, sell, or discard your, your mother's or even your grandmother's collectibles, you should know that the public's demand for these items has established a market and these items have value.

In your home you probably have many of these collectibles that you may once have overlooked but should now include in your inventory.

ℰ 8 ℛ

When Age
Isn't Enough

Now you know and understand some of the terminology of personal property, let's look at one last "myth" that needs some clearing up.

Antique = Quality = Value

To many people anything old, whether period piece or collectible, simply because it is *old* suggests quality, and quality equals value. Period pieces, old reproductions, collectibles, even this year's Christmas gifts all have value. And, I can assure you, that value mounts up rapidly if you lose your personal property and have to replace those items. The trouble is, there is so much talk about antiques being valuable today that people *assume* that antiques are more valuable than new items. This is not necessarily true. Age alone does not determine the value of any piece, whether antique or new.

Quality, or Why Hers May Be Better Than Mine

"Quality" is a difficult word to define because it has so many connotations. To some people, quality means "expensive." In reality, quality means, quite simply, a particular characteristic. Quality can mean good or bad. We speak of good qualities and bad qualities. But of course, when we speak of antiques of quality we are only speaking of the good.

Confusing Quality and Taste

When you first look at an item you see the total object—a chair, a picture, a highboy, a fork, a spoon. Then you begin to break the piece down into its component parts—the design, the proportions, the materials used to make the piece, the finish on the piece, etc. Actually, each individual aspect of the piece has its own quality.

Take a simple one-drawer nightstand, for example. It can be of fine design but made of poor materials. Or the finish can be excellent, but the piece can be squatty and poorly proportioned.

There are also degrees of quality within each classification of our personal property. Take, for example, a chest of drawers and a drop leaf table. The two pieces of furniture immediately produce different mental images. Most people hearing "drop leaf table" think of a simple table with four legs and two drop leaves.

On the other hand, a "chest of drawers" suggests a much larger piece, one that is more expensive.

In reality, a fine mahogany drop-leaf table can be of superior quality to a golden oak chest of drawers with applied machine-cut decoration. Quality in personal property is primarily determined by materials used, artistic design, and craftsmanship. Immense variations in quality exist in each category of personal property—furniture, silver, paintings, china, rugs, etc.

There are silverplated pieces that are more valuable than the same item made of sterling silver. A fine-crafted piece of pottery can be better in quality than an inferior piece of bone china. A fine machine-made rug can be of superior quality to a crudely handmade Oriental rug.

The Best and the Worst

You can learn to identify variations in quality by studying the two extremes, the best and the worst. You must remember that the best is the ideal, and often unobtainable. The best may already be in the museum. Or it may bring hundreds of thousands of dollars at auction. Or the best may simply not be to your liking. Yet, by studying the best you will learn what to look for in pieces that you can afford so you can make the best purchase possible.

It is easy to find pictures of the best. Most antiques books are full of museum-quality pieces. It is not so easy to actually *study* the finest pieces because museums do not want their pieces handled. In fact, they are in museums in order to preserve them from everyday wear and tear.

Speak Up

The best places to seriously study the varying quality of antiques are antiques shops and auction houses. In both places you should be able to wander about freely and closely examine the pieces you are interested in. But even more important, both places are learning grounds where you can *ask questions.* Do not be afraid to ask, "Why is this piece better than that one?" "Can you show me how this piece is constructed?" "Are there any replaced or repaired parts?" Or, the most general question of all, "Please tell me about this piece."

Don't be surprised if sometimes you receive an "I don't know" for an answer. Remember, no one can be an expert in all fields. It is not uncommon to hear antiques dealers discussing points that they have learned from their collector-customers. In fact, you should beware of the glib expert who has an answer for everything.

Not long ago I was in an antiques shop where I overheard another customer ask the salesclerk about an English writing desk that had a leather top and drawers that flanked the kneehole opening (the type you see in executive offices).

The desk was in perfect condition, the leather gleaming, the brasses polished, and the mahogany shining.

"About how old is this desk?" the customer asked.

"1820," was the specific reply.

"This leather certainly is in fine condition for a 160-year-old piece," the customer observed.

"Oh, that has been added recently. But it is hand-tooled English leather and appropriate to the piece," the clerk explained.

"And the wood is so beautiful. You don't expect to see a 160-year-old piece in this perfect condition."

"Oh, but you take care of pieces like this. There's no reason for it to be in other than perfect condition." (In my mind's eye I saw the weekly cleaning service in the executive's office banging the vacuum cleaner into the corners of the desk.)

The customer noted, "These look like new brasses," and started to open the drawers to further inspect the piece.

"Yes, most antiques have had their original brasses replaced. Brasses break and wear out over the years from constant use. No one considers a set of new brasses to be important as long as they are in the appropriate style." Just then the clerk was called away by another customer.

The customer looked further, then glanced up at his wife, "I wonder what his answer is going to be when I ask him about the plywood drawer bottoms?"

Buy the Best Quality You Can Afford

Ask questions, but use your own common sense, and remember, the ultimate value of a piece will show a relationship to its quality. Granted, the world's finest nineteenth-century pine cottage chest will never compare with a medium-quality eighteenth-century mahogany Chippendale chest of drawers when it comes to cost. But the value of a mediocre cottage chest is certainly less than the value of a fine cottage chest. This is why potential antiques investors are always told, "Buy the finest-quality piece that you can afford." If you can't afford the eighteenth-century mahogany chest but can afford the nineteenth-century pine one, then buy the very best nineteenth-century pine chest you can find.

The Quality of New Items

To learn about currently manufactured products, visit retail stores that carry a range of lines. Pick out an item like a bedroom set that is available in two price ranges, say medium and high. Then ask the salesperson a simple but demanding question, "Why is this bedroom set more expensive than that one?"

You should then learn about the material used in construction, the important but unseen parts (refer back to Chapter 3), and the finish the company uses. From the explanation you should learn what quality you can expect to find in currently manufactured items.

The same principles that apply to furniture apply to all decorative personal property. A knowledgeable salesperson can show you the difference in the quality of china, diamonds, rugs, lamps, etc.

You Can Learn to Judge Quality

Judging quality is difficult to the novice who has never paid close attention to his or her personal property. But once you begin to examine a piece closely and to make comparisons, you will find that you too can develop a sixth sense for distinguishing quality. You may begin looking without even knowing what you are looking for, but once you see the difference for the first time, a lasting impression will be made, which you will remember. This is how experts learn.

Let me assure you that museum curators are not born knowing why Rembrandt paintings are superior to other Dutch paintings of the sixteenth century. Curators study, ask questions, and observe.

Nor did the eighteenth-century furniture maker create a superior Chippendale chair the first time he tried. He had to learn about his materials, his tools, and discover how he could adapt the idea in his mind to his medium.

So you too, by reading, asking questions, observing, touching, comparing, and by making judgments both good and bad, can grow to learn the differences between poor quality and superior quality.

Condition—The Hard Facts

"This has to be valuable," I am told as I am handed a broken plate. "It's an antique, you know."

The only value a broken plate has, no matter how old it is, is its value as a study piece. If the plate was excavated at an historical site and has archeological importance, then yes, the plate is valuable—but as an artifact, not as an antique.

The same is true of the eighteenth-century silver porringer that has been extensively mended or altered. And what good is a country rocking chair, no matter who sat in it, if the splats are broken and split, one rocker is gone, and the other is splintered? Condition is of primary importance in determining value. The more damage there is, the lower the value.

First, remember that chances are, somewhere, there are other items just like the plate, the porringer, or the rocker, which are *not* broken, mended, or splintered. *They* have value.

Second, any object in bad condition is going to cost a lot to be put into repaired condition. Labor is expensive and hard to find these days. Once the broken piece is repaired, you are still going to have a repaired piece.

When You Can Make Poor Condition "Pay"

There are times, though, when you can buy a piece in "as is" condition, have it repaired at minimum cost, and end up with something worth more than your total investment. This is particularly true if you have a craft yourself and you can avoid the expense of paying someone else to repair a piece. But in order to come out with a repaired or refinished piece worth more than your total investment of cash and time, you need to know (1) how much the repair is going to cost (money and time), and (2) how much it would cost to buy a comparable piece *in good condition*. Only if there is *considerable* difference between these two totals is the item in poor condition a worthwhile purchase.

In making such a decision, if you can restore or repair the piece inexpensively for your own use, then do it. *But do not think that you can restore or repair a piece and come out with an investment-quality antique.*

Replacements

One question that is repeatedly asked is, "How much do changes affect the value of antique furniture?" To know this you must know what *kind* of change occurred.

Some major changes in furniture that *always* decrease value are:

Replacement of the original headboard and/or footboard of a bed (this has often been done to enlarge the bed to double or king size or to make two beds out of one.)

Replacement of chair legs (sometimes just the feet will have been replaced—either replacement is major).

Replacement of drawer fronts on chests, desks, and secretaries.

New doors hung on corner cupboards, secretaries, or linen presses (sometimes glass will have been replaced with wooden panels or vice versa).

Replacement of the original painted glass section (eglomise) in Federal mirrors and shelf clocks.

Replacement of leaves or the entire top on tables.

Alterations

In addition to replacement parts, there are also major alterations that can greatly devalue a piece. The excessive refinishing of any piece is always damaging, as is the removal of hand-planed or hand-crafted marks. It seems hard to believe that anyone would make these changes, but I have seen pieces that have been made to look "like new" by owners who did not want their friends to think they had to live with "old things!"

Other alterations you must also beware of are the "improvements" made on pieces of furniture in an attempt to make them appear to be "better," "fancier," or "more expensive." It takes a sophisticated eye to detect many of these improvements, so if you suspect that a piece has been altered you may wish to consult an expert. However, you should know that common improvements found on antiques today include:

Later carving of chair backs, legs, and arms.

Adding of inlay to any case piece—desks, secretaries, chests, breakfronts, sideboards, Pembroke and dining room tables, etc.

Reshaping of tops of tables, aprons of highboys and lowboys, cornices of secretaries, corner cupboards, pewter cupboards, etc.

Embellishment of desk and secretary interiors.

Just remember, most legs and arms can be carved, inlay can be added to most large pieces, and top surfaces often can be reshaped.

When Imperfect Condition and Repairs Are Worth Considering

Of course you may find a truly genuinely rare antique in poor condition, or that has had old repairs, that you may still wish to purchase. In the case of the rare piece that is in poor condition, the reason for buying it may simply be to preserve it as an artifact from the past. This goes back to my point about the value of the piece lying in its historical purpose.

But, more often, you will come upon a good-quality item that has respectable "old" repairs. Some such pieces are still very expensive. At this point you will want to find out (1) how much the repair depreciates the value of the piece, and (2) once again, what a comparable piece in pristine condition would cost.

For example, you may find a lowboy that is basically in its original condition—with the exception of having a new top. However, since the top was added seventy-five or one hundred years ago it may now almost be an antique. What you will learn from consulting an expert or from your own research is:

1. The replaced top is considered a major repair.
2. The value of the piece with new top is $5,000 to $6,000.
3. The value of a pristine piece of comparable quality, design, and age is $12,000 to $18,000.

With this information, you can make a sensible judgment about your choices.

Fashion

There is one final factor you should be aware of that will affect the value of your personal property—fashion. This fickle factor changes as regularly as the seasons.

We are familiar with the effect fashion has on our wardrobes as we discard last season's "fashionable" mistakes. We are even aware of the effect of fashion on our decorating habits as we change our ivory walls to magenta and replace our beige wall-to-wall carpeting with colorful geometric Oriental rugs. We realize when we discard the Spanish Provincial bedroom set for an Early American type pencil-post bed and Windsor style chair that fashion is expensive. But how many of us realize that *antiques* have distinct fashions that affect their value on the marketplace?

Yesterday's Passion

Years ago when I was working in an antiques shop, the single most requested item was an English sideboard. Everyone, it seemed, wanted a sideboard on which to place a silver service or Oriental bowl, flanked by silver candelabra or brass candlesticks. Naturally, when a sideboard sold, it was replaced with another sideboard, which always was more expensive than its predecessor. I watched the cost of sideboards creep up slowly from $1,500 to $2,500 to $3,500. Meanwhile, only occasionally would a lone customer come in looking for a mahogany corner cupboard. At the time they were selling for around $900 to $1,000.

Today, you can still buy an English sideboard comparable to the ones that were selling between $3,000 and $3,500 for $3,500 to $4,000. But corner cupboards have become the "hot" item and they are now selling for $3,000 to $4,000. Why has one remained basically the same and the other taken such a jump? Fashion. Supply and demand.

> When you can identify a particular item or type or period that is
> currently out of vogue, buy it at a low or stable price, and hold it
> until it becomes fashionable once again, you have identified the
> true "investment" antique.

What's in Fashion and What's out of Fashion

Some areas that were temporarily out of vogue but have made impressive,
sometimes even spectacular, comebacks are turn-of-the-century romantic
paintings, fine English furniture, decorative Oriental accessories from the
nineteenth century, and American nineteenth-century primitive furniture
and accessories.

On the other hand, nineteenth-century pressed glass, which was once
coveted by every antiques collector, has not been in vogue for twenty to
twenty-five years now. Tapestries and Medieval (or Medieval style) pieces
are in a current slump, though more interest is being shown in this area of
late. Luster ware is nowhere near as widely collected as it was in the first part
of the twentieth century. And whatever happened to the Pop Art movement of the 1960s? Wait a few years and all of these now passé items will
once again be the talk of the antiques and auction worlds.

Fashions, Antique Dealers, and Wheels

Geographic fashions also affect the value of antiques. Generally, the population of an area wants what its earliest settlers had. The older a geographic
area's history, the earlier the region's taste in antiques.

For example, New England antiques lovers want eighteenth-century
American pieces; Midwesterners prefer nineteenth-century or Victorian antiques.

When the buying public of an area wants early pieces—eighteenth-century Queen Anne, Chippendale, and Federal antiques, the later
pieces—nineteenth-century Empire and Victorian antiques—go underpriced and unpurchased. Yet these "rejects" are highly desirable in other
sections of the country.

The opposite is also true. Recently, a Texas dealer, who now lives in Connecticut, told me she buys her "early" antiques in Texas where they are less
expensive than they are in the Northeast. But, she added, she takes nineteenth-century porcelain pieces that she buys inexpensively in Connecticut
to Texas.

Smart dealers capitalize on these regional fashions. Southern and Mid-
western dealers buy Victorian pieces in New England at low prices and
transport them to Alabama, Texas, Ohio, and Wisconsin, where they sell at
high prices.

Home Sweet Home

At the same time, regional antiques and collectibles have their highest value in that specific region. The coin silver spoon made in Charleston, S.C., may be worth $300 there, but will sell in Boston for $20 or $30, the price of any coin silver spoon.

A log cabin quilt made and signed by a Wisconsin pioneer has much more value if sold and kept in Wisconsin than it ever would have in New York. Even a Philadelphia Chippendale chair that can find a home in Stuttgart, Tokyo, or Rio will bring a higher price when sold in the Philadelphia region.

How Fashions Are Started . . . and Finished

Fashions and fads in the antiques world are usually created by a series of coinciding events. First, there is a large show or exhibit or a particular collection or category of art objects at a major museum or restoration. For example, there might be a showing of silver snuff boxes or an exhibit of Eastlake furniture. Articles and books on the subject suddenly begin appearing. Next, magazines start running features about these objects.

As a result, the public begins going into shops and asking, "Have you any silver snuff boxes?" or, "I'm looking for an Eastlake chest." By now, someone who just happened to have a collection of silver snuff boxes or a houseful of Eastlake furniture, decides to sell these items at auction. Record prices and headlines follow, naturally, and by now a bull market has been created.

Until . . . the marketplace suddenly becomes saturated with either the real things (dragged out of storage), or reproductions, imitations, and sometimes fakes. At this point, the fashion is no longer fashionable and it fades away, or goes back into storage. . . .

Until . . . fifty or one hundred years later, when another generation rediscovers silver snuff boxes and Eastlake furniture.

Quality + Condition + Fashion + Age = Value

Learn to identify *quality* in your personal property. When you can distinguish it you will also be a wiser shopper and better investor in personal property.

Next, look carefully at the *condition* of your property before listing it on your inventory. Mint condition in an antique raises its value. You will also need to know the condition of your property in order to submit a fair insurance claim if the need ever arises.

Finally, all old things are not equally desirable at all times. But every year every piece gets older, and closer to being rediscovered . . . again.

9

Property Categories
and How to Use Them
to Save Time

If you will take my advice in Chapter 4 and make a preliminary survey of your property, dividing it into the pieces you know about and those you do not know about, you will have taken the first big step in avoiding unnecessary frustrations and wasted time.

Next, divide your property into the following four major categories, which cover the vast majority of personal property:

- Silver
- China and crystal
- Furniture
- Accessories and bric-a-brac

You may begin your appraisal with any one category and do the rest in any order. But keep to the categories.

I have chosen to begin with silver, since it is so frequently stolen today and has such a high cumulative value. If you have a lot of silver, it may also take you the longest time to inventory it.

The china and crystal category covers sets and groups of china and crystal including serving pieces, pressed and cut glass. Individual decorative items fit in the accessories and bric-a-brac category.

Furniture is a large and important category, but you can cover it quickly because, unlike crystal or silver, you will not have lots of "pieces" to count.

Accessories and bric-a-brac are saved until the end. These pieces generally are less valuable when viewed one at a time, but the final replacement figure for these "accent" pieces can be staggering.

"But why can't I just start in one room and list everything in that room in all categories and then move on to the next?" I am often asked.

You can. But do you always leave everything in exactly the same spot? Even museums change the pictures around. A good inventory is best made when it divides property into major categories. If you list your property with your insurance agent you will learn that insurance companies have one rate for silver and another rate for furniture. If you want to insure crystal and porcelain against breakage there is yet another rate. By organizing the categories ahead of time you will better know what kind of insurance you need.

Also, by using categories you learn how much of a particular item you have. For example, if you have your silver scattered throughout the house, from the dining room and kitchen to the bedrooms and living room, with some stored in the attic, you probably have a great deal more silver than you thought.

Movers and packers who specialize in shipping antiques always place items in categories. Crystal is packed together. Pictures are crated together. Figurines are wrapped individually and sealed in one box. This allows for better accounting at the end and for safer passage en route.

A categorical listing is also easier to work with when listing values. It is easier to "stay in gear" and work in one category than to shift from the cost of a silverplated round tray to a set of crystal liqueur glasses, to a den sofa, to your fireplace tools, back to a single German beer mug, and then on to the sofa table.

Accompanying each of the category chapters that follow are value charts to assist you. The value charts located at the end of each category are intended to be used as a *gauge* by which you can *approximate* the value of your personal property. We know that if a manufacturer makes twenty-five lines, each line will have a different price. Once the line is in the retail store, the store owner or manager makes the final decision as to what price to sell each piece for. If all prices were the same, there would be no reason to shop around for the good buy.

But because you have neither the time nor the resources to search out all the current prices for your personal property, I have compiled value guides to assist you in determining the *estimated* worth of your household furnishings. These value charts should be used with the understanding that the prices are compiled by combining several price lists of comparable quality. In no instance are the prices from one company's line used alone. The values given are replacement prices for products currently in production. In some instances additional charts are provided, that are relevant to some antique and collectible items. However, because antiques values fluctuate so widely, depending on condition, alterations, quality, location, and the knowledge and whims of each individual dealer, antiques values usually are omitted.

If you begin amassing total values that far exceed your expectations or current insurance you may wish to call in a professional appraiser. (Information on appraisers is found in Chapter 22.) Remember that these prices are *average* values for general *types* of personal property and are not to be considered the specific value, down to the last dollar, of a particular chair, china pattern, or sterling silver water pitcher.

I have not written another antiques price guide to add to the ever growing list, but I have included a short chapter (Chapter 23) on price guides.

🐚 10 🐚

Silver, Sterling, and Silverplate—All That Glitters Is Not Gold

Because retail silver prices fluctuate with the cost of silver bullion, prices quoted today may change tomorrow. However, because silver is a precious metal, it will always hold its relative value, even though its cash value will vary, depending on world economic conditions.

Bullion value bears no relation to the value of true antique silver. There is no relationship between the value of an eighteenth-century cake basket worth $50,000 and the cost of one troy ounce of silver mined yesterday.

Two basic types of silver are found in most homes, sterling and silverplate. Both are valuable, and a few silver objects can easily mount into thousands of dollars if it becomes necessary to replace them. If you don't know about your silver, you may let a wonderful treasure slip through your fingers or even out the door and never know the difference. This almost happened to a client of mine a few years ago.

When Cartier Was Upstaged by a Little Teapot

I was busily at work in her dining room, examining the silver, while she gathered up other silver pieces from around the house and brought them to me.

Suddenly she appeared at the dining room door and in a trembling voice exclaimed, "The cigarette box and teapot are gone!"

This has happened to me so often that my reaction is always the same. "No, you just don't remember where you've put them."

"Not this time," she insisted. "They were right there two days ago because I polished them. I didn't want you to see what a terrible housekeeper I am!"

(What no one realizes is what a terrible housekeeper I am. I can't be in your house and keep my home spotless too.)

None of my assurances convinced her that her pieces might be around. It seems she was also having some remodeling done.

"Any one of the workmen could have picked them up," she insisted.

"Well, if they're gone, let's get a good description of them so you can call the insurance company," I said.

"The little teapot didn't amount to much. Oh, it had sentimental value. My grandmother gave it to me [I never would have guessed!] ... but I know you can't put a price on sentiment. [How I wish all my clients knew that.] It's just a silverplate probably—all I can do is tell you what it looked like."

"But," she continued, "the cigarette box is quite valuable. It came from Cartier and had all our groomsmen's signatures on it. My husband is going to die!"

"Go ahead and call your insurance company. Tell them what's missing. But tell them you want to wait a couple of weeks before turning in a value, just to give the silver time to show up," I advised.

Sure enough, only a few days later they appeared—in her two-year-old's toy box, of all places—both filled with Lego blocks and coated with Play Doh.

The cigarette box was exactly what she had said—a current Cartier piece costing, at that time, about $250.

And the little teapot ... that little silverplated gift from Grandmother was a sterling silver Queen Anne pot, made in 1697 in London and the earliest piece of hollow ware I have ever seen in a private home ... with a value exceeding $5,000.

What You Need to Know About Silver

The following sections explain the marks found on silver so you may correctly identify your silver on your inventory.

American Sterling and Coin Silver

Sterling silver pieces are made of 925/1000 parts pure silver combined with 75/1000 parts of other metal, usually copper, added to make the silver durable and pliable. Sterling silver is easily detected when the words "sterling silver" are marked on the piece. At other times, the numbers 925 or 925/1000 will be present on sterling silver. By about 1860, sterling silver became the American standard used in "solid" silver (as opposed to silverplated) items, and most pieces dating after 1860 are clearly marked "sterling."

American sterling silver hallmarks most frequently found:

Alvin

Dominick & Haff

Durgin

R. Blackinton

International

Gorham

Manchester

S.Kirk & Son Inc.
Samuel Kirk & Son

LUNT
Lunt

Graff, Washbourne & Dunn

Reed & Barton

Schofield Company

Rogers, Lunt & Bowlen

TIFFANY & C<u>o</u>.
MAKERS
Tiffany

Frank Smith Silver Company

Stieff Company

Towle

Weidlich

Wallace

Frank M. Whiting

Whiting

Before that time, "solid" silver pieces only contained 900/1000 parts of pure silver, with 100/1000 parts of other metals. This silver was known as coin silver and was often marked as "coin," "pure coin," "standard," "premium," or "dollar." Sometimes the letters C or D were used. Just as often, coin silver was marked with only the maker's name, and sometimes there was no mark at all.

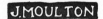

American coin silver dates from early colonial days. Seventeenth- and eighteenth-century coin silver was usually marked only with the maker's initials, last name, or first initial and last name.

Later, in the nineteenth century, complete company names were used and sometimes even locations were given.

Another common practice was to mark coin silver with "pseudo hallmarks." These marks implied that American silver was as fine as English silver, which was clearly hallmarked. (English marks are discussed further on in this chapter.)

PSEUDO-HALLMARKS

Because coin silver is not always clearly marked *coin* but may be
- unmarked
- marked C, D, standard, premium, or dollar
- marked only with initials or with a name, or
- marked with pseudo hallmarks,

it is often overlooked and even discarded as plated silver.

Better Than Sterling

I have picked coin silver spoons out of discarded shoe boxes filled with kitchen throw-aways. In fact, there are times when I almost have to force my clients to show me a piece I *know* is coin silver but which they think is silverplated.

One day I was working through the stacks of sterling silver on my client's dining room table when I spied a coin silver baby cup at the end of the table. The temptation was to jump ahead and look at the cup then, but I decided to save the best until last.

Just as I was coming to the cup, the owner walked into the room.

"Don't bother with that," she said, "it's only plated. I didn't even mean for it to be out here."

I insisted that I had to see the cup. Only when I told her I thought it was very valuable would she let me examine it.

And indeed it was. The cup was coin silver, made by an important regional silversmith in the 1840s, and is now housed in a museum for others to see and learn from, and insured for over $3,000. But because the cup was not marked sterling, the owner thought it was "nothing." The truth is, if the cup *had* been marked "sterling," it would have had only one tenth the value.

English Sterling

English sterling silver is collected by antiques connoisseurs. Fine English silver epitomizes the silversmith's art. It is displayed in museums, is the topic of $100 scholarly books and the subject of full-page color advertisements in expensive magazines. Sotheby's, Christie's, and the other auction houses devote entire auctions to English silver—sometimes issuing hardbound catalogues for the sales. But beware. Unless you can correctly read English hallmarks, you can let a wonderful piece of silver slip by unknowingly. Or you can be taken when you buy a piece that you are told is an English silver piece, but is not.

Bargain Box Cast-Offs

Once a young wife whose in-laws had sent her boxes of silver, china, and linen, asked me to go through her attic and tell her "what's what."

Silver, china, and linen were *not* what this couple wanted. They were a young family with a toddler and another baby on the way. If anything, they wanted fewer possessions.

"I think I'll just give most of this to the Medical Wives' Bargain Box," she explained. "But if they're going to throw it all away, I don't want to waste their time messing with it."

When I opened the first box I was literally dumbstruck. Here were beautiful Georgian silver pieces that she was going to *give away*.

"Have you ever heard of Hester Bateman?" I asked as I lovingly fondled a 1783 Hester Bateman cake basket.

She hadn't, of course.

Right there in the middle of a dusty, drafty attic I embarked on one of my silver lectures, until I realized she really didn't want to know who Hester Bateman was.

"Look," I explained, "the girls at the Bargain Box are just as likely not to know who Hester Bateman was as you. But these are wonderful pieces that a collector would cherish forever. Let me find these pieces a home where they will be loved for what they are—not resented because they have to be polished and stored and insured."

The young wife agreed, and within a few days I had found buyers for these pieces (unfortunately my code of ethics does not allow me to buy what I appraise—how easy it would have been to offer her a few dollars for the entire box!) and the couple was considerably better off financially. This is an example of almost losing money because of not knowing how to read English silver marks.

But just as often—perhaps even more often—silverplated pieces are passed off as English silver because they have "hallmarks" on them. This happens so frequently that later I have a section which shows some of these often misinterpreted marks. But for now, let's see what English hallmarks really do look like.

Identifying English silver is simple once you know how and have a reference book close at hand. But if you've never been told how to reach these hallmarks, you will be fooled every time.

English silver is marked with four and sometimes five important symbols.

First, look for the lion passant.

This mark, which denotes the piece is sterling or 925/1000 parts silver, can be thought of as "shorthand" or a "symbol" meaning sterling silver. The lion has been used continuously since 1544.

Second, there will be a guild or town mark. This tells where the silver was made.

London
1478–1821

For example, London is represented by a leopard's head. The crowned leopard was used between 1478 and 1821. The uncrowned leopard appears on silver from 1822 to the present.

London
1821 to present

Other town or guild marks frequently seen include:

Birmingham   Sheffield   Dublin   Edinburgh

For other towns' hallmarks see the English silver books listed at the end of this book.

Third, look for a letter. The use of a letter contained in a shield or cartouche can be matched exactly to the key provided in any English silver marks book. This letter tells the year the piece was made. The type of print used and the enclosing shield change with each alphabet cycle. Also, different cities use different letters in different shapes. Only after you identify the city (London, Birmingham, etc.) can you learn the year by matching the letter.

Birmingham 1780–1   Birmingham 1805–6   London 1823–4

Paul Storr

Fourth, the silversmith adds his hallmark (usually his initials) to the other marks. The value of English silver is greatly affected by the identity of the maker. The best known of the English silversmiths are Hester Bateman, Paul Storr, Paul de Lamerie, and Mathew Boulton. As you might expect, these makers' marks have been forged many times, and spurious pieces of their silver exist on the marketplace.

Finally, there is often, but not always, a fifth mark, that of the sovereign's head. This is the profile of the reigning king or queen and is found on English silver between 1784 and 1890. The mark reappears in 1934, 1952, and 1977—the years of coronations and the Silver Jubilee.

Thus a full complement of English marks and their "interpretations" reads like this.

London 1820–21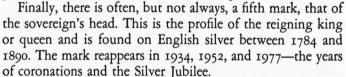

Hint: English silver hallmarks, unlike American manufacturers' marks which appear on the bottom or underneath surface of the silver piece, can appear any place on the silver. Look on the body, around the rims and edges and handles, as well as on the bottom for English hallmarks.

Now you understand how American coin silver pseudo marks sometimes "mislead" the public, as do the American marks that are used on silverplated pieces that closely copy English hallmarks.

Even some American *sterling* marks are confused with English marks.

One American sterling company often mistaken for English is Gorham. The Gorham sterling mark consists of a lion (remember the lion in English silver means sterling), a G (the letter is used to denote a year), and an anchor (Birmingham's mark). Though none of these marks as used by Gorham resembles the English marks, I have seen many a Gorham piece labeled—"English silver, fully hallmarked."

Here, then, are some of the marks most often misinterpreted as English hallmarks.

American manufacturer marks
commonly misinterpreted as English hallmarks:

Barbour Silver Company

Crescent Silverware
Manufacturing Company

Gorham Corporation

Reed & Barton

Sheffield Silver Company

Watson Company

E. G. Webster & Son

The Watson & Briggs Company

A final word—English silver remains of high quality in the 1980s. Even New York's most famous silver store, Tiffany, carries English silver today, as it has since the nineteenth century.

European or Continental Silver

Yet another type of "solid" (not silverplated) silver is the silver made in Europe and known as Continental silver. Just as each guild in England had its own distinct mark, so did all the silver centers of Europe, from Russia to Italy, from Spain to Switzerland. As you can imagine, there are thousands of Continental hallmarks.

Volumes have been written on Continental silver, and much of this silver has journeyed across the ocean to America. However, identifying the individual country of European silver is often difficult, and even experts sometimes do not know.

For your general information, the marks I most commonly find on Continental silver in homes in my daily appraisal work are as follows:

An ornate capital letter in conforming outline with a crown or fleur-de-lis at the top. France.

A half-moon or crescent and a crown, accompanied by the number 800. Germany after 1888.

A castle or other shaped center design encircled by numbers. Eastern European countries—Austria, Hungary, Czechoslovakia, Poland.

A Roman or classical type head pointing left and accompanied by other hallmarks. Italy after 1872.

Continental silver is also often marked with numbers. For example, "12" or "13" are German marks denoting the silver content.

Generally speaking, the silver content in European silver is 800/1000, or slightly lower than the 925/1000 content of

English and American sterling. However, the value of Continental silver lies in its age, quality, and design, and it is not considered inferior because of its lower silver content. Only when silver is melted down does the raw silver content affect its value.

South American Silver

Finally, much Mexican, Peruvian, and South American sterling is found in American homes today. This silver is usually immediately distinguishable because of its hand-hammered finish and distinct Latin American design. The silver is commonly marked "925," often accompanied by the word "sterling," with the maker's name and country of origin.

At one time, Latin and South American silver was considered vastly inferior to American silver, and indeed there is a great variety in the quality. Some is crude, poorly designed, and badly finished. Other pieces are refined and have a rich patina. Almost all of the silver is heavy in weight, as silver in these countries is plentiful and at one time was even cheap. Before sterling silver became so expensive, South American silver was valued only at its scrap, or melt-down, value. Today, with so much silver being melted down, and with the drastic cutback in silver production by the manufacturers, South American silver is being "reappraised." Most appraisers are now using comparable American prices for South American silver when insuring it for their clients.

Silverplate

Silverplating is the process whereby a thin layer of pure silver is placed over a base of another metal—sometimes copper, but more often a white metal. The oldest silverplate is known as Sheffield, named, of course, for the city in England where it originated in the eighteenth century. Unfortunately, the name Sheffield has turned into a generic term and is commonly given to any and all silverplated items. The term has even been adopted by the Sheffield Silver Company, a Brooklyn firm established in the 1920s. Your chances of having true eighteenth-century Sheffield silver are slim, *and you can be guaranteed that if the piece is marked "Sheffield" it is not true eighteenth-century Sheffield silver.*

The most common test for early Sheffield silver is the fingernail test: you run your finger across the bottom of the

piece, and if you feel a rolled-over edge and your nail catches on this irregular edge, you *may* have a piece of Sheffield silver. Unfortunately, imitations of eighteenth-century Sheffield have been made by copying this technique. True Sheffield silver can be as costly as sterling silver; a silver expert can further advise you about specific pieces.

> If your piece is genuine Sheffield, do not have it replated.

Victorian and Modern Silverplate

The majority of "antique" silverplate seen today was made either in England or America is the nineteenth century. It is distinguished both by its marks and its design. Just as South American silver was once scoffed at, so this nineteenth-century silverplate was once overlooked by collectors.

However, because silver from the 1870s and 1880s is now respectably old and fits into Victorian restorations and decor, it is once again in fashion. Many wonderful pieces that were common in Victorian times are no longer made—lemonade or water pitchers, epergnes and baskets, condiment sets and pickle jars. These are now being reevaluated for their design and historic context. And, oh yes—naturally, prices are rising.

Another reason for the increase in the value of antique silverplate is the cost of sterling silver today. Dealers tell me that customers who used to buy sterling pieces are now asking for fine-quality silverplate. "They don't want to worry about sterling being stolen, but they are not willing to give up the appearance of fine silver," one dealer explained.

Even new silverplate is more expensive than ever before because of the cost of the metal (both silver for the plate and the base metal) and the labor and manufacturing costs. A silverplated goblet can cost $25 today, the same price of a sterling goblet eighteen years ago.

To identify your silverplate, look for the following marks on the back:

| Triple plate Quadruple Plate Al Silverplate | All denote silverplated items |

NS	Nickel silver
EPC	Electroplate on copper
Silver on Copper	Just what it says, silver on copper
EPNS	Electroplate nickel silver
EPWN	Electroplate white metal
EPNS—WMM	Electroplate on nickel with white metal mounts (usually feet, finials, handles)
EPBM	Electroplate on Britannia metal (see below)

There are many other confusing terms associated with silverplate, including German silver, Nevada silver, Alaska silver, Argentine silver, Craig silver, and Inlaid silver. Each has its own "technical" meaning, but you should know these are all silverplated items—not sterling silver.

The most confusing term associated with silverplate is "Britannia." Britannia metal is actually a pewter type metal. The confusion comes about because pieces were made and sold that were Britannia metal, but Britannia metal was also used as the base metal for silverplating. Then to further confuse matters, "Britannia" appears in the name of the Meriden Britannia Company, which made silverplate and sterling silver. For your purposes, you may consider any "Britannia" pieces you own to have a value of silverplated or pewter pieces. All sterling silver made by the Meriden Britannia Company is clearly marked "sterling."

Silverplated items made today range in value from pieces that cost as much as some sterling silver to very inexpensive items. Many manufacturers have two lines of silverplate, one more costly than the other.

WARNING: Most of the silverplate coming out of the East—India primarily—is not fine quality. It may be marked to look like English sterling silver. While an expert can tell the difference, much of this silver is sold at flea markets as sterling. (Look carefully at the hallmarks.)

Inventorying Your Silver

A few snapshots of your silver are not going to do you much good if you lose it. You need to know what you had. In most states, unless you have insured your silver separately for its replacement value you are limited to $1,000 cash recovery.

You may use the value chart that follows later in the chapter to find an approximate value for much of your silver. It goes without saying that this chart is a *guide* and is not exact to the penny. I would have to come into each of your homes to make a truly accurate appraisal of your personal property.

But I have taken the time to make these guides to assist you in learning whether or not you have adequate insurance coverage, and whether you need the help of a professional appraiser.

The Format

Remember—name, describe, value.

Set up your routine before you start. Decide whether you are going to use index cards or lined paper (two or three columns).

First, enter the name of the piece, and if it is in multiples (twelve forks, two candlesticks, etc.), include the number.

Describe the object by telling what it looks like. Refer to the picture-description guide for help. Begin at the top or bottom of the piece, not in the middle. Always find out if your silver is sterling or plated by referring to the marks and record this. If you do not know, put the marks that appear on the piece on your page. A silver appraiser can read these marks and know what the piece is.

Be sure to list any peculiarities about your silver in your description. Just one unique characteristic may help you reclaim your silver if it is stolen and recovered. These peculiarities are especially important to note on silver because so much of it is exactly alike.

While I was viewing the thousands of pieces of flat silver on display at the police station at Fairfax, Virginia, after the infamous Halberstam murder in Georgetown, and the subsequent arrest of master thief Bernard Welch, the one comment I heard most frequently was, "You know that could be my silver—it's my pattern. But I don't really have any way of proving it's mine."

A few years ago, robbers entered a home in a nearby town. They were professionals. Their modus operandi was to fly into a town, rent a car, and "case" well-to-do neighborhoods, studying the habits of individual residents and noting prime houses for their burglaries. These thieves were highly successful, and the rash of burglaries that occurred in only two or three days was remarkable.

After they had left town—uncaptured, of course—I was called by one of the victims to help prepare her insurance claim. Luckily, the thieves had not taken everything, but they

Decorative motifs and techniques
frequently used in silver and china.

Acanthus

Adamesque

Beading

Egg & Dart

Etching

Foliage

Floral

Gadroon

Greek Key

Guilloche

Lobed

Reeding

Reticulated

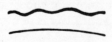

Scalloping

Scroll

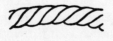

Spiral

Interloped

had made a substantial dent in the family's collection. They had taken two complete sets of flatware, sterling goblets, vermeil fruit knives ... over sixty lots of antique silver. At this time silver was being stolen but not melted down. Bullion was only selling for around $8 an ounce. Why melt down a sterling spoon for $7 worth of silver bullion when you could sell the spoon in an antiques shop or flea market for $12, $14, or $16, we reasoned.

The thieves thought the same way, because two years later my client went to a large antiques show in another city, where she spied her Strasbourg sterling silver flatware. She was sure this was hers. First, she recognized the silver chest it was in. Then, when she examined the silver, she saw her mother-in-law's monogram. Finally, when she asked the dealer how many pieces were in the set and he replied, "Too many to count," she was positive.

She then called the police. When they arrived at the armory where the show was being held, she told the police about her robbery, how she had seen the silver, and why she was sure this actually was her stolen silver.

"Do you have any foolproof way of identifying it?" they asked.

Suddenly she remembered.

"The end tine on one of the dinner forks is bent sharply outward," she stated. "I know because I always put this fork at my place when I had large dinner parties so none of my guests would be stabbed by a bent tine!" She also mentioned the monogram.

The police examined the silver and found one dinner fork with a tine bent at one end, and the monogram checked with family records.

The irony is that to this day my client has never recovered her silver. The silver had been fenced so many times before she finally found it that the police and insurance company can't decide who the rightful owner is.

Whether or not you choose to include the price, the careful listing of your silver is of utmost importance. Please do it.

Hints on How to Proceed

- List your flatware (knives, forks, vegetable spoons, etc.) separately from your hollow ware (pitchers, trays, etc.).
- *Sterling silver flatware.* Arrange your pieces according to patterns before you begin. Put all of each pattern together. If you know the pattern name, list it. If not, describe the pattern. Then match your pattern to the clos-

est class in the value charts for *approximate* current value. Try to identify the manufacturer by comparing that mark with the chart of those most commonly found.

- *Silverplated flatware.* Figure it at an average figure of $12 per piece for replacement with *new* silverplate. If your silverplated flatware is badly worn, figure it on replacement "in kind"—used silverplated flatware that would be purchased at a flea market or house sale at $2 to $3 each.

- *Coin silver flatware.* List the mark (initials, notation— coin, D, premium, etc.—or pseudo hallmark). Research these in a coin silver book (see the Bibliography). For coin silver made in the nineteenth century in the northern states, use the coin silver value chart. All other—seventeenth- or eighteenth-century silver and that made in other states—has historical and regional value and an expert should be consulted. Coin silver with a sheaf of wheat or flower basket motif is much more valuable.

- *Coin silver hollow ware.* Prices are rapidly increasing in this underpriced area. Consult an expert.

- *English silver.* English silver varies more in value than does most American silver because its value is based on its age and who made it. For nineteenth- and twentieth-century English flatware you may use the value charts provided for Class III as a *very general* gauge. English hollow ware and eighteenth-century flatware should be valued by a silver appraiser.

Hints on Fakes

Because silver is generally marked, once you know how to read the marks, you are not as apt to be fooled into buying fake silver pieces as you are glass or furniture fakes.

The faking of English silver is punishable by law, but of course this does not stop everyone. Before you pay a great deal of money for English silver, I would advise you to buy it from a reputable source or have the silver checked by an expert if it is offered to you as a "once in a lifetime chance."

Marks have been forged, especially the marks of the most famous smiths.

And marks have been cut out of old pieces and added to new ones. For example, it is relatively simple to cut the marks from the round bottom of a badly damaged eighteenth-century mug and place this bottom in a nineteenth- or even twentieth-century mug in pristine condition. Sometimes recent letter dates are rubbed so they become illegible and the silver is sold as eighteenth century.

You should also be aware of altered English silver. Fine Georgian silver was on occasion reworked into another piece that could be offered at a higher price. The meat platter that was given handles and turned into a tray, or the mug given a lid which it was never intended to have, are two such obvious "transformations."

There are also fakes and frauds in American silver, but once again these examples involve pieces and marks that bring a great deal of money. (Silver is too expensive to waste the time making fake 1820 spoons which would only sell for $20 to $30 each. But it *would* be worth the time to create a Paul Revere porringer.)

Mostly, you need to beware of silverplated pieces sold as sterling—just because they "have some hallmarks," and silverplated ware with a little copper showing through sold as "Sheffield."

Value Guides and How to Use Them

To effectively figure the approximate retail or replacement value of your American sterling silver flatware for your inventory, choose the pattern illustrated on Charts 1, 2, or 3 that most closely matches your pattern. Find the cost of each piece and enter that price on your inventory. Remember that the values stated in *Why You're Richer Than You Think* are average composite retail prices at the time of publication. (Many manufacturers and stores often feature promotional and discount sales on silver.) If you wish to use one price for all your sterling patterns, turn to Chart 4, which gives an average value for estate or used silver found in antiques and silver specialty shops and enter those values on your inventory.

The replacement cost of most sterling silver and silverplated hollow ware can be figured by referring to the values in Charts 6 and 7.

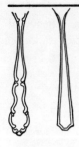

CLASS I Plain patterns, patterns with small scallop or scroll motifs

Examples: Rondo, Hepplewhite, Faneuil

Teaspoon	$43	Butter Serving or Cheese Knife	$50
Place Fork	$65	Cake, Pie, or Pastry Server	$60
Place Knife	$40	Cold Meat Fork	$150
Dinner Fork	$90	Cream Sauce Ladle	$55
Dinner Knife	$55	Flat Server	$125
Place, Dessert, Soup, Iced Tea,		Gravy Ladle	$100
or Grapefruit Spoon	$62	Jelly Server or Sugar Spoon	$50
Salad, Ice Cream, or Fish Fork	$62	Sugar Tongs	$50
Butter Spreader	$40	Salad Fork, Salad Spoon, Berry	
Cocktail, Pickle, or Lemon Fork	$40	Spoon, Large Vegetable Spoon	
Demitasse Spoon	$25	(all silver)	$150
Baby Feeding Spoon, Fork, or		Salad Set (silver and wood)	$100
Spoon	$40	Tablespoon (solid or slotted)	$100
Child's Fork	$40	Steak Carving Set	$200
Child's Spoon	$40	Roast Carving Set	$250
Child's Knife	$30	Punch Ladle	$350
Bonbon Spoon	$50		

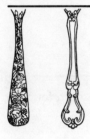

CLASS II More elaborately ornamented patterns

Examples: Steiff Rose, Repoussé, Strasbourg, Buttercup, Chantilly, Pointed Antique, Prelude

Teaspoon	$53	Butter Serving or Cheese Knife	$55
Place Fork	$85	Cake, Pie, or Pastry Server	$72
Place Knife	$52	Cold Meat Fork	$175
Dinner Fork	$105	Cream Sauce Ladle	$65
Dinner Knife	$55	Flat Server	$150
Place, Dessert, Soup, Iced Tea,		Gravy Ladle	$110
or Grapefruit Spoon	$68	Jelly Server or Sugar Spoon	$56
Salad, Ice Cream, or Fish Fork	$65	Sugar Tongs	$56
Butter Spreader	$43	Salad Fork, Salad Spoon, Berry	
Cocktail, Pickle, or Lemon Fork	$45	Spoon, Large Vegetable Spoon	
Demitasse Spoon	$30	(all silver)	$185
Baby Feeding Spoon, Fork, or		Salad Set (silver and wood)	$130
Spoon	$45	Tablespoon (solid or slotted)	$120
Child's Fork	$50	Steak Carving Set	$230
Child's Spoon	$45	Roast Carving Set	$275
Child's Knife	$35	Punch Ladle	$425
Bonbon Spoon	$58		

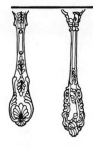

CLASS III Ornately decorated, elaborate, and heavy silver patterns... for Jensen patterns double these prices

Examples: Malvern, Grand Baroque, Melrose, English King

Teaspoon	$66	Butter Serving or Cheese Knife	$60
Place Fork	$100	Cake, Pie, or Pastry Server	$85
Place Knife	$65	Cold Meat Fork	$180
Dinner Fork	$120	Cream Sauce Ladle	$85
Dinner Knife	$70	Flat Server	$200
Place, Dessert, Soup, Iced Tea,		Gravy Ladle	$150
or Grapefruit Spoon	$80	Jelly Server or Sugar Spoon	$82
Salad, Ice Cream, or Fish Fork	$80	Sugar Tongs	$82
Butter Spreader	$50	Salad Fork, Salad Spoon, Berry	
Cocktail, Pickle, or Lemon Fork	$60	Spoon, Large Vegetable Spoon	
Demitasse Spoon	$35	(all silver)	$200
Baby Feeding Spoon, Fork, or		Salad Set (silver and wood)	$150
Spoon	$50	Tablespoon (solid or slotted)	$150
Child's Fork	$60	Steak Carving Set	$250
Child's Spoon	$50	Roast Carving Set (large)	$325
Child's Knife	$40	Punch Ladle	$500
Bonbon Spoon	$67		

CLASS IV Average cost of used silver pattern found at antique and specialty shops

Teaspoon	$35	Butter Serving or Cheese Knife	$35
Place Fork	$42	Cake, Pie, or Pastry Server	$45
Place Knife	$35	Cold Meat Fork	$85
Dinner Fork	$50	Cream Sauce Ladle	$35
Dinner Knife	$38	Flat Server	$100
Place, Dessert, Soup, Iced Tea,		Gravy Ladle	$85
or Grapefruit Spoon	$45	Jelly Server or Sugar Spoon	$40
Salad, Ice Cream, or Fish Fork	$45	Sugar Tongs	$40
Butter Spreader	$35	Salad Fork, Salad Spoon, Berry	
Cocktail, Pickle, or Lemon Fork	$30	Spoon, Large Vegetable Spoon	
Demitasse Spoon	$22	(all silver)	$175
Baby Feeding Spoon, Fork, or		Salad Set (silver and wood)	$75
Spoon	$30	Tablespoon (solid or slotted)	$125
Child's Fork	$35	Steak Carving Set	$100
Child's Spoon	$30	Roast Carving Set (large)	$150
Child's Knife	$25	Punch Ladle	$375
Bonbon Spoon	$35		

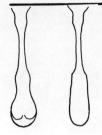

COIN SILVER FLATWARE—plain pattern from
1820-1850

Teaspoon	$30	Mustard Ladle	$40
Dessert or Soup Size Spoon	$50	Salt Spoon	$25
Luncheon Fork	$45	Tablespoon	$60
Dinner Fork	$65	Serving Pieces (Cake Knife, Fish	
Butter or Breakfast Knife	$40	Knife, etc.)	$250
Sugar Spoon	$40		

STERLING SILVER HOLLOWWARE—
Replacement Value Chart Guide

Prices will vary according to weight, design, manufacturer, age, and quality. These prices are to be used as a guide to currently manufactured sterling silver items.

	Low	High
Baby Brush and Comb	$40	$75
Juice Cup	$80	$125
Milk Cup	$100	$300
Rattle	$60	$120
Porringer	$110	$300
Wine Goblet	$100	$175
Water Goblet	$270	$500
Cordial Glass	$50	$75
Sherbet	$125	$275
Bonbon Dish	$60	$195
Compote	$125	$260
Low Candlestick (pair)	$80	$175
Tall (plain) Candlestick (pair)	$200	$500
Three-Branch Candelabra, Plain (pair)	$850	$1,400
Five-Branch Candelabra, Ornate (pair)	$1,900	$5,200
Cake or Sandwich Plate	$275	$575
Water Pitcher, Plain	$1,000	$1,800
Bud Vase, 7", Elaborate	$55	$70
Julep Cup	$225	$350
Bread and Butter Plate	$115	$175
Salt and Pepper Shakers, 4"	$50	$150
Sugar and Creamer Sets	$300	$500
Cigarette Box	$600	$900

	Average
Dresser Set (mirror, brush, and comb)	$500
Military Set	$200

Tea Service:

	Low	High
Plain Design		
Tea Pot	$1,200	$2,400
Coffee Pot	$1,200	$2,400
Covered Sugar	$500	$1,200
Creamer	$400	$800
Waste	$350	$775
Scrolled Motif		
Tea Pot	$2,000	$3,000
Coffee Pot	$2,000	$3,000
Covered Sugar	$1,200	$1,700
Creamer	$825	$1,200
Waste	$700	$950

	Average
Repoussé	
Tea Pot	$3,800
Coffee Pot	$3,800
Open Sugar	$1,900
Creamer	$1,800
Waste	$1,800

	Low	High
Revere Bowls:		
12-inch	$1,725	$3,800
10-inch	$1,050	$2,300
7-inch	$400	$1,000
5-inch	$250	$575
3½-inch	$125	$225

Pieces Not Frequently Found in Sterling Silver:

Well and Tree	$6,500–$12,500
Large Trays, or Waiters	$4,500–$10,500
Covered Entrée Dishes	$2,000–$ 5,000

Silverplated Items:

	Low	High
Bonbon Dish	$7.00	$45
Open Serving Bowl	$25.00	$125
Covered Butter Dish	$30.00	$75
Bread Tray	$18.00	$70
Bread and Butter Plate	$12.00	$40
Chafing Dish	$95.00	$350
Covered Entrée Dish	$35.00	$165
Compote	$7.00	$50
Well and Tree	$50.00	$225
Water Pitcher	$30.00	$250
Sandwich Plate	$35.00	$85
Silver Service, 4-piece	$150.00	$1,200
Tray or Waiter	$45.00	$550
Water Goblet	$15.00	$65
Baby Cup	$5.00	$45
Trivet	$5.00	$35

🎭 11 🎭

China and Crystal—
Replacing the Broken Plates
Can Break You

China—The Way It Was

For years you could go to a jewelry store or china department in a department store, buy a plate to match your set, and pay the same price for the new one that you paid the year before, or the year before that.

No longer.

China prices are increasing as steadily as furniture prices and only slightly less erratically than silver prices.

A major cause for this increase is our present energy crisis. The ovens in which china is glazed must be kept at constant temperatures twenty-four hours a day. Since you know how expensive it is to heat your home, you can imagine how expensive it is to maintain a consistent high temperature in a china factory.

A few years ago I overheard a conversation in New York's Royal Copenhagen shop on Madison Avenue. A salesperson was explaining that if the oven furnaces ever were shut down, it would require a great deal of time and money to bring them back to the temperature necessary to achieve the unique glaze on the beautiful Royal Copenhagen figurines and china.

This consistent increase in overhead costs has brought about many changes in the porcelain market. It wasn't more than three or four years ago that a bank hired me to act as the agent for a large collection of pre-World War II Meissen china that had been purchased in Germany in the 1930s. The bank needed to get the most money possible to settle the estate but had had little success in locating a local buyer.

I contacted both Sotheby's and Christie's and requested a pre-auction estimate on this large Meissen "Onion" pattern service. At that time neither auction house appeared interested in selling the china. In fact, one house suggested that I could figure out a pre-auction value myself by multiplying the total number of pieces by $3.

"Even the large tureens?" I asked, knowing full well that these brought several hundred dollars in antiques shops.

"Even the large tureens," was the reply.

Multiply a 225-piece set of Meissen "Onion" china, including rimmed soup bowls, nut dishes, covered vegetable dishes, egg cups, knife rests, a mustard pot, hors d'oeuvres serving dish, lozenge-shaped serving dishes, a water jug, and wine funnel by $3 and you come up with a measly $675!

Three years later, in 1980, just such a set of "Onion" pattern Meissen, in fact 227 pieces, sold at auction for $10,000. In 1981, yet another "Onion" pattern service consisting of 226 pieces also sold for $10,000. A far cry from $675.

Obviously, as the price for new china has gone up, the desire for fine antique and even semi-antique china sets among dealers and collectors has greatly increased. What this means for you and me is that the cost of replacing a china service, whether it be Meissen, Lenox, Haviland, or even Bavarian china, has now reached astronomical proportions.

The Types of China and How to Distinguish Them

For the purposes of your inventory you need to know that there are two major categories of china commonly found in your dining room and kitchen—porcelain (or china) and semi-porcelain or ironstone (or pottery).

One distinction always made between porcelain and semi-porcelain is that porcelain is translucent, meaning you can see through it. The usual way to test your china is to put your hand at the back of a plate, then hold the plate in front of a strong light. If you can see the outline of your hand, it is porcelain.

On the other hand, pottery is opaque; you cannot see through it. Semi-porcelain is actually pottery-based but with a porcelain-type glaze that makes it more durable than pottery, which is easily broken.

Porcelain

"Porcelain" is often used interchangeably with the term "china" to mean high-quality and expensive dinnerware. Porcelain collectors know that there are two classifications of porcelain—hard paste, the porcelain made with kaolin as its main ingredient, and soft paste, which is largely bone ash. But since you are using this book as a guide to identifying and inventorying your property and not as a scholarly work to research museum-quality porcelain, the more specific details of hard and soft paste are not relevant here.

What You Will Find in Your China Cabinet

Relatively little porcelain is of American origin. Until the mid-nineteenth century almost all china in America was imported. William Ellis

Tucker is considered the first American china maker, but Tucker china is extremely rare and seldom found in private homes. In fact, the majority of porcelain called "Tucker" is actually French nineteenth-century china generically termed "Old Paris."

But even after American china companies were established, French, English, and German china remained so popular in America that we did not develop many large and important porcelain manufacturing companies. Lenox and Pickard are two of the exceptions. Today, if you walk into a china department and look around, you will see that the majority of the fine porcelain displayed is still imported from England, Germany, and Denmark, and bears the names Minton, Wedgwood, Rosenthal, Royal Copenhagen, etc.

Granny Again

Proof of Americans' preference for European china is established the moment you mention grandmother's china. I have never heard of a grandmother yet who did not have at least one set of Haviland china. There is so much Haviland china around that it will require several volumes for author-appraiser Gertrude Tatnell Jacobson to catalogue the hundreds of Haviland patterns.

The Haviland factories in Limoges, France, manufactured china that was decorated in the French style for the American market. Everyone is familiar with the usual Haviland dinner sets decorated in pastel floral motifs. But not everyone knows that the Haviland factories also produced such diverse pieces as terra-cotta vases and sculptured busts.

Haviland china is highly treasured and widely collected today. Those fortunate enough to have inherited a set are always seeking individual pieces to replace broken or damaged ones. On the other hand, serious Haviland collectors are always looking for the rare items to enhance their collections. The wise investor in Haviland china knows it is often possible to buy an entire set for less money per piece than it costs to buy the individual pieces to assemble a set.

Knowing the Age of Your Porcelain

Much of the mystery surrounding the age of your china can be cleared up by knowing two dates, 1891 and 1914. If the name of a country, such as England, China, Japan, or France, appears on the bottom of your china, it dates after 1891, in accordance with the McKinley Tariff Act passed in 1890, which required that the name of the country of origin appear on porcelain imported into the United States. If the additional words "made in" appear, the plate is of even more recent vintage and post-dates 1914. The majority of the china you will find in sets, whether your grandmother's or even great-grandmother's, will date from the end of the nineteenth century or into the twentieth century.

A Thing of the Past

Just as sterling silver has become expensive and sometimes even extinct, so some porcelain has become rare, and certainly out of the reach of the average buying public. Notable among such porcelain are the patterns decorated with rich cobalt blue and bold gold borders. Cobalt, a pigment made principally of cobalt oxide and alumina, has become so expensive to extract that it is prohibitive to use it in manufacturing china. Rich gold borders are also becoming decorations of the past. When a china pattern is made in the 1980s with gold and cobalt, resembling the patterns of twenty, forty, or sixty years ago, the price can range as high as $150, $200, and even $250 for a single dinner plate!

The Second Best—Semi-Porcelain

And your second-best china or kitchenware—what should it be called? Many choose "semi-porcelain," while others prefer "ironstone." Ironstone ware was first made in England and became immediately popular because of its strong (or ironlike) properties combined with its colorful decoration on the porcelain-type glaze. English ironstone of the nineteenth century is widely collected—particularly large serving pieces such as soup tureens, covered vegetable dishes, and cake plates.

The ironstone made in America by the end of the nineteenth century was made in both an off-white glaze and decorated patterns. This "second-best" china is now also highly collectible. For example, pieces made by the Homer Laughlin China Company are now being snatched up by collectors. Some collectors concentrate on buying dinnerware made by one particular company, while others collect specific patterns, often made by many companies.

Perhaps the most famous and most often collected dinnerware is the "Willow" pattern, which has been made by companies from England to Japan and back again to the United States. It exemplifies the kind of semi-porcelain china you may find in your home that now has "collectible" value.

Made in U.S.A.

Among the currently popularly collected American china is that made by such companies as Buffalo Pottery Company, Castleton China, Fulper Pottery, W. S. George Pottery, Hall China Company, Hull Pottery, Knowles, Taylor & Knowles, the Homer Laughlin Company, McCoy Companies, Pickard China, Roseville Pottery Company, Salem China Company, Sebring Pottery Company, Shawnee Pottery Company, Stangle Pottery Company, Steubenville Pottery Company, Syracuse China Company, Universal Potteries Incorporated, Weller Pottery, and Russell Wright. Check the bottom of your china to see if you possibly own "collectible" kitchenware.

Confusing Names and Marks

Just as the nineteenth-century American silversmiths imitated English hallmarks, so American china companies freely drew upon English and European names and hallmarks. For example, you find Chelsea, the name of one of the most famous of the eighteenth-century English porcelain companies, used by the Chelsea Pottery Company of West Virginia. The American companies also liberally copied English ironstone marks and used such typically English symbols as the unicorn, lion, crown, horse, and hybernia in their American marks.

One company that adapted a foreign name and symbol was the French China Company, an Ohio firm, which used a fleur-de-lis and the term "La Française" on its products at the turn of the century. They later became the French Saxon China Company and used as a hallmark an armored head, coat of arms, suit of armor, and crossed swords in a cartouche. Under this they placed the term "French Saxon China." I cannot tell you how many times this particular china has been brought to me to be appraised as Sevres or Limoges china.

In fact, even Sevres, the French china literally fit for a king, was imitated in East Liverpool, Ohio, when a company called itself the Sevre China Company and marked its wares with a fleur-de-lis. No matter how fine their line of hotelware dinner sets, bowls, plates, and toilet sets, only the person unfamiliar with the true French Sevres mark and china could think that this American semi-porcelain is the "real thing."

The China Syndrome—Fakes and Frauds and Just Stupid Mistakes

While these misnomers are examples of copying and imitating they are not truly fakes. The majority of the fakes come out of Japan and the other Oriental countries.

One of the most blatantly copied and falsely sold chinas is the type known as "Jasperware," made after the famous English Wedgwood Jasperware. This china, easily identifiable by its pottery body in blue, green, yellow, lavender, etc., and decorated with classical scenes executed in white, originated in eighteenth-century England. However, both the type and the name have been copied numerous times. The correct spelling is Wedgwood. Counterfeit Wedgwood is often spelled "Wedgewood." Twentieth-century factories in both Germany and Japan freely copied Jasperware type glaze and style, and these copies are often passed off as nineteenth-century English Wedgwood.

Unfortunately, china marks can be removed from the bottom of plates and saucers with the help of either a grinding wheel or hydrochloric acid. These methods of removing marks are often used on nineteenth- and twentieth-century china made originally in Japan or China and now sold in the United States either as being older than it really is, or as examples of English, French, or German china rather than Oriental copies of English, French or German china. And as I mentioned earlier, marks can also be added.

Frequently, china is sold for something it is not, due just to plain stupidity. You have to be very careful when buying china in antiques shops and flea markets because it so often is wrongly marked. (The seller may not know what the china is, but always seems to know what price to put on it.)

Only a week or so ago I wandered into an antiques shop located in a large shopping mall. The majority of furniture in the shop was from the 1900s and 1920s, and I was beginning to wonder whether or not the shop could rightfully claim the name "antiques shop." Then one item particularly caught my attention. Perched on top of a pie safe (once again of questionable age), was a blue and white plate with a historical scene at the center. The plate was badly cracked, but on the sticker I read the following,

Antique blue and white plate.
"As is" condition. $16

I was shocked. Only two or three years ago I bought that identical plate in the A & P for 49 cents. In fact, I have a stack of these plates in my kitchen cabinet which I use every single day, none of which is cracked, and none of which is worth $16. I wondered if the crack made the plate worth $16. Perhaps I was mistaken. Was this really the same plate? Knowing full well it was, I nonetheless took it from the rack, turned it over, and read,

Original copper engraving of Historical
Colonial Scenes printed on Staffordshire
Ironstone. Detergent and Dishwasher safe.

Dishwasher safe? It would seem to me that anyone would know that an *antique* plate would not have the words "Dishwasher Safe" on it. I know time is flying, but I don't think it is passing that rapidly.

Common Confusions

While speaking of fakes and frauds, I would like to try to clear up some of the confusion surrounding two china companies.

Very often a piece of china that has two marks, "Pickard" and "Haviland," will be brought to me. The Pickard China Company, founded in Chicago in 1894, had its beginnings as a china company that decorated china imported from France. Thus the china was imported bearing the Haviland mark (remember the 1890 law) and once it was decorated, the Pickard mark was added. Much of the china was exceptionally well painted, and early pieces of hand-decorated Pickard china are now collected. Those pieces bearing any of the following artists' signatures are particularly sought after:

E. S. Challinor, Leonard Kohl, Podlaha, Hessler, Vokral, and Klippon.

Then there is the matter of the most misunderstood of the generic china terms—Dresden. Dresden is actually a town in Germany where the Meissen factory was located (just as Limoges is a town in France where Haviland China was manufactured). But the term "Dresden" is commonly used by the layman when speaking of the floral spray motif that often appears on Meissen china. This general term is then interpreted to mean that any china with this floral decoration is Meissen china. In reality, this floral spray motif was and is still used by many china manufacturers, and Meissen made many patterns of china aside from this one. This floral-patterned china was particularly popular in the 1930s, and many eastern European china companies made patterns imitating the original eighteenth-century Meissen floral design. ("Louise" is one particular pattern made in the 1930s, and another current popular adaptation is the "Empress" pattern.) Yet, I am often handed a plate clearly marked *Bavaria* or *Czechoslovakia* and told, "This is Meissen china."

Hints on China

Look carefully at the backs of dinnerware china. That china made in popular patterns and sold in sets in the late nineteenth and twentieth century will be clearly marked. Fine early English china by such companies as Rockingham, Minton, Coalport, and Worcester can be identified by studying scholarly books on porcelain and by learning the appropriate markings. This fine china, like Sevres and Meissen, frequently has been imitated. Unless you know how to distinguish the real from the fake, do not invest in this china without buying it from a reputable firm that will guarantee to refund your money should the china be other than what it is stated to be.

Even when buying fairly inexpensive china in flea markets and antiques shops, take the time to inspect the back for marks. Before spending your money, look for the words "made in," or the country where the china was made, and compare what you now know—that this would be nineteenth- or twentieth-century china—with what the tag or the shop owner tells you about the china.

When purchasing china, buy only that in the best condition. Sometimes repairs, even major ones, will not show up under normal light. If possible, use a black light for a quick check of both condition and authenticity of the mark. If that is not possible, use your fingers. A small hairline crack, which may be invisible to the naked eye, can be detected by "thumping" or ring-ing porcelain with your finger. Porcelain has a distinct clear ring and if you notice a dull thud there is damage somewhere.

Inventorying Your China—How to Proceed

Organize your china before entering it on your inventory. Group all the pieces of the same pattern together, just as you did with your silver. In the left-hand column note a general description, such as, "Large dinner set of English bone china" or, "Group of dessert plates."

Next, in the center, or description column, enter the pattern name and company, if you know it. For example, "Kutani Crane by Wedgwood." If the specific name of the pattern is not given, but the manufacturer's name or mark is present, enter this. (Remember to draw the mark if the name is not stated.) Even if you know the pattern name, make some descriptive comment so you or a future generation can distinguish one pattern from another.

To describe the pattern, start at the outside rim and move toward the center. An example of a simple description might read like this: "Having a gold band and floral border; the center is decorated with one large floral de-sign." (You may want to refer back to the silver chapter for additional de-scriptions of motifs.) Also note the colors of the china, such as "blue, green, pink, and yellow predominating" or "the china is decorated in an all-over pastel floral motif."

Now list how many of each item there are in the china set—twelve din-ner plates, eight cups and saucers with two additional saucers, one teapot, two round open serving dishes, etc.

If you wish to enter prices based on the value charts that follow, state both the cost of the individual item and the total unit cost. For example, twelve plates at $25 each, total $300. Finally, add up the entire value of the set and list it. You will be amazed at how rapidly your china mounts in value.

Notes on Using Values Charts

There are as many china patterns as silver patterns, and the china patterns go out of production even more rapidly than do silver patterns. The charts that I have provided will help you *estimate* the replacement value of your china. Three classes are provided.

The first class is for the usual "inexpensive" kitchenware you use every day. Use this category to determine the value of both collectible dinnerware from the 1920s and 30s and today's current semi-porcelain dinnerware. Needless to say, patterns vary in price, but this chart will help you arrive at an approximate value.

The second class relates to good-quality bone china, or porcelain, usually found at the lower end of the English and American company lines and sold in jewelry stores and good china departments. In this category will fall some familiar china patterns made by King Albert Bone China, Lenox, Noritake, and Wedgwood. *This category may be used to figure an approximate or rough value of the usual Haviland patterns.*

The third class relates to elaborately decorated fine china with gold borders. In this category will fit such manufacturers as Lenox, Minton, Crown Derby, etc. Match your pattern to the closest class by comparing the illustrations.

CLASS I

"Pottery," "Semi-Porcelain," "Ironstone," including that available in department stores and the newly collectible 1930s dinnerware patterns such as Fiesta Ware

	Low	High
Dinner Plate	$ 4	$15
Salad Plate	3	9
Bread and Butter Plate	2	6
Cup and Saucer	5	15
Rimmed Soup Bowl	3	10
Cereal Bowl	3	10
Fruit or Dessert Bowl	2	6
Platters:		
Oval, small	9	20
Oval, medium	15	35
Oval, large	18	40
Round, medium	14	32
Round, large	16	40
Vegetable Bowls:		
Open, round	6	28
Open, oval	8	32
Covered, round	20	50
Covered, oval	23	55
Tureen, covered	30	65
Tureen, covered with stand	50	85
Tea Pot	20	50
Coffee Pot	20	50
Sugar, covered	12	25
Creamer	8	16
Gravy Boat	12	30
Gravy Boat with stand	18	36
Celery, Butter, or Pickle Dish	12	18

CLASS II

Simply decorated English Bone China, American porcelain by Syracuse, Lenox, Pickard, Noritake, "Queen's Ware," and commonly found Haviland patterns

	Low	High
Dinner Plate	$ 12	$ 20
Salad Plate	8	12
Bread and Butter Plate	6	10
Cup and Saucer	14	20
Rimmed Soup Bowl	12	18
Cereal Bowl	11	18
Fruit or Dessert Bowl	8	12
Platters:		
Oval, small	30	50
Oval, medium	35	60
Oval, large	45	80
Round, medium	35	55
Round, large	50	75
Vegetable Bowls:		
Open, round	20	40
Open, oval	25	50
Covered, round	45	90
Covered, oval	50	100
Tureen, covered	70	110
Tureen, covered with stand	100	160
Tea Pot	45	70
Coffee Pot	45	70
Sugar, covered	30	40
Creamer	20	25
Gravy Boat	20	40
Gravy Boat with stand	25	45
Celery, Butter, or Pickle Dish	15	22

CLASS III

Fine English and American porcelain, gold-decorated patterns

	Low (Simple, gold rims, floral motif)	Medium (More richly decorated patterns)	High (Elaborate, extremely fine China)
Dinner Plate	$ 25	$ 54	$ 120
Salad Plate	20	38	80
Bread and Butter Plate	15	24	50
Cup and Saucer	40	54	120
Rimmed Soup Bowl	35	52	110
Cereal Bowl	30	50	100
Fruit or Dessert Bowl	25	30	95
Platters:			
Oval, small	90	140	350
Oval, medium	120	170	475

	Low (Simple, gold rims, floral motif)	Medium (More richly decorated patterns)	High (Elaborate, extremely fine China)
Oval, large	140	225	520
Round, medium	85	140	300
Round, large	120	180	475
Vegetable Bowls			
Open, round	65	100	200
Open, oval	75	115	250
Covered, round	160	280	550
Covered, oval	180	300	600
Tureen, covered	225	350	900
Tureen, covered with stand	375	500	1,400
Tea Pot	112	220	475
Coffee Pot	112	220	475
Sugar, covered	60	115	250
Creamer	50	70	150
Gravy Boat	100	115	225
Gravy Boat with stand	125	185	350
Celery, Butter, or Pickle Dish	35	45	75

Crystal

Had I written this book seven or eight years ago, I would have treated household crystal in a paragraph or two, and only then because crystal, like china, is a staple item in most households. At that time, crystal prices seldom changed. If you had gone to the store to buy new crystal, you would have found that, like china, the price for your water goblet was the same, or within 50 cents or $1 of what it had cost a year or so before.

And had you gone to an auction of household property and bid on a complete set of fine lead crystal, you could easily have bought it for 50 cents to $2 per stem, sometimes less. Crystal sets, like china sets, just were not considered valuable. They are today. The rise has been radical.

Once again, the change has been precipitated by the increased cost of buying the new. When Irish cut-crystal goblets cost between $30 and $45 per stem, buyers are rushing to buy older crystal—not yet antique, but of equal and sometimes superior quality to that being sold in stores today. So, before you throw out the crystal because you don't have any place to store it, you should realize that this one-time "give-away" can now stand on its own merits and demand its own price.

The Types of Household Crystal and Glass

Basically I find three categories of glass or crystal in most homes. First is the everyday drinking glass, which may even have come from Hardee's or McDonald's with the purchase of a fast-food order. Believe it or not, these will become collector's items someday. In fact, if you really wanted to start investing in collectibles for the next generation (or the one after that) you would carefully pack all these glasses away and never allow them to be touched by human lips again.

Investment aside, most homes have a variety-store quality collection of glasses, from jelly jars to inexpensive parfait glasses, which only need to be photographed or quickly noted—if that.

Machine-Made and Depression Glass

Next, I usually find a group of glasses comparable to the semi-porcelain or ironstone dinnerware just discussed. This is machine-made glassware produced in modern factories and considerably less expensive than fine lead or hand-blown crystal. Machine-made stemware is usually referred to in crystal departments as "casual stemware." But before you throw this glassware out or neglect to list it on your inventory, you should realize that even this glassware can easily run as much as $10 and more per stem.

In the same category you can list your mother's or grandmother's stemware which she bought for only a few pennies in the 1920s, 30s, and 40s. This glassware, which is often pastel-colored (green, pink, blue, or yellow), is a popular collectible of today commonly called "Depression glass." Depression glass, which was sold in large sets, is the equivalent of much of today's machine-made glass.

Once the fashion for this colorful and decorated glass died, the goblets, sherbets, and lemonade pitchers were packed away in attics, given to Goodwill charities, or simply thrown away. But during the 1960s so much interest in Depression glass was rekindled that articles written on the subject appeared in magazines, price guides were published, and suddenly Depression glass became a hot collector's item—usually bought or traded at flea markets.

Depression glass is still not an expensive item in terms of antiques values. But once again, if you take twelve water goblets that can be sold for $6 each, you end up with $72 for twelve. And if you have twelve sherbets, twelve juice glasses, and twelve ice tea goblets to go along with the twelve water goblets, multiply $72 by four and you quickly total $288 for a group of glasses you might be ready to toss in the junk pile.

Collectors of Depression glass buy both specific patterns ("Open Rose" and "American Sweetheart" being only two of hundreds of patterns) and glassware made by specific companies. Among the most familiar of the glass companies were the Cambridge Glass Company, the Imperial Glass Company (known for its famous Nuart and Nucut lines), the Jeanette Glass Company, and of course, the Fostoria Glass Company, which is still operating in Moundsville, West Virginia.

Fine Crystal

The third category is the finest glassware—hand-blown or hand-cut lead crystal. Fine crystal is called "lead crystal" because it contains lead oxide, the ingredient which makes the glass clearer in color and gives it the bell-like

Glass and crystal decorative terms

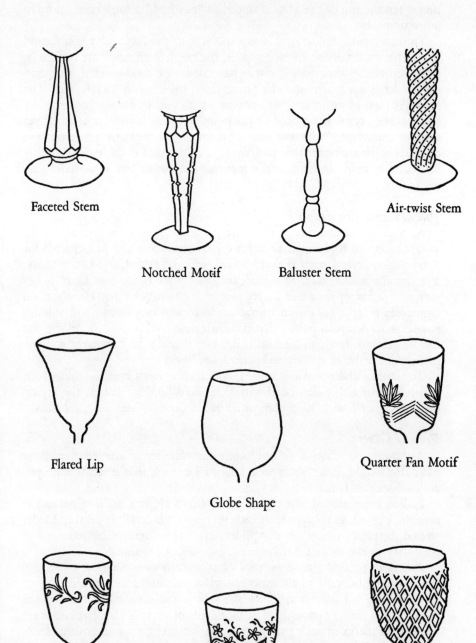

Faceted Stem

Notched Motif

Baluster Stem

Air-twist Stem

Flared Lip

Globe Shape

Quarter Fan Motif

Scroll Motif

Etched Floral Motif

Diamond Motif

ring when the rim of the glass is tapped or "pinched," a sound not found in other stemware.

To understand why crystal is so expensive to produce today you should know that each portion of each goblet, the bowl, stem, and base or foot, is made separately. Each part is either handblown or hand-molded, and then the goblet is assembled and the pieces fused together by a craftsman. The goblet is then given to another craftsman who cuts or etches the design by hand. If the crystal has a gold or platinum rim, this is hand-painted by yet another craftsman. With the cost of labor and manufacturing what it is today, it is little wonder that the cost of a goblet that is finely cut or richly decorated in gold can equal and sometimes exceed the cost of a sterling silver spoon.

Quality and Condition

As with china and silver, there are grades of quality in crystal. In the value charts you find two listings for crystal stemware. The first chart is for good-quality crystal, such as that sold by Noritake, Astral, and Lenox today. *You can also use this chart to estimate the value of the Heisey glass which you or your mother bought for $2 or $3 per stem in the 1930s and 40s.* However, do remember to take condition into consideration when listing and valuing your crystal. A crystal goblet that is nicked in several places around the rim can be ground down to a smooth lip, but this can be expensive and the piece will not be in its original perfect condition.

The second chart provides value guides for the finest crystal—that which is hand-cut or richly decorated with deep gold borders. This is the crystal often associated with such companies as Baccarat, Waterford, and Stuart.

Pressed Glass

Although most homes do not have a complete set of nineteenth-century pressed glass, this is such a broadly collected favorite that it seems appropriate to discuss it here.

Earlier, I mentioned that pressed glass values are in a holding pattern at present. The values go up a little each year, and it is certainly getting harder to find the pieces you want. But prices have not suddenly escalated the way they have in the area of Art Nouveau bronzes, for example.

American pressed glass presents a capsule study of antiques fashions and values that is relevant to all antiques—glass, furniture, and art alike.

When pressed glass was first made in the mid-nineteenth century the public could not get enough of it. Hundreds of pressed glass patterns were made with pieces in each pattern, ranging from egg cups to covered compotes. To be fashionable, a complete set of pressed glass for the dining room was essential.

The popularity of pressed glass reached its height at the end of the nineteenth century when suites and sets were "in." Just as you wanted a suite of matching furniture in your bedroom, so you wanted a set of matching pressed glass, a set of Gorham sterling silver flatware, and a set of French Haviland china adorning your dining table.

Pressed glass was also so inexpensive that you could literally buy it by the barrel. It was purchased from dry goods stores, five and dimes, and the wonderful new phenomenon, the catalogue store. Eventually, however, the passion for pressed glass died out, and the covered compote, cake stand, and forty-eight goblets were relegated to storage.

But by the late 1920s the public once again became enamored of the nineteenth-century's pressed glass, and by the 1930s *research* on early American pressed glass patterns was begun, notably by Ruth Webb Lee, whose numerous books and articles on the subject (which led to the collecting boom at that time) are still read today. In her *Handbook of Early American Pressed Glass Patterns,* Mrs. Lee wrote,

> It is not so many years ago that collectors of American blown glass and writers on the subject attached little importance to later commercial glassware which flooded our markets during the decades immediately preceding and following the Civil War. Collectors of rarities found no pleasure in acquiring anything so plentiful as glass made in America from 1840 to 1890, but the urge to buy essentially American antiques grew stronger ... Today discriminating collectors are as keenly interested in matching sets of this popular glass, both crystal and colored, as they used to be in acquiring the rare forms of blown glass.

The moral is, just wait long enough and everything comes back into fashion. Now, it is almost time for pressed glass to be rediscovered—once again.

Cut Glass

Almost every house has one or more pieces of cut glass, ranging from a simple bonbon or nappery to an elaborate punch set or even a cut glass lamp. The American cut glass that is most frequently found comes from the Brilliant period of the 1880s to the 1900s, when cut glass was the rage of the day, the way pressed glass had been a few years earlier. But unlike pressed glass, very fine, heavy, large cut glass items, such as lemonade pitchers, decanters, and large punch bowls, were very expensive when first made and are equally expensive now. Many factories produced cut glass, and the patterns of cut glass were almost as numerous as sterling silver patterns. Each pattern has a name, and there are many pattern books which list these for you. The decorations most frequently used in cut glass are the hobstar, quarter fan, ribbed, diamond, and caned motifs. These appear separately and in various combinations on every type of cut glass item made. By the late nineteenth century, cut glass was made on an assembly line rather than by an individual craftsman who completed the design from the original etching of the design on the glass mold to the final cutting and polishing of the glass.

> Cut glass is always a collector's item, and you will find the com-
> bination of cut glass and sterling in powder jars, occasionally on
> pitchers, and even on bonbons, where a silver frame and handle
> make a basket motif.

Cut glass was often decorated in a combination of deep cutting and pictorial cutting frequently referred to as "intaglio" cutting. The combination
usually includes the quarter fan or diamond deep cuts with an intaglio floral
motif, which has the quality of being engraved and is less deep than the geometric line deep cutting.

One of the big confusions in cut glass is distinguishing it from the
pressed glass that was copied after cut glass patterns. Pressed glass is made
by pressing the pattern into a mold, while cut glass involves the mechanical
cutting of the glass by a wheel. *Molded edges are rounded and irregular; cut
edges are sharp and angular.* Your fingers can quickly learn the difference
once you have handled enough of each type of glass. However, to confuse
matters further, there are "Nucut" and "Nearcut" and "Presscut" glass,
which more closely resemble cut glass than the usual pressed glass. Just the
use of the word "cut" in the name is confusing.

Cut glass is currently being produced in the European countries, primarily Czechoslovakia—and, once again, marked by a simple, removable
label. However, the new cut glass is made in more "contemporary" shapes,
and the motifs of the cuttings are differently interpreted. I haven't found
much confusion between old and new cut glass.

Distinguish Pressed and Cut Glass

If you have difficulty deciding whether a piece actually is cut or pressed
glass, compare it to another piece which you know to be cut glass or pressed
glass. Cut glass has a much clearer, crystal-like color due to the high lead
content used in making the form or blank. Cut glass is also considerably
heavier than pressed glass and has a higher ringing tone.

Signed Cut Glass

It is now quite fashionable to speak of signed cut glass, although it has
been said that perhaps only 10 percent of cut glass made during the Brilliant
period was signed. Looking for the signature on cut glass is like knowing
the hallmarks on English silver—once you know what you are looking for,
it's easy. Signatures on cut glass are usually in oval or circular forms and are
very faint. They were applied by dipping a pre-cut die of the trademark or
emblem into acid. This die was then pressed into the glass at a smooth
point. To find a signature on cut glass, be sure to look on the uncut surface,
usually the interior. Shift the piece around in different light until the very

faint impression is caught. However, so little cut glass was signed that most of the time you are looking for a needle in a haystack.

The value of cut glass is dependent upon the condition of the piece, the brilliance of the cutting, the rarity of the piece itself—usually even a simply cut pitcher will be more expensive than most finely cut tumblers, simply because there were more tumblers made than pitchers. Also look for unusual shapes. A fine heart or cloverleaf-shaped bonbon dish will be more valuable than a simple round bonbon dish.

> The more spectacular pieces of cut glass are now showing up at some of the larger auction houses, thus indicating the viable interest in cut glass in the marketplace.

Hints on Glass Fakes and Copies

Glass is one of the most commonly copied and faked of all antiques. I believe this is because there are so many glass collectors. Tourists, antiques shop browsers—everyone wants to buy a small memento or to have a collection that can be added to bit by bit. Not only can a piece of glass easily be carried home, it can be set out on display after a quick rinsing-off. Furthermore, since glass is fairly inexpensive to make, it is worth the time and trouble to "copy" or "fake" antique glass which can be sold for a large profit.

Pressed glass patterns have been copied for years. Many companies claim that these newer pieces are made "from the original molds," but glass experts tell us there is a difference in the weight and color between the old and the new.

Now even Depression glass is being reproduced. An excellent guide to reproductions of Depression glass is found at the back of the Kovels' *Illustrated Price Guide to Depression Glass and American Dinnerware*.

However, most sets of *crystal* that you find in homes today are just what they appear to be, wedding presents from the twentieth century, and they should be included on your inventory.

Describing and Inventorying Your Crystal

Follow the same procedure in listing your crystal that you followed when you entered your china. Categorize each pattern and list the number of individual pieces you have, such as goblets, sherbets, juice glasses, etc.

Because so little glassware is marked and most pattern names are forgotten, describe the design as best you can. If you find yourself stuck for words

CASUAL STEMWARE Current machine-made glass to include the usual Depression glass patterns. It should be noted that some rare Depression glass serving pieces are now selling for hundreds of dollars.

	Low	High		Low	High
Goblet	$ 6	$12	Creamer	$ 5	$ 15
Iced Tea	6	12	Bud Vase	3	15
Sherbet	5	12	Salt and Pepper Shakers	2	10
Wine	5	12	Pitcher	10	35
Tumbler	6	12	Vinegar Cruet	5	20
Juice Glass	4	10	Cake Plate	5	25
Salad-Dessert Plate	5	10	Open Bowl	6	30
Candlesticks, 4" pair	5	40	Relish Dish	4	15
Sugar	5	20			

 **CRYSTAL STEMWARE I** Good-quality lead crystal, including much Heisey glass.

	Low	High		Low	High
Goblet	$14	$ 25	Creamer	$10	$ 25
Iced Tea	14	25	Bud Vase	10	30
Sherbet	14	25	Salt and Pepper Shakers	20	40
Wine	14	25	Pitcher	40	100
Tumbler	14	25	Vinegar Cruet	25	40
Juice Glass	14	25	Cake Plate	30	45
Salad-Dessert Plate	14	25	Open Bowl	32	95
Candlesticks, 4" pair	45	95	Relish Dish	18	40
Sugar	10	25	Decanter	60	150

 **CRYSTAL STEMWARE II** Excellent quality—hand-cut—usually imported. To include the highly decorated crystal by Stuart, Orrefors, Baccarat, Waterford, and crystal with a rich gold band.

	Low	High		Low	High
Goblet	$28	$ 62	Creamer	$25	$ 75
Iced Tea	28	62	Bud Vase	35	70
Sherbet	28	62	Salt and Pepper Shakers	60	95
Wine	28	62	Pitcher	85	200
Tumbler	28	62	Vinegar Cruet	45	70
Juice Glass	28	62	Cake Plate	85	150
Salad-Dessert Plate	32	62	Open Bowl	90	250
Candlesticks, 4" pair	72	140	Relish Dish	45	90
Sugar	30	70	Decanter	125	275

even after referring to the description aid below, sketch the basic style of your goblets beside the listing, or attach a photograph to your inventory.

To verbally describe crystal stemware, note the shape of the bowl (globe-shaped, flared at the top, etc.) and any pattern or design on the bowl (floral band, swirled motif, gold rim, etc.). Next state whether the stem is short, long, notched, round, etc. Almost all stemware has a round base if it is in goblet shape.

Finally, total up the number of pieces in each pattern, the same way you did with the china, and estimate an approximate replacement cost by using the accompanying value charts.

12

Furniture—Chip Off the Old Block or Chipboard?

Your Biggest Investment

Unless you have an exceptionally fine collection of silver or jewelry, or a specialized collection such as coins or guns, the single largest investment in your household personal property is probably your furniture. Whether it is antique, old reproductions, or new, doesn't really matter. It is expensive to buy these days.

Volumes, encyclopedias, and entire series of books have been written on furniture, and I would be foolish to think I could educate you completely in all facets of furniture styles, construction, and values in one chapter. (No one person knows everything anyway.) So, based on observations made in my clients' homes and the questions I am most frequently asked, I am sharing the information I think will be most helpful to you. This chapter concentrates on the styles and types of furniture I see most often in your homes and in antiques shops, furniture stores, and at auctions.

I will not deal with exceptionally early sixteenth- or seventeenth-century furniture. Chances are you do not have this. But I will deal with furniture *styles* made in the twentieth century, which you may well have. I will not delve into rare Newport blockfront secretaries or Philadelphia highboys. But I will tell you about the reproductions and copies of these rare and extraordinarily valuable antiques. After you have read my comments, if you examine your highboy or secretary and believe it to be a period piece, call in an expert.

Let's begin then with the *styles* and *types* of furniture most commonly found in homes and shops today, so you can correctly identify the pieces on your inventory.

Pilgrim Furniture—There Isn't Much Around

During the 1920s Wallace Nutting brought the public's attention back to what he termed "Pilgrim" or "Colonial" furniture, the furniture of the seventeenth century, including Brewster and Carver chairs, trestle tables, joint or joined stools, butterfly and gateleg tables and Hadley chests. Few of these pieces actually survived from the 1650s, so the majority of joint stools and butterfly tables found today are indeed nineteenth century or even Nutting's 1920 reproductions, or, as in the case of the Brewster chair, a modern fake.

Not only was there not much furniture made to begin with (there were many fewer people living here), but period seventeenth-century furniture tended to be big, cumbersome, and uncomfortable, and quickly passed out of fashion. Thus it has not survived. However, the seventeenth-century *style* of tables—butterfly, trestle, and gateleg—have frequently been copied and are often found in today's homes.

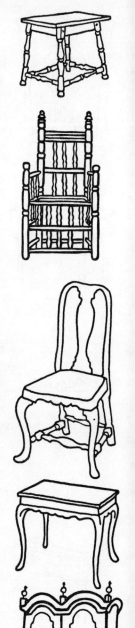

Queen Anne—A Graceful Lady

By the eighteenth century one of the most popular of all styles, Queen Anne furniture, emerged with its lovely curves and graceful lines replacing the large, bulbous furniture of the seventeenth-century. The style can be identified by looking first at the legs and then at the top of the piece in question. The cabriole leg curves outward at the knee and then tapers at the ankle. The foot may be a slipper foot, a padded foot, a trifid foot, or, once the Chippendale influence begins, a ball-and-claw foot.

The top of Queen Anne furniture also usually repeats the graceful curve. A Queen Anne secretary is identified by its domed, curved top, and Queen Anne chair backs repeat the graceful curved line at both the crest rail and the back splat.

Queen Anne furniture may be totally plain or embellished with carving—the shell motif is most frequently used. While Queen Anne period furniture is scarce and expensive, it is not rare. The style of Queen Anne furniture was frequently copied in the nineteenth century and continues to be manufactured today.

Chippendale—The Gentleman Cabinetmaker

Chippendale furniture became stylish in the second quarter of the eighteenth century and lasted in America until almost

the end of the century, or around 1785 or 1790. There are many variations of the basic Chippendale style, with Chinese Chippendale, characterized by its fretwork, being the most familiar.

Chippendale furniture retains some of the characteristics of the Queen Anne period, but it is generally distinguished by its straighter lines and heavier feeling. These characteristics are most easily seen by comparing a basic side chair, a table, and a secretary from the two periods.

Yes, you will find curved lines in the Chippendale chair back splat, but they are framed by a boxier and straighter outline. The curved leg of the Queen Anne table is replaced by the straight leg characteristic of the Chippendale period. (You also find straight legs on the chairs which often end in ball-and-claw feet.) The top of a Chippendale secretary will be straight across or have a broken swan-neck pediment, which is characterized by its triangular or scroll outline.

Fine Chippendale furniture is considered by many to be the epitome of grand elegance. It is more imposing than Queen Anne furniture. English Chippendale furniture is often classified as "Georgian," and it is the English Chippendale style, both antiques and later reproductions, that is most often found in America. Because of the great popularity of Chippendale furniture, as well as its size, which requires large boards of wood and greater labor costs, even reproduction Chippendale furniture can be as expensive as antique, if not period, pieces.

Adam Furniture—An American Hiccup

Following the Chippendale period, at the end of the eighteenth century or around 1780, America jumped right into the Hepplewhite period. But in England, which is the predominating influence in American furniture styles, the mid-eighteenth century saw a new development, the Adam style.

During this time the model English home was one in which the architecture, furniture, wallpaper, fabrics, silver, even furniture arrangements were perfectly coordinated. The Adam period is characterized by circles, ovals, urns, and garlands, and the furniture begins to be lighter in feeling.

However, during this time—the 1760s and 1770s—Americans were more involved in political unrest and pioneering than they were in developing new high fashions. Thus, little of the Adam influence is found in American furniture.

Hepplewhite—A Chance to Express Ourselves

As the 1780s arrived, Americans were looking for new styles to show off their newfound independence, both political and economic. The Hepplewhite period dominates American taste from the 1780s until the turn of the century, 1800.

The motifs of the Hepplewhite period—inlaid shields and urns—and the lighter, more delicate feeling of the furniture had actually evolved from the Adam style, which of course had developed from the Chippendale style. Thus when you compare the evolution of English furniture from Chippendale to Adam to Hepplewhite, the change seems more gradual than when you go from the American Chippendale period straight into the American Hepplewhite period.

American Hepplewhite furniture can often be distinguished from English Hepplewhite furniture by the ornamentation added to the basic style. By the 1780s Americans were proud of their country's accomplishments, and typically American symbols were used in furniture ornamentation. Eagles, crossed arrows, the American shield, even stars appear on tables, chair backs, clock cases, and secretaries. (Of course, to incorporate these designs in the furniture, inlaying and carving were refined and perfected.)

Because of the American motifs found during this time, many scholars call the era from 1780 to 1810 in America the Federal period. You will hear Hepplewhite, Sheraton, and Federal used interchangeably.

Hepplewhite furniture has experienced a resurgence of popularity in recent years. The smaller, daintier proportions of the style make it more suitable for many smaller homes, apartments, and townhouses than the large Chippendale (or later Empire or Victorian) furniture. Many reproductions of Hepplewhite furniture were made in the twentieth century.

Sheraton—Moving into the Nineteenth Century

By the end of the eighteenth century, the Industrial Revolution was picking up steam and styles were changing more rapidly than they had at any previous time in history. Developing simultaneously at the end of the Hepplewhite era was the Sheraton style, which began around 1790 and extended into the first decade of the nineteenth century, or around 1810.

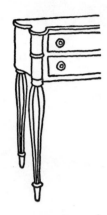

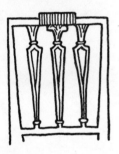

Remember that the Sheraton period is often included in the broad term, "American Federal Period." In fact, Sheraton is a much maligned word in the antiques world. Many people simply consider the Sheraton period an extension of Hepplewhite, and they refer to all Sheraton furniture as "Hepplewhite." There are still others who insist upon calling Sheraton furniture "Duncan Phyfe." In reality, Sheraton furniture has its own special style, which I illustrate here, but don't be surprised if you hear it called Federal, Hepplewhite, or Duncan Phyfe.

The easiest way to distinguish Sheraton furniture from Hepplewhite furniture is by comparing the legs and the wood. The characteristic Sheraton leg, whether on a chair, table, or chest of drawers, is rounded and may be turned or fluted. (The Hepplewhite leg is square and tapering.) The characteristic use of inlay in the Hepplewhite period is replaced with plain drawer fronts and table tops of either solid wood or veneer during the Sheraton period.

Sheraton chairs are distinguished by their backs, of which there are two major types. One has an angular or squared-off back (when contrasted with the Hepplewhite shield back) with either an open carved center splat design (this may be similar to the Hepplewhite style) or with vertical splats, which sometimes almost resemble chair legs or columns.

The other type of chair is the one often called the Duncan Phyfe style, which is recognizable by the wider, horizontal crest rail. The rest of the chair back may be totally open with only another plain horizontal slat, or there may be a carved, often lyre motif, back splat.

(Reading along, you have already learned a lot of furniture terminology which you can use in writing your descriptions. For example, you now know that a *splat* is the vertical back, which runs up and down from the crest rail to the seat. A *slat* is the horizontal back, which runs across from one side (or stile) to the other.)

The Sheraton chest of drawers is easily distinguishable from the Hepplewhite chest because of the shape of the legs and the higher, or raised, aspect of the piece. Also, the inlay found on sophisticated Hepplewhite sideboards or Pembroke tables is replaced by fluting, reeding, or turning on fine Sheraton pieces.

Sheraton furniture is not as popular as that of the Hepplewhite, Chippendale, or Queen Anne period. It is therefore often less expensive than other, more favored styles. Many fine Sheraton period pieces are available on the marketplace.

But be careful: the style was copied and reproduced in the late nineteenth century, as it continues to be today.

Poor Duncan Phyfe

Duncan Phyfe's name has become associated with a style of furniture, when, in fact, Phyfe, who worked in New York from 1780 to 1840, made furniture in *several* styles. It is not at all uncommon to hear a Sheraton, Empire, or Victorian chair called a Duncan Phyfe chair. This would have been fine (Chippendale, Hepplewhite, and Sheraton had styles named after them) except that Duncan Phyfe's style *changed* following the changing tastes of his time. Thus, while other cabinetmakers followed Hepplewhite's *designs,* for example, Duncan Phyfe's designs followed the tastes of the Sheraton and Empire styles. It is best to leave Mr. Phyfe's name out of styles and go by Sheraton, Empire, and Victorian instead. But remember the name if someone tries to sell you "a true Duncan Phyfe" piece. The "Duncan Phyfe" style was mass-produced in the 1930s through the 1950s.

Empire? What's That?

You leave one area of confusion and step into another. But these can all easily be cleared up. Just as "Duncan Phyfe" is misused to denote a style which was really Sheraton or Empire, so Empire furniture is ignored as if it never existed at all.

American Empire furniture is actually the furniture made from about 1810 until the beginning of the Victorian period, or 1840. Very high-fashion Empire furniture is carved, gilded, and quite unlike any other style you will see. The decorative motifs come from architecture (the Greek key and palmette), nature (cornucopias and serpents), and classical mythology (dolphins, griffins, and caryatids). The furniture is heavy, bold, and richly ornamented.

The American Empire furniture found in today's homes is often mistakenly called Victorian furniture because Empire furniture, like Victorian furniture, is big, heavy, and dark. It also looks more like Victorian than it does like Hepplewhite or Sheraton. As a result, Empire furniture is generally lumped in with the rest of the nineteenth-century furniture, and the style of almost one hundred years becomes termed "Victorian."

The usual Empire household furniture is characterized by its straight lines, mahogany veneer, and basic plainness. You

have seen hundreds of Empire chests and tables, but perhaps you called them Duncan Phyfe or Victorian pieces.

By the Empire period, furniture was being manufactured and shipped throughout the country, and thus a lot of Empire furniture looks alike. This is the era of the Hitchcock chair and mantel clocks—also mass-produced.

Empire furniture is the most underpriced furniture around these days. Because it is veneered and was often heavily varnished (as was popular in the late nineteenth and early twentieth centuries), much of the furniture has missing veneer and a grungy crackled finish. Empire furniture is also oversized for many of today's homes. But just wait ... the prices are already beginning to creep up as the cost and quality of modern furniture astound the public. Empire is on the verge of being rediscovered.

You need to know that there were reproductions of Empire furniture made in the twentieth century. Look for the signs I list under reproductions and fakes to tell the difference.

Queen Victoria—A Much Abused Lady

Queen Victoria ascended the English throne in 1837 and did not descend until her death in 1901. Every *dominant* style of furniture made during those sixty-four years bears her name. The era began quietly with a gradual change from the plain but big Empire furniture into a more decorated style with the "embellishment" of Empire pieces. A rose was carved on the back of a sofa, the horizontal splat of a chair was made to resemble a Gothic arch, and soon the Victorian era was in full swing.

There are five major "sub-styles" of Victorian furniture and great overlapping of their years of popularity. But once you learn what motifs characterize each style, the styles become distinctly different.

The first two sub-styles are the Gothic (1840–1860) and the Rococo (1845–1870). *Victorian Gothic* furniture is characterized by the architectural motifs found on the great European cathedrals built during the fourteenth century. There are arches, trefoils, quatrefoils, and rosettes all intertwined and conjoined. Gothic Victorian furniture is not as popular or as frequently found as the next style.

The *Victorian Rococo* style is the most familiar of the Victorian sub-styles and uses the same decorations that the original

Rococo period (eighteenth century) used but interprets them differently. The word "rococo" comes from the French word *"rocaille"* and means rock or shell. So Victorian Rococo furniture is an intermingling of flowers, shells, grapes, foliage, all brought together in curved, flowing, even "rocky" lines. Some of the furniture is more elaborately decorated than others, but the flowing, curved line is consistently present. Into this large sub-style are included characteristics of the French Louis XV furniture—also characterized by the cabriole line, scroll and floral motifs. This is the most popular of all the Victorian sub-styles and has been expensively priced for quite a while. Several reproduction lines of Victorian Rococo furniture are currently in production. Watch out!

The *Victorian Renaissance* came into fashion around 1850 and lasted through the 1870s. By this time, furniture manufacturers in New York and Michigan could easily meet the public's demand for the latest fashions, and these new pieces were quickly bought to replace old, out-of-style furniture.

The public got what it wanted—large, heavily decorated furniture with strong European overtones. Scrolls and flowers were still used, but in a more geometric fashion. Bulls' eyes and shields frequently appear, but the most distinguishing motif of the Renaissance style is a cartouche used as the center decoration on chairs, beds, mirrors, and sideboards or buffets. The entire shape of this style departs from the Rococo rounded shape and the Gothic pointed or turreted shape. Renaissance pieces are more rectangular or squared and geometric in total perspective. The large size of this style has limited its popularity. Victorian Renaissance furniture can still be found and usually is priced in the middle line of the Victorian styles.

Following the Renaissance, and incorporating some of its characteristics, is the fourth sub-style, *Victorian Eastlake* furniture (1870–1900). Inspired by the English architect, Charles Locké Eastlake, this style is identifiable by two main characteristics: burl wood or veneered panels appear on drawer fronts, cupboard doors, and chair backs. If this decoration is not present, you can almost bet that an incised motif (carved into the wood) will be in its place. Pilasters on chests and table legs were reeded during the Eastlake period.

The Eastlake style was once passed over in favor of the other Victorian sub-styles. This is now changing. Eastlake furniture is becoming quite fashionable and, naturally, finding its way into antiques shops with appropriate price tags, showing three numbers before the decimal point, where two used to be. Because the furniture is generally less imposing than other Victorian styles, usually made of walnut (instead of the later golden oak), has some style (the burl panels in particular), and is still affordable, it is logical that this should be the new discovery. If you like it, you'd better buy now. To my knowledge, unlike the other "sleeper"—Empire furniture—Eastlake furniture has not been mass-reproduced.

Finally, the fifth sub-style is known as the *Victorian Cottage* style (sometimes called Spool style). Introduced around the middle of the century (1840), this fashion lasted until the end of the nineteenth century and has never really been out of style. This furniture is everywhere, from Cape Cod cottages to crossroads stores in the Midwest, and is characterized by its simple style and spool (or Jenny Lind) turnings. The furniture was mass-produced and was inexpensive when it was made. In fact, it is probably more expensive now in relation to its value than it was when it was first made. The furniture was often sold in suites and painted or stenciled. Much that you find today has had the paint removed.

Because one of today's looks is the country look, even though this cottage furniture is neither terribly old nor of fine quality, it is in great demand and prices are creeping up as the demand continues to increase.

Belter—A Star Is Born

Before concluding with Victorian styles and moving onto Golden Oak and Mission furniture, a comment should be interjected on Belter furniture.

Ten years ago if you wanted information on John Belter, you would have searched to find a scant bibliographical entry or a sentence or two about his furniture under "Victorian furniture." Today Belter furniture is pictured on the cover of slick-cover magazines, in auction house catalogues, and in expensive full-page magazine ads. At least one new article about Belter appears every month.

During the 1850s John Belter developed revolutionary techniques that allowed wood to be curved, shaped, and carved. His laminated furniture, mostly of rosewood, exemplifies the Victorian Rococo style. While Belter's name is not yet as familiar as Chippendale's, the prices paid for his furniture now equal those of fine eighteenth-century furniture— and a few years ago you couldn't give it away.

Oak—Gold Is Right

Most books stop with Victorian styles. Nothing else follows, I have been told. Maybe yesterday nothing else followed, but today we can come right up to the present.

At the end of the nineteenth century and during the first quarter of the twentieth century, oak was the favorite of the great American middle class. My own father has told me many times of the day in his childhood, in 1918 or 1919, that the Golden Oak secretary arrived at his home. He helped move the new secretary in and the 1800 cherry Chippendale secretary up to the attic for storage (Thank goodness they kept it in storage until my mother rescued it in 1938! Unfortunately, however, the golden oak secretary was given away in the 1950s.)

"I really couldn't figure out, even in my child's mind, why they wanted to replace the beautiful, heavy cherry secretary with that ugly light oak piece," he still recalls today.

Today's generation looks át oak differently. They consider it to be "antique," although it was retailed new through the 1930s. There is much speculation as to why this inexpensive furniture is back in fashion—but probably the respectability of its increasing age combined with its durability when compared to some of today's chipboard furniture are as good reasons as there need to be.

Golden Oak furniture is easily recognizable by its wood grain alone. The major styles concentrate on large, oversized pieces reminiscent of Empire furniture (which, you see, was just about one hundred years before Golden Oak furniture— remember it is said that styles go in one-hundred-year cycles) and the angular, straight, almost barren furniture associated with Mission furniture.

> **Warning.** Golden Oak furniture became so popular again so quickly that entrepreneurs have dug up old catalogues and are making copies and reproductions literally overnight. It is not uncommon to see an 1880 Golden Oak table with 1980 Golden Oak chairs sold as a group in antiques shops.

Arts and Crafts and Mission Furniture—Ad Men Have Been Around a Long Time

Once the furniture manufacturers had thriving businesses, they learned they had to keep the public buying. If fashions never changed, there would be no reason to buy new furniture once a house was furnished.

The end of the Victorian era, the 1880s and 1890s, saw a reaction to the ornate furniture of the mid-nineteenth century. In resistance to the trefoils, flowers, cartouches, burl woods and oyster veneers, incised grape leaves and turned spools of the previous fifty years, a new austere style developed. Known as the Arts and Crafts Movement, the style was extremely linear and mostly devoid of superfluous decoration. In America the style was interpreted by Frank Lloyd Wright and Gustav Stickley. The less expensive mass-produced versions of this furniture made by the Grand Rapids, Michigan, companies became dubbed Mission Furniture, after the austere Spanish style associated with New Mexico and Texas. Since this section of the country held much fascination for the far away East Coast, it caught on, both as a name and a style.

And it has caught on again. Some seventy years after the Stickley companies published their catalogues, *Craftsman Furniture Made by Gustav Stickley* and *The Work of L. and G. Stickley,* they have been reprinted by Dover and their names are once again famous.

The current vogue is in higher swing in New York and California than in other sections of the country. But interior decorators are looking for this furniture to combine with Tiffany Studio lamps and Rookwood Pottery to create a total look.

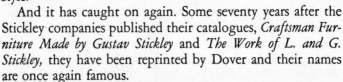

If you find any labeled Stickley furniture and don't buy it, you'll regret it later. It's already being sold in New York by Christie's and Sotheby's for thousands of dollars.

Art Deco—Fred and Ginger, Enter Right

Coming in on the coattails of the understated, austere Arts and Crafts Movement but with the new worldly sophistication sired by the First World War, the 1920s and 30s gave birth to a new style, Art Deco. The straight lines and geometric design of the Arts and Crafts Movement were elaborated upon by using bleached and burl wood combined with chrome hardware and legs. Furniture of this period is still hovering in limbo. The accessories of the period—everything from Lalique perfume bottles and Chiparus figurines, which sell at the international auction houses, to Depression glass and Fiesta Ware, which sell at flea markets—are now *hot.* The exceptionally fine furniture by Louis Majorell, Thonet, and Josef Hoffman is being sold at auction for thousands of dollars. The mass market boom can't be far behind.

What's Next—We've Only Just Begun . . .

Danish modern, Eames chairs, plastic chair frames with naugahyde-covered cushions, Parsons tables, modular units, even redwood and mesh-style wrought-iron patio and porch furniture . . . each will have its day.

The Also's: Windsor and Wicker

Windsor chairs became Americanized around 1725 or 1730 and have been made continuously since then. The two major kinds of Windsors that I see frequently are the New England versions with either turned legs or with bamboo type legs. The third type of Windsor, the distinctive Philadelphia version with ball or bulb feet, is less common. The biggest problem with Windsor chairs is that they were made for such a long time—through the eighteenth and nineteenth centuries—in the same style and same method that even experts can be fooled into thinking that an 1830 chair that has had excessive wear dates from 1790. Windsor chairs are riding the high tide right now, and even chairs labeled "Wallace Nutting" and sold as twentieth-century reproductions can be expected to bring over $500. An exceptional eighteenth-century museum-quality Windsor chair with elaborate turnings and the maker's stamp can be expected to bring $7,500 or more.

Wicker furniture, as we know it in our homes today, was first made in the mid-nineteenth century. Because of its combined properties of strength and pliability, wicker can and has been made into every style conceived by the human imagination. The most popular wicker style embodies the Victorian Rococo, and the more elaborate the piece, the greater its price tag. Like Windsor chairs, wicker pieces are being made today,

and it is difficult to distinguish some reproductions from some antique (the word is used loosely) wicker. I have been told that old wicker is much heavier than reproduction wicker, which, in comparison, is very lightweight. Obviously, condition must always be considered in valuing wicker, as broken parts weaken the entire piece and repairing broken wicker furniture can be both costly and time-consuming.

Our Total Look

The two other major furniture styles I see most frequently in private homes which I have not covered already are French styles and American country furniture.

America's divergent background has always been seen in our home furnishings. French Provincial is mixed with American gingham and highlighted with a touch of Oriental bronze and porcelain. This mélange makes our interior design international to some, eclectic to others.

Our preference for styles goes in cycles as dictated by current events (when President Nixon went to China, our interest in Oriental styles was rekindled), museum exhibits (the reopening of the American Wing at the Metropolitan Museum of Art created new reproduction lines), major auction sales (the Christie's sale of Mrs. Prescott's English collection was followed by many articles on the increasing interest in English furniture), and advertising (as orchestrated by the furniture manufacturers and Madison Avenue).

Fashion Abroad

The two major French styles most often reproduced are Louis XV and French Provincial. The Louis XV is characterized by curved legs, delicate proportions, and typically French embellishments (brass or bronze doré galleries, beading, foliage mounts, and inlaid motifs), parquetry (geometric designs), and marquetry (floral and classical designs). These are the sophisticated motifs so frequently associated with the court of Louis XV. French Provincial is just what it says—the French style but with a provincial, country, or less sophisticated flair. The same lines and many of the same motifs as the Louis XV style are used—particularly the floral designs—but the interpretation is simpler and less elaborate than when found in Louis XV furniture. Also, in French Provincial furniture these motifs are part of the furniture itself, carved in the wood, rather than being added to the furniture, as the sabots and chutes of the Louis XV style were separate parts and made of different materials. Most French furniture found in homes and the usual antiques shop is *not* period furniture but later reproductions—some imported, some American-made.

Fashion at Home

American country furniture is easily identifiable but difficult to date. The actual furniture pieces are mostly utilitarian—chairs, storage pieces (corner cupboards, pie safes), and tables. The lines are angular and the decoration simple. The wood is that of the region—pine, ash, maple, oak, poplar and, for the better pieces, cherry and walnut. Country craftsmen made the same pieces—tables, beds, desks—in the same styles, with the same tools, and out of the same materials for years.

In contrast, the city craftsmen were always seeking the newest styles, latest inventions, and imported materials (mahogany being the favorite wood, of course). Thus, you may find a simple Chippendale secretary made of walnut, with panel doors, a molded straight top, and shaped bracket feet, which you would normally date 1780, but discover in a family inventory or history that the piece actually was made in 1830, when you would have expected the family to be buying Empire fashions. This is why most country pieces are broadly dated—a pine corner cupboard may be dated circa 1800–1850, or a ladder-back chair may be simply called nineteenth century. I remember one museum exhibit of country furniture which labeled some of the chairs circa 1800–1900!

Country furniture is highly sought after and our renewed interest in ecology and the natural life has heightened its popularity. Country styles also evoke dreams of the bucolic life with warm apple pies, a cheery kitchen and a blazing fire as we commute to the city for another day's work in the skyscraper.

City Chest and the Country Cupboard— A Few Specifics

The big investors, dealers and collectors alike have always sought out the finest authentic antiques. Money is not an object for them. They have paid $100,000 for a Newport, Rhode Island, Chippendale drop-leaf table, c. 1765, made and signed by John Townsend, and $360,000 for a Chippendale block-and-shell carved mahogany chest of drawers, also from the same maker and time. Fine and rare pieces always bring top dollar. But there are other thoughts on the relative value of antiques.

Some investors are noting that the highly formal antique pieces, while they are terribly expensive, do not show the percentage increase that some of the less expensive items do. For the $100,000 table to show a 50 percent increase in its auction price, it would have to sell for $150,000, and the $360,000 chest of drawers would have to bring $540,000. But the pine corner cupboard, which you bought last year for $1,400 in the country antiques show, will see a 50 percent increase when it reaches $2,100, and the simple walnut drop-leaf table, which sold for $325 two years ago, already has a replacement value of $500, or a 54 percent increase. Furthermore, the corner cupboard and the drop leaf table are within the reach of many buyers, while very few people can seriously compete for a $360,000 chest.

Reproductions, Frauds, and Fakes

There are plenty of fakes around. But you really don't need to be too concerned with furniture fakes, at least not the rare, expensive ones. For the faker to earn enough money to make faking worth his time, he has got to sell the piece either to a museum or to an "uptown" dealer. If the piece is good enough to get by the museum curator or this class of dealer, chances are it may go undetected until it indeed is an antique. And anyway, if the fake is of that superior quality, it is probably worth what you paid for it. *Instead of worrying about fake antique furniture, the general public must learn to beware of buying furniture that is not as old as it is purported to be.*

At least two or three times a week I go into a private home and am told, "This is a Chippendale desk," as I stand in front of an 1890 lady's writing desk with machine-cut dovetails, mahogany veneer drawer fronts, and machine-cut screws attaching the sliding brass hinges to the writing surface.

"Chippendale style," I suggest.

"No, real Chippendale . . . The dealer told me this could have been made by Chippendale himself!"

If it has been an unusually rough week I am often tempted to say something like, "How many women had their own writing desks in 1760, especially ones with brass hinges screwed into the sides that are marked 'Pat. Applied for, June '95'?"

But the appraiser who puts it that way isn't going to stay in business for long, and anyway, if the desk gets burned up, I want the owner to receive a justified $450 for the desk—not get either ripped off for $75 or paid $5,000.

Only when you become knowledgeable about antiques can you keep from falling for such dealer sales pitches—especially if you like the piece anyway.

In just a few pages I am going to tell you specific signs to look for—both good and bad—when you are examining the furniture in your own home to identify on your inventory list and when you are antiques shopping. But here, I want to share with you some extra hints and facts that will make you more astute.

Before you Learn the Specifics, Hints to Always Remember

> First, always remember that there are thousands of reproductions made for every antique.

The fine reproductions of one hundred, seventy-five, and even fifty years ago are being sold as "period" pieces by unknowing dealers. If you keep this fact in the back of your mind, you will be less gullible.

Second, almost every local area had a craftsman (back in the 1920s, 30s, and 40s) who used to sell antiques and make reproductions. These men would comb the countryside and backwoods, buying antiques—many of which had been discarded for "finer" new pieces. They would bring these antiques into their shops and make copies to sell to customers who wanted "old-looking" new pieces.

Sometimes such a vendor would sell the antique itself— once it was copied—but usually not before he had "improved" it a little. If the craftsman liked inlay, he would add a little inlay to the walnut chest of drawers. Or if he thought an eagle would look nice on the card table apron, he would add an eagle.

And about those feet. Our craftsman tried sitting at the secretary, but it was just too high, so before he sold the eighteenth-century cherry Chippendale secretary, he removed the ogee feet and added a shorter bracket foot.

Every antiques dealer or appraiser who is truly knowledgeable about furniture has seen literally hundreds of these pieces. These are often the desks, secretaries, and chests that end up being catalogued and classified in New York auction sales as "restored." These are also the same desks, secretaries, and chests that may turn up in antiques shops labeled as "period" pieces.

Third, if you are going to buy and invest in antique furniture, learn not only how to identify the periods and styles, but also what pieces of furniture were made in what time frame. Take the "Chippendale lady's writing desk. " Not only was this obviously not a period piece because of the reasons already stated, but this form, a small desk on raised cabriole legs, *in these proportions* did not exist in eighteenth-century England.

The same can be said for the wicker rocking chair that came over on the *Mayflower.* A wicker chair with rockers had not been conceived in 1620.

And there is no such thing as a period Queen Anne sideboard. Sideboards were not designed and made until the 1760s—some forty years after the Queen Anne period.

Fourth, and this is particularly important if you are going to *invest* in antiques, learn what prices should be paid for what pieces. This will take study and an investment on your part of both time and money spent for catalogues and books, but it will save you thousands of dollars in the long run and keep you from buying antique items that are something other than what they are purported to be.

Let me illustrate how important it is to know *how much* to pay with the following story.

A few years ago I found I had some time between appointments in another city, and as I drove down the road I saw a tempting antiques sign. The automatic pilot took over, and suddenly I found myself inside an antiques shop.

The owner was nowhere around, but I thoroughly enjoyed browsing undisturbed through a collection of English brasses, German porcelain, and a mixture of English and American furniture—mostly old reproductions and Victorian pieces. Then a pair of chairs caught my eye. "English, twentieth-century makeups," I thought matter of factly (appraisers never take holidays, I've decided).

I started past the chairs, and then I wondered, how much does the shop owner get for this type of chair? I wandered over and began reading the ticket which was attached to one chair by a daintily tied ribbon.

"Pair of rare maple Chippendale arm chairs, Philadelphia, 1780."

Furniture Vocabulary—Motifs and Terms

Acanthus

Bellflower

C-Scroll

Chamfered or
Canted Corner

Cartouche

Conch Shell

Crest Rail

Cross Banding

Dentil Molding

Egg & Dart

Escutcheon

Finial

Fret

Garland or Swag

Paterae

Quarter Fan Inlay

Shell or Fan

Slat

Splat

I thought I was dreaming. The wrong ticket got on the chair, I reasoned. I looked at the ticket on the other chair. Identical.

To begin with, the chairs were not maple. They were a combination of oak and burl walnut. Second, Philadelphia chairs are usually walnut or mahogany—rarely maple, to say nothing of English oak and veneer. They were not Chippendale—they were Queen Anne—but some people do call those chairs Chippendale, no matter. Third, the chairs no more dated from 1780 than I did. Everything was wrong—the proportion, the tool marks, the wood combination.

Then I looked at the price, $1,500 for the pair. The last time a pair of 1780 Philadelphia arm chairs went for $1,500 would have been three or four years earlier. I didn't doubt that *these* chairs might sell for $1,500, but Philadelphia 1780 arm chairs were then bringing $1,600, $1,800, and $2,000 apiece at Sotheby Parke Bernet and were retailed at $3,500 to $5,000 a pair in many shops.

Just about this time the shop owner appeared.

"Aren't they lovely chairs," he began. "And so rare. I was extremely lucky to get them. Do you know how much they would cost in New York?" he continued.

"How much?" I asked.

"Oh, at least $2,000 or $3,000 apiece."

"But that would be $4,000 or $6,000 for the pair! Why are you selling them for $1,500?" I couldn't resist asking.

"I don't really have that much equity in them," he said a little apologetically. "You see, they belonged to an old family friend and she asked me to sell them for her."

Where was the logic? Why not tell the friend to send them to New York and make a couple of extra thousand dollars? Because, of course, they were *not* rare Philadelphia Chippendale chairs dating from 1780; they were English 1920s chairs, and if they had been auctioned off in New York that year the pair would have brought $300 or $400 top dollar!

> If you know prices you will keep from being "taken" many times, particularly if the dealer has mistaken and often grandiose ideas about his merchandise.

When you walk into an antiques shops and see a stylish Hepplewhite chest of drawers beautifully inlaid and in pristine condition with a tag reading, "New England, 1790, $800," be ready to find machine-made dovetails or plywood drawer bottoms. But if you examine the chest and are convinced that it is a 1790 chest and you can afford it and you like it, buy it. After all, a really fine chest of drawers of comparable quality bought today from a retail furniture store would have a price tag 50 percent to 100 percent higher than the one you're looking at!

Fifth, and finally, never buy antique furniture without asking yourself the most basic of all questions, "Does it *look* old?" Follow this question up with, "Does it *feel* old?" and finally, "Does it *smell* old?" It is amazing what you sometimes find if you let your mind and senses rule your eagerness to get a steal.

The Truth About Old Furniture

Before reviewing the signs that distinguish old furniture from new, let me repeat what Michael Gordon wrote about "fakes" recently in *Antiques Monthly,*

> Being a world center for fine arts and antiques, London is also a world center for conservators and reproducers. I have been shown examples of restoration that were simply flabbergasting, especially when I was told how little it cost to have the work done. Therefore, don't assume because the piece you are buying seems "so cheap" it has not been worked on; also, don't assume that because the shop you are buying it in is reputable it could not be a reproduction. The person selling you the piece may just not know what has been done to it or just when it was made.

We are alert to new "fakes," but are we ready to accept nineteenth-century "fakes?"

I will never forget one such, a highboy. It was an imposing piece with a closed bonnet, large cabriole legs, and whorl feet. It was carved, crossbanded, and had a large cartouche at the top center. The highboy was obviously a Victorian interpretation of many styles and fashions, but it was such an unusual mixture of Queen Anne and Louis XV styles, English and European influences that I asked the owner what she knew about the piece.

She opened a drawer and handed me a fragile letter dating from the 1890s. The highboy, the letter stated, dated from the 1680s, descended through several notable families, and was brought into Baltimore by a finely titled gentleman who sold it—to the present owner's ancestors.

I had been prepared for the owner to say she thought the piece was an eighteenth-century piece. This happens frequently, and actually when I had asked my question I was stalling for time while figuring out how to tell her that the highboy was not as antique as she perhaps thought. But the written statement threw me.

I carefully explained why the piece could not be a seventeenth-century one—the highboy, cabriole legs, and whorl feet had not even been conceived of in 1680 for starters.

The owner now cheerfully shows off the bogus letter when asked about the highboy. But the truth is, there have always been gullible antiques lovers who have bought with their emotions, helped along by a glib seller's "documentation."

How can you avoid being such a victim? You can't always. But there are some precautions you can take.

Examining Furniture—Some Specifics

First, approach each piece of furniture with great suspicion. Expect something to be wrong.

Look for the following signs:

- Circular saw marks. These are a sure giveaway that a piece was made after 1830 or 1840. Look along the piece of wood where it would have been sawn—the end of a board—for example, at the back of a drawer in a chest of drawers, along the bottom of a chair frame, or the flat edge of a table top. Once you see and can identify circular saw marks, you will always recognize them.

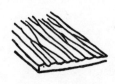

- Plane marks. These are a good sign that a piece is earlier than 1840 or 1860. Plane marks can be seen, but they can also be felt. Because they are usually on interior surfaces, you will want to learn how to *feel* them as well as know what they look like. I always ask my audiences to rub their fingers over the inside of their hands, both the fingers and palms. The rolling indentations that you feel are similar to the feeling of irregular plane marks. It is these irregular ripplings that experts are feeling for when they run their fingers under the top of a chest or along a drawer bottom. You want to find these plane marks on drawer bottoms and the underneath surface of top boards of chests made before 1850. Always check the top—replaced tops are frequently found.

- Round circles and clean feet. As I explained, old wood that was cut "green" shrinks. Furthermore, if regularly rubbed against another surface, all wood is eventually going to wear down. Look for obvious signs of wear on the bottom of all feet, and on country style chairs, which might have been sat in and tilted back (and even rested against a wall or porch railing), see if the back legs are worn at the back and look for signs of wear across the back. Look at chair stretchers to find possible wear from constant rubbing. Examine drawer side bottoms for signs of wear from opening and closing the drawers—they should be *smooth* from wear. If all circles are round and all interior surfaces are sharp, ask yourself, where are the signs of normal wear?

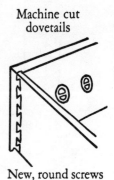

Machine cut dovetails

New, round screws

- Handles and screws. "I bought this piece because it had the original brasses," one owner told me. Yep, she got new brasses *and* a new chest! There is much to-do about replaced brasses. But ask anyone who owns an old chest with the original brasses or hardware and he will tell you—they break! The constant pulling on a drawer or door by the same handle year in and year out weakens the handle and often it breaks—it's that simple. If a piece has "its original brasses," and they are secured by a rounded head screw with wide grooves, be suspicious—the whole piece may be new, or else you've got some old parts combined with new drawers or doors, or some such combination.

Interior view of drawer

Old post holes, new replacement screw

Do not worry if you find that the antique chest or desk has had more than one pair of brasses. This is the norm, not the exception. But *do* check all the drawers to make sure that these postholes (the holes where the earlier brasses had been) match in all drawers and that the interior holes match with the drawer fronts. Often new drawer fronts have been added to an old backing—particularly in English pieces and any veneered piece.

Good: evidence on front of drawer of first set of post holes

While examining the handles and screws, remember to check the locks. This is one place where even the expert craftsman, who made a very fine reproduction using hand-cut dovetails, wooden pegs, and the proper dimensions in copying an antique, may have become careless. First look at the lock itself. Many eighteenth-century locks had two or more bolts and are held in place by handmade screws or hand-forged nails. Very often these locks are large and may take up almost the entire depth of the drawer ledge. By the nineteenth century, smaller locks predominate, but once again look for old nails and screws used to attach the locks to the drawers in early nineteenth-century pieces. Many locks of the later nineteenth century will have the manufacturer's name or a

Warning! No evidence of post holes — newly veneered drawer front

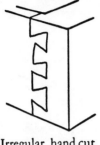

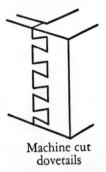

Irregular, hand cut
dovetails

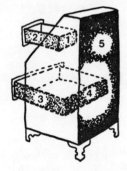

Machine cut
dovetails

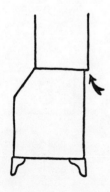

patent designation imprinted on them. When you find a "period" Chippendale desk with a perfectly fitted lock labeled "Yale," begin looking the entire piece over again.

• Dovetails. Early hand-cut dovetails have slight irregularities to them. If you compare the perfect machine-cut dovetail with an irregular hand-cut one, you can see the difference immediately. Remember, though, that by the mid-nineteenth century furniture is manufactured, and thus you can have an "antique" Victorian piece with machine-cut dovetails. What you do not want to see are machine-cut dovetails in a "1780 Chippendale chest of drawers."

• Patina and color. Some experts claim that they can tell by the patina or finish of a piece whether it is old or not. I have seen many eighteenth-century pieces with twentieth-century finishes which I had written off as "old reproductions" until I looked inside. Don't stop with the outside color—look inside. The unfinished backs of corner cupboards, chests, sideboards, grandfather clocks, etc., turn dark from constant exposure to air. Contrast this darkness with the unfinished drawer interiors inside a slant-front desk where little air ever reaches. These drawers look like new—light and often almost shiny. Now look at the drawers in the bottom of the desk (or any chest of drawers). The sides should be "cleaner" or lighter than the dark back board of the desk, but the back board of the drawer will be darker where air has circulated between the protective desk back and the drawer backs than the sides—but not as dark as the board at the back of the desk.

• Marriages—for better or for worse. While you have the drawers open, check the interior sides of all the drawers for similar dovetailing and coloration. Chests and desks are often made up of composite "old pieces," and if there are distinctly different dovetails or colors between the drawers, think twice. This test should *always* be given to chest-on-chests and highboys. The two separate pieces may have been put together at different times, or, in antiques terminology, "married." If there are distinct differences, you can be fairly sure that the pieces were not originally intended to be together. Even if the color and dovetails match up, check the depth of the two pieces and make sure that they align correctly at the back. A distinct difference in depth is a warning sign. And, of course, this is the test to give a secretary or breakfront or any case-piece which has two parts but where the top may have doors and the bottom drawers.

• Feet, legs, and aprons. Just as the constant wear on handles and knobs leads to breakage, feet and legs take the brunt of wear on any piece of furniture. In days of heavy spring and fall cleaning, secretaries, chests, corner cupboards, etc., were tugged and dragged out of their niches, often causing damage to their feet and legs, especially delicate, thin legs. Even today I often see considerable damage to the feet and legs of furniture caused by our modern invention—the vacuum cleaner. To tell whether or not feet have been replaced or changed on chests and desks you need two tools—your hands and your eyes. Just as you *feel* drawer bottoms for hand-planed marks, feel for this same undulated unevenness on shaped aprons that connect the legs and feet on Hepplewhite and Sheraton pieces. An absolutely sharp, rough-edged apron is a warning sign. Always check for the same signs, which may indicate a new molding or frame on a Chippendale chest or secretary.

Next, learn to recognize with your eyes the correct perspective that a period case-piece should have. Furniture made during the eighteenth-century Chippendale and Hepplewhite periods had taller feet, whether they are ogee or bracket feet, than the later copies of this style. Once you can *sight* the correct perspective of a period case-piece, the copies will immediately be identifiable because of their "cut-down" proportions, which begin with the feet. By learning that a Chippendale foot should be approximately five to seven inches tall on a period desk, for example, when you see a short or truncated three-to-four inch foot, you will be suspicious and either look for cut-down or replaced feet, or question the age of the entire piece.

Just as feet and legs can reveal the age of a person, they can also indicate the age of a piece of furniture.

The Obscure and the Obvious

In addition to these general clues to look for when examining a piece of furniture, you should know that there are other, often obscure characteristics that can be telltale signs of age. In the bibliography, I have listed books that go into more specific detail about detecting furniture fakes and frauds, but

Feet & Legs

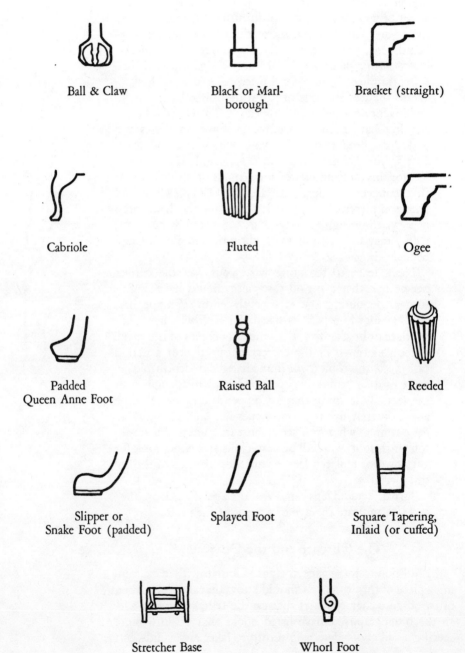

Ball & Claw

Black or Marl-
borough

Bracket (straight)

Cabriole

Fluted

Ogee

Padded
Queen Anne Foot

Raised Ball

Reeded

Slipper or
Snake Foot (padded)

Splayed Foot

Square Tapering,
Inlaid (or cuffed)

Stretcher Base

Whorl Foot

two of the very best are Moreton Marsh's *The Easy Expert in American Antiques* and Nancy Smith's *Old Furniture, Understanding the Craftsman's Art.*

Misery Loves Company

I have made my own share of mistakes, but one of the most frustrating ones involved another expert, which at least gives me comfort.

I was called in to help an elderly client price some objects for sale. Most of the pieces were ordinary household furnishings. There were a few Victorian pieces, an oak table, and a couple of interesting beds. But there in the corner was the piece you hope to find, but seldom do—a fine Hepplewhite or Federal side chair, crisply carved and wonderfully proportioned. Next to it was a matching arm chair which was just as "right."

When I asked the owner about the chair, everything she told me was what I wanted to hear. She had found the chairs in an 1830s house in her small home town. One of the chairs was in bad condition—the stretcher broken, the back loose—but she bought them and took them both to a cabinetmaker. The year was 1938. He fixed and tightened them but did not refinish the chairs or alter them in any way.

I told her that I thought the chairs were worth a good deal of money—$1,500 at the minimum if sold to the right dealer. If she wanted, she could sell them for more, but that would take time. She needed the money. Since she was going to the hospital she asked me to take the chairs home and ask the dealer to come and see them.

I took the chairs home, put them in my living room, and went straight to my library. There they were, illustrated in all of the right books—Nutting, Miller, Sack!

I called a dealer I knew would be interested and he agreed to drive several hundred miles to see them. Meanwhile, my husband came in, took one look at the chairs, and said, "Those old chairs look good for reproductions. Where are you going to put them?"

Blasphemy! And worse—blasphemy from a layman. "Just wait until you see them advertised in *Antiques* magazine!" I retorted.

The dealer arrived the next day and when he saw the chairs became as excited as I. We examined the chairs carefully. No saw marks, good signs of wear, wonderful carving, perfect proportions. You couldn't ask for much more. We'd done our homework. We were satisfied. We settled on a price above the one quoted to my client. The dealer drove away.

Late that night the phone rang. While unloading his truck, the dealer had pulled one chair out by its top rail. The old glue was loose, and the crest rail slipped out. There, for the expert to see, was a perfect, round machine-cut dowel connecting the crest rail and stile—the sign to the knowing eye of a fine old reproduction made around 1920. "And I was deciding which of my customers to call first," he sighed.

Of course the chairs were returned. They were sold as handsome reproduction chairs for $500.

The moral of this story is that anyone can—and most people do, sometimes at least—make a mistake. If you think you have a genuinely rare piece, ask a true expert. Do not take the word of a neighbor or antiques hobbyist. If the expert believes you do have an exceptionally valuable piece, a rare find, *don't believe him or her.* Ask another expert. If they both give the same verdict, independently of one another, then you may *begin* to raise your hopes.

The Obvious and the $50,000 Dream

One snowy night I drove a distance to look at a ball-and-claw sofa which the owners described to me as an "eighteenth-century Chippendale piece." They had been told by a knowledgeable expert—but knowledgeable in another area of antiques—that their sofa was worth $50,000.

"Mrs. Jenkins, he told me he didn't know if it was English or American, but he said that didn't matter. That sofa is worth $50,000," the husband eagerly exclaimed over the phone.

I genuinely wanted to see an American ball-and-claw Chippendale sofa in a private home. I had only seen them at Winterthur and the Metropolitan Museum of Art's American Wing.

But the moment I saw the sofa I knew I would have to be the bearer of sad tidings. The sofa, if indeed it were eighteenth-century, was English, I explained, thus making the $50,000 price unrealistic. To support my explanation I carefully showed the owners pictures of English and American pieces and cited the differences in perspective, styling, and proportions between the two.

But then I asked a very basic question.

"Have you looked for a label or tag under the seat?"

They hadn't. We pulled the sofa out, tilted it over, and

there was the answer. "Kittinger Company, Buffalo, New York." Even so, the owners were doubtful (and more than a little embarrassed that they had never seen the label).

"Kittinger? Don't they make Williamsburg reproductions? This sofa was inherited. It's not a new piece," they protested.

What they did not know is that the Kittinger Company has been making very fine furniture for over one hundred years. In fact, some of their old reproductions are, by definition, antiques. But not worth $50,000.

The husband shook his head sadly, "You don't know how many times I've spent that $50,000."

Describing and Inventorying Furniture

To list your furniture, proceed in a logical room by room progression. Inspect each piece and classify it as period, antique, or reproduction as best you can. Use the pictorial guide for descriptive terms. This, combined with the textual illustrations in this chapter, should make your descriptions accurate and informative. For estimates of replacement prices for reproductions refer to the value charts.

Value charts for currently manufactured furniture styles.
These prices are not for antique or period pieces.

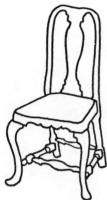

	Good Quality	Exceptional Quality (Hand-rubbed finish, hand-carved motifs, often custom-made)
QUEEN ANNE STYLE		
Side Chair	$ 325	$ 1,325
Arm Chair	370	1,500
Lowboy	800	3,700
Highboy	1,500	6,000
Tea Table	450	1,275
Drop-Leaf Table		
(Sofa arm size)	350	1,575
Candlestand	200	500
Secretary	1,500	8,000
CHIPPENDALE STYLE		
Sofa	1,200	3,500
Side Chair	400	1,300
Arm Chair	450	1,700
Wing Back Arm Chair	650	2,250
Breakfront	3,600	12,500
Chest of Drawers	700	2,500
Serpentine or Block-front Chest	1,000	3,500
Desk, slant front	1,700	5,750
Secretary	2,500	11,250
Pembroke Table	450	1,400
HEPPLEWHITE STYLE		
Pembroke Table	$ 400	$ 800
Shield-Back Side Chair	300	950
Shield-Back Arm Chair	350	1,300
Martha Washington Chair	500	1,600
Sideboard	1,500	6,500
Dining Table	1,200	2,800
Secretary	1,400	8,000
SHERATON STYLE		
Card Table	600	1,250
Pedestal Dining Room Table	1,350	2,600
Beds:		
Four Poster	650	1,850
Four Poster, carved		
with canopy	1,200	3,000

EMPIRE STYLE

	Good Quality
Side Chair	235
Arm Chair	300
Sofa	1,050
Carved Sofa	1,700
Sewing Table	400
Rocking Chair	320

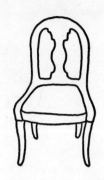

VICTORIAN STYLE
(*floral carving*)

	Good Quality
Arm Chair	$ 500
Sofa	1,000
Side Chair	200
Rocker	425
Chest	1,300

GOLDEN OAK STYLE

	Good Quality
Side Chair	95
Arm Chair	125
Round Table	375

FRENCH STYLES

	Good Quality
Louis XV Side Chair	350
Louis XV Arm Chair	400
French Provincial Side Chair	325
French Provincial Arm Chair	375
Dresser	600
Armoire	2,000

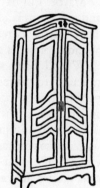

COUNTRY STYLE FURNITURE

	Good Quality
Ladder-Back Side Chair	$ 125
Ladder-Back Arm Chair	150
Windsor Side Chair	110
Windsor Arm Chair	160
Hitchcock Side Chair	125
Hutch or Cupboard	1,400
Corner Cupboard	1,000
Bedside Table	225
Occasional Table	425

13

Bric-à-Brac and Accessories—Little Things Mean a Lot

I t's the little things in life that get you," my mother always told me.
When it comes down to remembering all of your possessions, the little things are certainly the hardest to recall—yet the value of the accessories you have sitting around on bookcases, coffee tables, shelves, and stuck away in corner cupboards and hall closets can truly be astounding.

"But they didn't cost very much to begin with," I am often told.

Maybe. But have you noticed the price tags on "little things" in antiques and gift shops lately? A simple ashtray is now $12 or $18 instead of $1 or $2. The Beatrix Potter figurines you used to buy for nieces' and nephews' birthday presents are now almost $30 each.

We all have spent hundreds, often thousands, of dollars on "little touches" to make our homes attractive. These accessories often express our personal tastes more than our furnishings do. You walk into a crafts shop and choose a basket you would like to use in the kitchen. You stroll through an antiques shop, intending only to browse, until you fall in love with a vase you can't live without. You save all your Christmas checks until you can afford a pair of Williamsburg reproduction candlesticks and hurricane globes. Just a few dollars here and there, yet these purchases mount up rapidly. But you know how much they cost. You bought them.

What about the Staffordshire figurine that you loved as a child and now treasure as an adult? Or the pair of vases willed to you by your husband's aunt? These are now antiques, and their value may surprise you.

Even appraisers can have their own share of surprises. Among my own treasures is a miniature Staffordshire poodle, only one inch tall. When I was a child it was always kept on a shelf in the corner cupboard, and now I keep it on a shelf in my corner cupboard. I knew it was valuable, but its value to me was much more sentimental than monetary. Had I been forced to state a value, I probably would have said $100, followed by a big question mark.

Well, I saw one for sale at the 1981 Seventh Regiment Armory Show. In fact, I was tempted to take it home as a companion for mine until I inquired, "How much?" It was $400!

You genuinely need to include your accessories on your inventory, and once you discover more about them and their value you may wish to ask your insurance agent about breakage coverage.

The values of bric-a-brac and accessories vary radically according to where they are sold—from 57th Street galleries to back-road shops. In fact, one reason why people so often purchase small accessories in antiques shops and flea markets and at auction is because "they're too cheap to pass up." If you've seen a set of Haviland china plates priced at $30 each and you walk into a store and find the same design selling for $12 per plate, you are often tempted to buy the plates just because they are $18 cheaper than the ones you saw first.

The prices for antique accessories are greatly affected by both the tastes of each geographic region and the rarity of the item. Nineteenth-century European china—R. S. Prussia, Royal Bayreuth, and Beehive, for examples—are avidly collected in the Midwest but politely overlooked on the East Coast. Fiesta Ware is the rage in Texas and almost unknown in Maine. A Satsuma cup and saucer may sell for $35, but a Satsuma vase can easily bring $700. A Depression glass plate in a common pattern may sell for $5, but a Depression glass plate in a rare pattern can cost $25. Thus, it is almost impossible to assign accurate values to all the variations in all the classifications of accessories and bric-a-brac you have in your home. But you need to learn to identify what you have and know its approximate age.

Following is a list of accessories and bric-a-brac that I have compiled from the thousands of accessories that I see in private homes. Use this list to identify and approximately date your pieces. Before buying new accessories—especially antique accessories—learn what the "current activity" is in the marketplace. Are the particular pieces that you wish to buy now in vogue? If so, you may end up paying top dollar. Are they being reproduced? If so, you may be taken.

Knowing what is currently fashionable can help you know when to buy and when to sell and learn what to avoid as a possible fake, fraud, or reproduction if you are not an expert in the field.

Among the numerous accessories used as accent pieces I often find English ironstone and porcelain pieces. The majority of these date from the nineteenth century, though many of the factories or potters began in the eighteenth century. The following list covers some of the most frequently found English makers and information on specific types of popular accessories.

Dating English Pottery and Ironstone

As you begin looking at your porcelain accessories, you may discover a diamond-shaped marking with letters, numbers, and Roman numerals. These are known as registration marks. You can discover the exact date of many English pottery pieces if you know how to read an English registration mark. There were two designs used in the nineteenth century, and if you find one of these marks, compare the mark to those on the accompanying chart. (Incidentally, this marking was also used on some metal items in England.)

This mark was used between 1842 and 1867. Match the year letter at the top to the following chart.

This mark was used from 1868 to 1883. Match the year letter at the top to the following chart.

YEARS
1842–67
Year-Letter at Top

A = 1845	N = 1864
B = 1858	O = 1862
C = 1844	P = 1851
D = 1852	Q = 1866
E = 1855	R = 1861
F = 1847	S = 1849
G = 1863	T = 1867
H = 1843	U = 1848
I = 1846	V = 1850
J = 1854	W = 1865
K = 1857	X = 1842
L = 1856	Y = 1853
M = 1859	Z = 1860

1868–83
Year-Letter at Right

A = 1871	L = 1882
C = 1870	P = 1877
D = 1878	S = 1875
E = 1881	U = 1874
F = 1873	V = 1876
H = 1869	W = (Mar. 1–6)
I = 1872	1878
J = 1880	X = 1868
K = 1883	Y = 1879

Months for both series.

A	= December	K = November (and
B	= October	December 1860)
C or O	= January	M = June
D	= September	R = August (and
E	= May	September 1–19
G	= February	1857)
H	= April	W = March
I	= July	

After 1884 the mark changes to a simpler form which used the abbreviation "Rd." and accompanying number.

Rᴰ No.   1 registered on 1 January 1884.
Rᴰ No. 19754 registered on 1 January 1885.
Rᴰ No. 40480 registered on 1 January 1886.
Rᴰ No. 64520 registered on 1 January 1887.
Rᴰ No. 90483 registered on 2 January 1888.
Rᴰ No. 116648 registered on 1 January 1889.
Rᴰ No. 141273 registered on 1 January 1890.
Rᴰ No. 163767 registered on 1 January 1891.
Rᴰ No. 185713 registered on 1 January 1892.
Rᴰ No. 205240 registered on 2 January 1893.
Rᴰ No. 224720 registered on 1 January 1894.
Rᴰ No. 246975 registered on 1 January 1895.

Rᴰ No. 268392 registered on 1 January 1896.
Rᴰ No. 291241 registered on 1 January 1897.
Rᴰ No. 311658 registered on 1 January 1898.
Rᴰ No. 331707 registered on 2 January 1899.
Rᴰ No. 351202 registered on 1 January 1900.
Rᴰ No. 368154 registered on 1 January 1901.
Rᴰ No. 385088 registered on 1 January 1902.
Rᴰ No. 402913 registered on 1 January 1903.
Rᴰ No. 425017 registered on 1 January 1904.
Rᴰ No. 447548 registered on 2 January 1905.
Rᴰ No. 471486 registered on 1 January 1906.
Rᴰ No. 493487 registered on 1 January 1907.
Rᴰ No. 518415 registered on 1 January 1908.
Rᴰ No. 534963 registered on 1 January 1909.

The following marks identify the day, month, and year of many English products, especially porcelain goods.

English Semi-Porcelain

English semi-porcelain or ironstone has always been very popular for accessories. Though originally made as large dinner sets, breakage and division by families have broken up these sets. Today the individual pieces, particularly tea pots, pitchers, cream pitchers, decorative plates, and serving pieces are highly prized items. The English ironstone products are often called Staffordshire.

Staffordshire

Staffordshire refers to the district in England where pottery factories flourished during the eighteenth and nineteenth centuries. (Remember Dresden and Limoges are both names of towns rather than the name of a specific company.) Originally, Staffordshire was used when referring to the eighteenth-century work of Ralph and Aaron Wood. But now Staffordshire is used to refer to literally any English figurine or decorative semi-porcelain that has a "nineteenth-century" appearance, particularly the popular historical-view dinner sets in the 1810–1850 period. Among the popular Staffordshire factories are Ridgway, Clews, Adams, and Mason.

Staffordshire Animals

During the nineteenth century, Staffordshire figurines, both of living personages, such as Queen Victoria and Prince Albert, and historical figures from life and fiction, such as

MacBeth and Uncle Tom, George Washington and Benjamin Franklin, were popular mantelpiece or chimney decorations. The Staffordshire potters also made figure groupings of dramatic scenes, such as Romeo and Juliet or St. George Slaying the Dragon. But most popular of all were the Staffordshire animals, particularly the spaniels, whippets, and poodles. (There were many more Staffordshire animals made than are commonly known, including zebras, gazelles, foxhounds, and Dalmations.) The extreme popularity of these figures led to the inevitable copies, and these have been faked as frequently as any single item in the antiques world. Staffordshire animals were reproduced in Germany and the Orient, and even current manufacturers are still turning out Staffordshire animals, which often are sold as nineteenth-century ones. Currently produced "Staffordshire" animals that I have seen in innumerable gift shops include whippets resting on cushions.

Notable and Frequently Found Potters and Factories

William Adams. This Staffordshire, England, firm dates from the eighteenth century and is still in existence. This company is particularly noted for the Adams' Rose design and Dr. Syntax plates. Early Adams' Rose pieces are not marked, but the later pieces are; the very late ones will be labeled "England." Prices for Adams' Rose plates begin in the $50 range, and prices for the fine early and larger Adams' Rose pieces can range into the hundreds of dollars. Most Adams' ware is moderately priced semi-porcelain. Be particularly wary of the Dr. Syntax plates as these were forged in the later nineteenth and early twentieth centuries.

Mason-Ashworth ironstone. One of the most popular of the Staffordshire pottery companies was that founded by Charles James Mason. The most popular of the Mason china is brightly colored in blue, orange, green, and rust colors, often copying Oriental floral motifs. In the mid-nineteenth century the company became associated with Ashworth and Brothers Company. Like the Adams ware, both Mason and Ashworth pieces are highly desirable, but the bright coloration characteristic of the Mason designs adds to their current popularity (and value).

Ridgway. Note that the spelling here, just like the Wedgwood spelling, does not have an *e* in it. Much of the Ridgway ware of the 1830–1850 period is not marked and can be confused with other English companies. A typical Ridgway decoration is in the same Oriental style and coloration as that of the Mason Company. However, the factory is perhaps even better known for the Flow Blue style decoration.

Flow Blue

This is another generic term which refers to the ironstone china manufactured from the 1830s to 1890s. The term came about when the cobalt color flowed out of its lines and covered large areas of the decoration. However, flow blue can also refer to green, sepia, and purple wares, which also "flowed" in the kiln. Much flow blue is decorated with a historic scene, such as "Lafayette's Landing," or landscape scenes of famous buildings, "Mount Vernon," "Independence Hall," etc. Be warned that fakes and reproductions abound!

Blue Chelsea

One of the popular patterns made by the ironstone or semi-porcelain companies is "Blue Chelsea," also called "Chelsea" and sometimes "Grandmother's Chelsea." Once again, the name has become a generic term which refers to any of the ironstone ware that is white and decorated with a raised blue sprig. The pattern was made by many English potters and was very popular in the nineteenth century and then again, with collectors, during the early twentieth century. Presently Blue Chelsea has fallen into relative obscurity when compared to the much more popularly collected Haviland or Nippon china.

Luster Ware

Luster ware had its origins in the ancient East, and there is evidence that Italians and Spaniards used luster ware in the fourteenth and fifteenth centuries. However, the luster ware we are most familiar with today is English luster ware of the nineteenth century. Luster is created when a very thin layer of gold is applied to a pottery base. The resulting color or "luster" varies from a copper to pink. When a very thin layer of platinum is placed on pottery, the resulting color or "luster" is silver. The silver luster provided the middle class with "silver" tableware, by imitating the fine English sterling and Sheffield wares found on more affluent tables. Unfortunately, luster ware has been reproduced as frequently as the Staffordshire animals. Tremendous amounts of copper luster were

made in the first part of the twentieth century when luster ware was highly regarded as a collector's item. It can be hard to distinguish between the old and the new unless two pieces can be held and compared one against the other. However, I have found that the newer luster has a much thicker and heavier feeling than the almost translucent glow of nineteenth-century luster. Luster ware is not as popular now as it was in the earlier part of the twentieth century. Perhaps the preponderance of fakes will keep it from suddenly skyrocketing in popularity.

Later Nineteenth Century and Art Nouveau English Pottery

The whole decorative world of the later nineteenth century and twentieth century designs is being rediscovered. Included in this is English pottery from such companies as Ault, Ruskin, Doulton (Lambethware), Plinkington, and Moorcroft. But just as these highly collectible items are coming back into vogue, it must also be remembered that for each of these fine-quality period designs there were literally thousands of inferior-quality copies made, many of the type that were sold in dime stores or by catalogue.

English Figurines

Very popular during the twentieth century were figurines, particularly those depicting beautiful women. These figurines were developed in two major styles. One embodies the romantic image of ladies in long flowing skirts and large hats depicted in a pastoral or countryside setting. These figurines are still made today by Royal Worcester and Royal Doulton. The extreme opposite of the romantic embodiment of innocent womanhood was the sophisticated and alluring Art Deco female figure, often depicted as scantily dressed or even partially nude (in the "September Morn" tradition) or in a sophisticated masquerade motif. These Art Nouveau female figures were not only ignored but even thrown away during the middle part of the twentieth century. Now the cycle has turned around, and these figurines are collector's items. In addition to porcelain, these figurines were also executed in metals (bronze, often in combination with ivory, and spelter).

Other popular English figurines include Toby jugs, which had their beginning in the eighteenth century. Not only are the Toby jugs still in current production (even these are more expensive than they used to be, with the cost of a medium-size Toby jug now in the $50 range), but they were greatly copied in the Orient in the early and mid-twentieth century. I remember being quite surprised when I discovered that a Toby jug that had been in my grandfather's room, which I had always assumed was a Royal Doulton piece, was clearly marked "Japan" on the bottom. Remember this mark could be removed by the use of hydrochloric acid or a grinding wheel and the piece sold to the unknowing person as an "unmarked English nineteenth-century character jug" by an unscrupulous dealer.

Many articles and books have been written on English figurines. The Kovels' *Illustrated Price Guide to Royal Doulton* is an indication of their newfound popularity and value.

Fine English Porcelain

Many of the English companies that made earthenware or ironstone also produced magnificent fine porcelain. Among these companies are Spode, Ridgeway, and Wedgwood. Collectors of fine English porcelain seek wares by Derby, Worcester, Rockingham, Swansea, and Minton. Each of these companies has specific marks used to denote their wares of different times. Numerous books have been published that include a full compliment of the porcelain hallmarks. Great confusion exists among these companies because some of the decorators of the china ware moved from one company to the other, and some of the companies even imitated European marks. For example, the famous Meissen crossed swords appear on some Minton porcelain. Incidentally, Minton china from the nineteenth century is highly collectible.

Complete sets of English porcelain now command a king's ransom. Recently a set of Worcester china, consisting of several hundred pieces including large serving pieces, was offered wholesale to a dealer for $9,800.

European Porcelain

European porcelains are found so frequently in American homes because they were brought into the country by the immigrants who could bring a treasured pot or favorite cup and saucer but could not bring large furniture. What better testimony to how greatly we value the little antique pieces we have sitting around. How often my clients say, "I could stand to lose everything except my great-grandfather's mug," or "I cherish the blue vase brought from Austria by my grandparents more than any piece I have ever bought."

Another reason for the predominance of European porcelain in America is the absence of any American porcelain manufacturers until late in the nineteenth century.

Most of the European porcelain found in homes today is from the nineteenth rather than the eighteenth century, but to see why eighteenth-century porcelain is so highly treasured and expensive, let's look first at a typical eighteenth-century European porcelain company.

Herend

Founded in 1839, the Herend factory has produced fine porcelain for almost a century and a half. Located near Budapest, Hungary, the factory is surrounded by the Bakory woods. Until 1970 the porcelain was fired in wood-burning kilns heated by timber from the surrounding forests. The first firing took 30 to 32 hours to complete. Inside the kiln the wood fire was built up to 1,740° Fahrenheit and was then allowed to subside slowly. During these long hours any draft from a crack in the kiln door or from the factory chimneys could crack or warp the entire firing. Only in 1970 were these kilns replaced by more efficient and better controlled gas-burning ovens.

Actually, little nineteenth-century Herend is found in this country, but modern Herend china is very desirable and is carried by fine jewelry stores everywhere. Herend is noted not only for its dinnerware with very fine large serving pieces but also for its charming figurines. Just as your grandmother wanted to set her table with Heisey glass and Bavarian china, so today many people want Waterford crystal and Herend china.

Delft

Delft ware is commonly defined as tin-glazed pottery. The most familiar Delft was made in Holland, but it was also made in England during the seventeenth and eighteenth centuries. Unlike many of the other porcelain or pottery factories that you have read about, several Delft factories actually died out in the very first part of the nineteenth century and Delft ware was not revived until the 1870s when the factories once again began making the blue and white Delft that is generally recognized today. Earlier Delft was frequently polychromatic as well as blue and white. The difference between the value of the eighteenth- and the nineteenth- or twentieth-century Delft is astounding. A modern Delft 15-inch plate may cost around $200, but an eighteenth-century 15-inch Delft plate easily sells for $1,000 and more.

> There is little eighteenth-century Delft around, and you can be sure that if "Delft" or "Holland" appears on the bottom, the piece is post 1891.

Quimper

Another pottery that is currently popular is Quimper, but like Delft, the pieces that we are familiar with are primarily those made in the nineteenth and even twentieth century. Records show the Quimper potters in existence as early as the fifteenth century; Quimper, like Limoges, is the name of a place in France. Quimper ware is characterized by its bright polychromatic paintings of French peasants and farm animals. Quimper is being manufactured and imported today, but it is much more expensive than the usual pottery available in gift shops and department stores. An average price range for your new Quimper could be determined by using the low end of the Class II good-quality porcelain items.

R. S. Prussia

After reading about the bogus R. S. Prussia mustache cups in Chapter 4, I'm sure that every time you see an R. S. Prussia piece you're going to put it down and run away. Don't. Just keep your wits about you. But you also need to know that R. S. Prussia *type* china has been heavily reproduced by Oriental companies, including some rather attractive pieces made by Nippon. This, combined with the availability of the fake R. S. Prussia seals, should make you extremely cautious. But true R. S. Prussia is highly collectible, so if you like it, take the time to learn about it, and if you own true R. S. Prussia pieces, you can sell them for a lot of money.

The original porcelain was made by two brothers, Erdman and Reinhold Schlegelmilch, who each operated factories in an obscure little German town. R. S. Prussia reached its height of popularity at the end of the nineteenth century, at which time the wares were imported into the United States. In 1911 a chocolate pot could be bought for 69 cents and a seven-piece celery set, consisting of the tray and individual relish dishes, cost $1.25. A dozen bread-and-butter plates were $2.10, and a 10¾-inch urn-shaped vase was $1.35. Today the celery dish by itself would easily sell for $125 to $150. Sugar and creamers can range in the vicinity of $150 to $250, and vases usually start at $150 and go as high as $1,000. Anyone want to say anything about investing in personal property?

It should be noted that the Schlegelmilch china that is marked R. S. Prussia is considered to be of better quality than the other products from the same factory. R. S. Germany, for example, can be bought for only a quarter of the price of R. S. Prussia pieces.

Royal Dux

Another china which has taken astronomical jumps in value is Royal Dux porcelain, made in Bohemia and imported at the beginning of the twentieth century. This was inexpensive ware at the time, and even today when a Royal Dux figurine is compared, for example, to a Royal Doulton figurine, the difference in quality can be noted. However, collectors are out there, and the Royal Dux figurines often bring over $100 each, as do some of the vases and bowls.

Royal Bayreuth

If you have an unusually shaped ashtray or sugar or creamer around the house that you know isn't too old but is unlike anything you have ever seen—let's say that the ashtray is in the shape of a crab, the covered sugar looks like a tomato, and the creamer is in the shape of a shell—these may well be products from the Royal Bayreuth factory of Bavaria. These novelty pieces date from the very end of the nineteenth century, up to approximately the time of the First World War. To some, these are inexpensive novelty pieces. To others, they are the basis for an entire collection. Under no circumstances should they be casually thrown away. Another interesting product from the Royal Bayreuth factory is known as Tapestry ware; it was made by stretching a piece of fabric over the china body, which was then decorated and glazed, thus resulting in the slightly irregular or granulated surface that characterizes the floral and scenic pieces of Royal Bayreuth. Tapestry-type pieces are even more valuable than the novelty ones. Ironically, the Bayreuth Company is known in Europe as the manufacturer of extraordinarily fine-quality porcelain of the eighteenth century, which can be compared to the products of the Meissen factories.

Royal Austria

A commonly found mark on later nineteenth-century china is that of a beehive, associated with Royal Vienna or Beehive, Austria, china. As was true of so many of the European factories, this mark and china had its origin in the eighteenth century, but most that we see today consists of nineteenth-century portrait porcelain plates, vases, or cups and saucers, many copied after the eighteenth-century designs of Angela Kauffman. Royal Austria is sometimes mistaken as Sevres because many of the shapes and even type of designs that were used by the finer Sevres factory in France were also used by the Austrian factory. The china remains desirable but moderately priced when compared to the much more expensive Sevres pieces.

Sevres

Sevres is perhaps the most famous of all porcelain. Yet Sevres is little different from any other product of the European factories that have been discussed so far. During the eighteenth century Sevres produced the finest of porcelain wares, but in the nineteenth century the wares became less expensive and mass-produced. Needless to say, the fakes, frauds, and reproductions of Sevres porcelain are too numerous to count. The marks have been copied, the style has been copied, the shapes have been copied, the decorations have been copied—all to such an extent that now you often see a listing in an auction catalogue of "Sevres-type" porcelain. This description is the same used by the auction houses to differentiate period furniture from furniture in the *style* of a period. Thus, if you see a piece labeled "Sevres-type," know that it was made by another company but is of good quality and was copied after the Sevres designs. The difference in cost between a Sevres-type urn and a real Sevres urn will be the same one that exists between the value of a Georgian *style* chest of drawers and an eighteenth-century Georgian *period* chest of drawers.

To distinguish between the real and the copy you must study the fine Sevres pieces in museums very carefully and look at the quality of the painting. Once, while handling an estate appraisal, I came upon a basically good three-piece mantel set known as a garniture. "Could they really be Sevres?" I wondered. I decided not; the painting was not sufficiently good. I concluded that they were of the Sevres-type. I explained to the heirs of the estate the difference between

Sevres and Sevres-type and predicted that a reasonable sale price for the three pieces would be in the $1,000 to $1,500 range. The group eventually was sent to an auction house, where it was catalogued as a "highly important three-piece Sevres cobalt blue mantel garniture" and given a pre-auction estimate of $3,000 to $4,000. However, when the actual auction time came around, the group had been correctly identified as "Sevres-type" and sold for $1,500. But if sold in a fancy shop specializing in nineteenth-century French decor, this group could easily bring $3,000 to $4,000.

Scandinavian Porcelain

Mention should be made of two Scandinavian factories, Bing and Grondahl and Royal Copenhagen. Both Danish factories originated in the nineteenth century and still operate today. Both factories produce very fine quality figurines characterized by a very clear, bright glaze. Both companies primarily use blue and white coloration and are well known for their dinnerware as well as for Christmas and other commemorative plates. The figurines of both factories are valuable and will eventually, I believe, have the sort of following that the Hummel figurines do now. Meanwhile, the famous Christmas plates are widely collected. As you would expect, the glaze and type of this fine porcelain have been widely imitated.

Hummel

Almost every house has at least one Hummel figurine. The figurines may have been bought in Europe as souvenir items or from American stores as christening or birthday gifts. Little matter where they were purchased. The truth of the matter is, Hummel figurines are expensive, even the currently made Hummel figurines available in gift shops and department stores. There are collectors' clubs devoted exclusively to the Hummel figurines, and numerous books have been published for the Hummel collector. As you would now expect, because of this great popularity, fakes abound. Most of the imitations have come from Japan, and have been marked with a simple paper label to be brought into the country. The label is later removed. There is a distinction in the glaze and material used in the imitation figurines, but to be able to make the distinctions you should know both the genuine Hummel markings, which are explained in each of the Hummel books, and also the specific designs and characteristics of the figurines.

When valuing Hummel figurines, the rarity of the individual piece and its particular size are always taken into consideration, as well as the age of the figurine. Since some of the figurines have been in production for forty years or more, the earlier ones obviously bring more money. Many people do not realize that Hummel figurines were also made into ashtrays, candlesticks, and lamps—and even Nativity scenes.

Oriental Porcelain

A particularly hot subject in antiques today is the fine Oriental porcelain of the various dynasties. These pieces are bringing thousands of dollars in the international marketplaces and attracting headlines. It has been my experience that the majority of the truly valuable Oriental porcelain from the later centuries B.C. and earlier centuries A.D. are in European collections rather than in America. The pieces that do exist in America generally have been brought through one of the international auction houses or elite shops specializing in Oriental porcelain, or came from famous collections when they were dismantled. Thus, the owners know what they have. Most Oriental porcelain that you find in American homes as accent pieces can be broken down into two large groupings: Export china, and nineteenth- and twentieth-century Japanese china.

Export China

Export china was primarily made in China in the second half of the eighteenth century and throughout the nineteenth century for import into America. Of course, that made prior to the McKinley Act of 1891 is seldom going to be marked, and thus there can be a question about its age—is it eighteenth century or nineteenth century? A careful study of the style of the painting characteristic of the two different centuries, plus an understanding of the shapes that are typical of the different times helps the student of Export porcelain to date these pieces.

The oldest of this china, once called Lowestoft, now generally referred to as Chinese Export, is distinguished by the light gray or blue cast to the glaze and the distinctive floral motif. Much of the china is very simply decorated, but the most highly prized is the Armorial Chinese Export china, which was made specifically for families and exported from China. Armorial china was shipped to the European countries as well as America, and these pieces are always valuable.

There are two very popular patterns of Export china often found in today's homes. The first is Canton, recognizable by the center decoration of a pagoda-type house with mountains and trees in the background and painted blue on white. There are variations in the border that surrounds the center motif, but most common is the raincloud band. Condition is always important in valuing china, and there is no exception when considering Canton or any other Chinese Export. Remember, a broken dish has only an archaeological value, not an antique value. However, because collectors are so anxious to assemble whole sets of Canton these days, there is more market for a chipped plate or nicked serving dish than ever before. Value also depends on the rarity of each piece. Fewer large covered serving dishes were made than dinner plates and even fewer candlesticks or inkwells than table china.

The market for Canton is large and thriving, but Canton is most popular in the New England areas, where it was originally imported.

The other extremely popular Export china is Rose Medallion. This china is distinguished both by its rose motif and the rose coloring. Usually the china has a group of four panels which alternate flowers, birds, and butterflies with groups of people, usually depicted in a house. When *only* flowers, birds, and butterflies appear, the china is referred to as "Rose Canton." On the other hand, when only the people are used, as they sometimes are at the center of a plate, the china is referred to as "Rose Mandarin."

Everything said about the blue-and-white Canton applies to Rose Medallion. Probably more unusual pieces and a wider variety of shapes were made in Rose Medallion than in Canton, and pieces of all ages, even those marked "made in China," can be found for sale in fine antiques shops. Both patterns, Canton and Rose Medallion, are being reproduced. In fact, the Canton pattern is reproduced by Mottahedeh as part of the Historic Charleston line.

Other Chinese Export patterns of the nineteenth century include Tobacco Leaf, Fitzhugh, and Nanking. Export china is valuable both because it is old and because it is appropriate to period restorations and museums. Chinese Export was the favorite of American Presidents and is once again in great favor. While this means you can quickly find a buyer for any you wish to sell, you must also beware of cheap imitations, all of which are rather garishly painted when compared to the old.

Japanese Porcelain—Imari

Imari china originated in Japan in the seventeenth century, but that which we most often see today is nineteenth- and of course twentieth-century Imari. The characteristic Imari china is distinguished by the unmistakable deep orange-red color, cobalt blue, and gilt highlights, often combined with turquoise and yellow. Imari patterns often depict floral decorations, birds, and symbols of the Japanese culture. As in the Rose Medallion pattern, panels often are used that alternate one decoration or motif with another. Imari bowls are widely collected, as are plates and chargers. The more unusual pieces, and therefore the more valuable ones, are candlesticks, tall vases, and pieces with unusual shapings. Imari continues to be reproduced today, but once again the paintings seem a little too bright and too clean when compared to nineteenth-century Imari.

The charming, colorful floral motif of Imari china was adapted by English potters and used in both porcelain and ironstone, notably in the extremely expensive Royal Crown Derby Imari pattern and the ever-popular Mason ironstone Imari patterns. A very liberal translation of the Imari floral motif and coloring is found on some "Gaudy Welsh" china.

The price for Imari seems to have no limits. Only a few years ago you could buy a simple scallop bordered Imari plate in perfect condition for $20 to $25. Today if you can find that plate for under $100, you consider it a steal, and I have seen prices for that item as high as $200.

Satsuma

Satsuma was manufactured in Japan in the seventeenth, eighteenth, and nineteenth centuries, but the majority of that seen today dates from the later nineteenth century. Satsuma can be difficult to describe, and yet once you see a piece of it you never forget its characteristics. The china often depicts brightly dressed Japanese figures in red, blue, green, orange, and gold, and the china itself has an almost brocade-like appearance. There is so much movement in the design and so much contrast between the gold and the other colors that Satsuma takes on a three-dimensional aspect. The gold is often raised or even beaded. Not long ago Satsuma went unappreciated. Many people once considered the overall decoration gaudy—the bold, rich colors and crowded details are just too much. Today others love these very same details, and Satsuma ware is now very sought after and widely collected.

Kutani

Kutani ware is a stepchild. It originated in Japan in the seventeenth century and lasted for only a short time. But dur-

ing the nineteenth century, when Japanese porcelain became popular in the western countries, Kutani was once again produced. Connoisseurs refer to the nineteenth-century ware, which is found in so many homes, as "revived" Kutani. If you look for the term "Kutani" in many scholarly encyclopedias of antiques, you will find only mention of the seventeenth-century factory. And yet if you go into homes on a daily basis as I do, you know that nineteenth-century Kutani abounds.

Kutani is perhaps more like Satsuma than it is like any other of the Japanese designs. It is characteristically decorated in deep red-orange with much gold highlighting, and it usually depicts a landscape scene with birds in the air and generally has a floral border. Kutani china was extremely popular in the 1880s and 1890s, and sets, demitasse cups and saucers, chocolate sets, and dessert sets were frequently given as wedding presents.

I have a Kutani chocolate set that was a wedding present to my great-grandparents in the 1880s. I discovered this china packed away in the basement one day and asked my father if I might have it, since he wasn't using it.

"Yes, you may have it," he replied, "on one condition— that when I come to your house I don't have to look at it. I never did like the stuff, which is why it's packed away in the basement!"

This only goes to prove once again the adage that our parents have questionable taste, our grandparents acceptable taste, but our great-grandparents had superlative taste. My father never did like his grandparents' things particularly, but a generation later I find them extremely attractive.

The simpler Kutani is moderately priced and can be roughly compared in value to the more common Haviland patterns. Of course the more richly decorated and highly gilded pieces are more expensive.

Noritake

Running neck and neck with Kutani in popularity, and much better known to the general public, are Noritake and Nippon. Both companies produced their wares primarily in the twentieth century, and both are growing in popularity and value.

Noritake ware is best known by the red or green letter "M" encircled in a wreath. Above the wreath is often the word "Noritake," and below it "handpainted." The designs are generally simple, mostly depicting landscape scenes, and Noritake is found both in the usual dinnerware pieces—cups and saucers, plates, etc.—and also sets such as nut bowls and tea sets. The Noritake Company is still in existence today and makes a combination of kitchenware, glassware, and dinnerware, as well as the more expensive lead crystal and porcelain dinner sets. The "Azalea" pattern by Noritake is so popular that you will often find it listed in separate categories in the mass-produced price guides.

Nippon

The Nippon ware of the later nineteenth and early twentieth century can be compared to Depression glass in the new surge of its popularity. In fact, Nippon has become so popular that hardcover books are devoted to its proper indentification. It should be noted that many Nippon pieces, when viewed from a distance, can be mistaken for English or European china. I remember being quite taken aback when I discovered that a dish I had positively identified, from across the room, as very fine quality Royal Crown Derby in the Imari pattern turned out to be Nippon. Nippon successfully imitated Belleck, R. S. Prussia, Wedgwood, and Limoges, among others.

Unusual and well-executed pieces of Nippon china now bring hundreds of dollars. It is not unusual to find a biscuit barrel or cracker jar with a price tag of $250 or more, and humidors have now reached the $200 to $300 figure. But the average plate, colorfully decorated in the Oriental styling with perhaps a touch of a Victorian floral motif, is still reasonably priced in a $25 to $50 range.

Occupied Japan

Last are those frequently found 10-cent store items marked "Occupied Japan." These were the porcelain wares made in Japan during the years of the Allied occupation immediately following Japan's surrender after World War II. These pieces, which cost 15 to 25 cents in the 1940s are now collectibles and are bringing anywhere from $3 to $4 in an inexpensive flea market to $12, $15, and $20 among collectors.

Other Oriental Accessories

Cloisonné

When I give talks to groups, I usually provide a bibliography for my audience, just as I have included bibliographies in this book. No one book can tell you everything, and resource materials are invaluable. One of the best general books on antiques is the Kovels' *Know Your Antiques,* and it is always included in my bibliography. One day after giving a talk, I received a long-distance call when I returned home.

"My dear," the caller said, "I just want to tell you not to recommend that book, *Know Your Antiques,* any more. I rushed right out and bought it and got it home and found out that there was not one word about cloisonné. Do you think that the Kovels don't know about cloisonné?"

Of course the Kovels knew about cloisonné when the book was published in 1967. To begin with, not every topic can possibly be covered in a general book on antiques. I certainly have not covered everything here. But there's another side to the omission of cloisonné in *many* books that were published in the 1950s and 1960s. Cloisonné was not in fashion.

You could find it in antiques shops, and you would even see pieces in people's homes. But American buyers were not actively going out and seeking cloisonné until the mid 1970s.

Basically, cloisonné is made by soldering small strips or wires of metal, sometimes true gold and silver, onto a copper or brass base. Enamel paste in a variety of colors is then applied within these wires to create often beautiful and colorful designs. Cloisonné is commonly used in combination with bronze in vases, many of which have been converted into lamps.

> Always examine cloisonné carefully, as it may have been dropped and dented. The dents can be hard to see from the outside. The best way to check, if possible, is to feel around the interior of the piece for these defects.

As with porcelain, damage to cloisonné depreciates the value. However, since many cloisonné pieces are purchased primarily for decorative purposes, if you don't mind a dent, you can get a damaged piece for less money. The different quality of cloisonné also affects the value.

Cinnabar

Oriental accessories often are made of cinnabar, the red lacquer or "vermillion" ware made by applying hundreds of coats of vermillion one on top of the other. Once hard, a design is carved into the lacquer. The cinnabar process has been known for centuries, but the majority that you see today is either from the nineteenth century or may even be very recently made. There is usually a difference both in the color of new cinnabar and in the quality of its design. Even the new cinnabar can be costly. The cinnabar pieces most frequently found are covered boxes, small snuff bottles, and vases.

Art Nouveau and Art Deco Accessories

At the end of the nineteenth century a new art, or the "Art Nouveau" style of design, emerged. The style is characterized by a freely curving, flowing line. The graceful curve was very adaptable to natural forms—flowers, swaying trees, the female figure—and artists used these lines and forms in every medium of the decorative arts—from furniture to jewelry to lighting fixtures to stained glass. The most famous American artist who worked in the Art Nouveau style is, of course, Louis Comfort Tiffany.

However, the Art Nouveau movement was internationally popular, and the finest work was created in Europe, particularly France. We are all familiar with the famous French bronze statues which epitomize the Art Nouveau period.

Actually, the popularity of sculpture and statuary was a boon for the nineteenth-century artist who could finally support himself financially through sculpture. An artist could create a piece of sculpture, have his design cast in molds, and then "pour" as many figures in the molds as he wished and as the public would buy.

These decorative sculptures soon appeared in turn-of-the-century foyers, parlors, and music rooms, as the expanding middle class demanded these latest accessories. As a result, spelter, an inexpensive white metal, was used to make the figures, which were then given a bronze-type finish. They were now affordable for the masses.

Art Nouveau bronzes are currently immensely popular and are selling for thousands of dollars at the international auction houses. However, even the less expensive spelter figurines and statuary carry price tags ranging from a few hundred dollars into the low thousand-dollar range.

You must remember in dealing with all of the products of the Art Nouveau era that they were mass-produced in factories, foundries, workshops, and galleries. Because the entire Art Nouveau and later Art Deco styles were so unpopular during the 1950s and 1960s, it is easy to forget how plentiful pieces in these styles are.

Less expensive and poorer quality interpretations of these styles were also made and sold through mail order catalogues and in dime stores to the masses in the early 1900s.

However, every time a style becomes fashionable—usually starting with the rediscovery of the very finest quality pieces by a museum, the vogue creeps slowly but surely into all of our lives, and even the originally very inexpensive pieces become collectible. Just as an investor may pay $100,000 for a signed Tiffany lamp, so a collector with more modest means will buy a Tiffany-style lamp, made originally for a modest 1900s home, for $500.

The Art Deco style of the 1930s contradicts the Art Nouveau style. The flowing lines are replaced by straight angles, and natural forms—flowers and the human body—are discarded in favor of geometric and orderly motifs. But the medium remained the same, and the Art Deco style appears in furniture, jewelry, lamps, and glass.

Art Nouveau and Art Deco Pottery

In America the artistic movement of the 1880s through the 1930s is perhaps most commonly expressed in Art pottery. The Kovels have once again pioneered in this area, and their *Kovels' Collector's Guide to American Art Pottery* provides rich illustrations of the pottery and the marks of the companies that made it.

> When cleaning out the back closet filled with flower-arranging materials, be particularly on the lookout for vases, pitchers, and bowls bearing these companies' marks: Buffalo Pottery-Deldare, Cowan Pottery, Dedham Pottery, Fulper Pottery, Grueby Faience Company, Newcomb Pottery, Ohr Pottery; Owens Pottery, Rookwood Pottery, Roseville Pottery, Van Bringgle Pottery, Weller Pottery.

Rookwood is now commanding prices in the thousands of dollars for individual pieces, and even flea market values on Rookwood pottery can now reach into hundreds of dollars.

Art Nouveau and Art Deco Metal and Leather Accessories

The most familiar of the Art Nouveau accessories, and the ones I most frequently see in private homes, are the silver dresser sets adorned with blossoming flowers and romanticized ladies. Mirrors, brushes, pin trays, covered powder jars, and hair receivers, along with perfume vials and picture frames, are commonly found in both sterling silver and silver plate. Sterling silver brushes, which must have their bristles replaced, are often no more valuable than the weight of the silver, but large sets and richly decorated picture frames bring hundreds of dollars. Of course silverplated accessories are less valuable.

In reaction to the Art Nouveau style, and in keeping with the stark furniture styles exemplified by Stickley and the Mission style, many fine workshops and factories turned out metal (mostly copper and brass) and leather accessories. All Art Deco accessories have some value today as the style becomes increasingly popular. However, among the most prized items are those bearing the Roycroft name. The Roycroft shop existed between 1895 to 1938 and produced many of the accessories found in homes during this time, including candlesticks, sconces, desk sets, lamps, bowls, etc. Their leather goods included pocketbooks, match cases, and even book bindings. While all Roycroft pieces are collectible, those made between 1895 and 1915 are the most desirable.

Art Glass

During the mid-nineteenth century and later, corresponding with the Art Nouveau movement, art glass became immensely popular. Art glass was made in every European country and America, and was copied the world over. The art glass designers vied to produce new types of glass, and once the newest technique and style gained popularity all the other designers and factories immediately copied it.

For these reasons, the general category of art glass and glass accessories is the most dangerous area for the non-expert in the antiques field.

> No other medium has been imitated more times
> and in greater degrees of varying quality than
> glassware.

To complicate matters, remember that according to the
McKinley Act of 1891, which I have mentioned often, glass
that was imported into the United States had to be marked
with the country of origin. However, a simple paper label was
often attached to glass items, sticking only long enough to
get through customs. (Even today when you buy glass in the
jewelry store often the only sign identifying the manufacturer
is a gummed label, sometimes almost too small to see, which
comes off the first time the glass is washed.)

> Most glass is unmarked; therefore you should be
> particularly cautious when you are offered a piece
> of glass that is "signed." Many fake examples of
> glass have been signed with the name of a presti-
> gious company to sell the fake.

Often when the fake piece is compared with the authentic
one, the *absence* of a signature is noted on the *real* piece!
Most fake and reproduction glass is imported from either
Central Europe or Mexico. One reason that glass is so easily
faked is because so much of it was made originally that when
more pieces appear on the market, no one is immediately suspicious. However, a proliferation of *one design,* which begins
showing up at each auction and in every antiques shop,
should make you suspicious.

The other point to remember about glass is that while the
finest art glass was originally made for the wealthy connoisseur, once the rest of the population demanded this new fashion, imitations of art glass appeared in mass production.
These inexpensive vases, glasses, pitchers, etc., were purchased
through dime stores. In fact, it was the public's demand for
art glass that gave birth to Carnival glass, known as the "poor
man's Tiffany." But wouldn't you know! Even the poor man's
cheap Carnival glass has now been cheapened further by the
current reproductions.

The difference in period glass and reproduced glass is often
similar to the differences in china—the weight and color of

the newer pieces are considered to be giveaway characteristics. The best book on the new copies of glass is Dorothy Hammond's *Confusing Collectibles*. In it she discusses such popular patterns as amberina, Burmese glass, cranberry glass, hobnail, and, of course, the often copied Mary Gregory glass and Peachblow.

Glass copies are frequently sold today through museum and restoration gift shops. Even though these are sold as reproductions, when you mix the reproductions in with the old collections, just a piece or two at a time, it is easy for the new to become confused with the old and eventually passed off as antique pieces.

If the art glass in your home is genuine, of the period, in perfect condition, and of superior quality, you do indeed have something of value. However, if you are looking for an area in antiques to invest in and you are just beginning, my advice would be to stay away from art glass.

Lamps

Entire books have been written on individual lighting devices from Betty lamps, to night lamps, to Tiffany lamps. Lamps exist in profusion, and why not? Without proper lighting our night hours are wasted. Therefore, from the earliest times, a lamp was a necessity, even in the most primitive of homes.

Lamps have been made out of every conceivable material— from metal to glass to porcelain. As we in America know them, the earliest lamps are the crude oil or fat-burning lamps used by the pioneers and commonly called Betty lamps.

I wondered for years why the lamps were called Betty lamps, asked many knowledgeable people, but received no answer. However, according to Carl W. Dreppard, the word "betynges" refers to the crude fat used as fuel in early torches or lanterns. Thus, the small metal lamp with an extended handle, which could be hooked over and hung from a mantelpiece, is referred to as a betynges or Betty lamp. There were originally countless numbers of these lamps in existence, as the type continued to be used by the pioneers in their humble cabins and homes through the nineteenth century.

Nineteenth-century lamps were made in a variety of materials, many in the fancy glasses made by the famous New England glass companies. Both oil-burning lamps and then, later, gas lamps are available in all varieties of glass and brass and in every conceivable shape. And, of course, these have all been reproduced. To identify nineteenth-century lamps correctly you must first be able to identify the product they are made of—Sandwich glass, end-of-day glass, milk glass, etc.

Later, the lamps of the nineteenth century and early twentieth century were carried to new heights by the famous Tiffany Studio products. These lamps were so rapidly copied and reproduced that now all lamps of this era (unless *marked* by Tiffany, Handle, or Hubbard and Bradley, to name a few of the lampmakers of the time), are referred to as "Tiffany style." While most "Tiffany" lamps turn out to be reproductions and copies, occasionally you will find the real thing, and what a find it is!

As I completed finishing an appraisal one day, my client called me back.

"There's one other thing I'd like you to look at. It's a Tiffany lamp," she said in a very matter-of-fact way.

Of course I did not expect to see a Tiffany lamp—I had been disappointed so many times, but I reluctantly followed her into her basement. There she unpacked a lamp with two broken glass panels, but labeled "Tiffany."

"About eight years ago I bought this lamp at a white elephant sale for $1. We needed another lamp, and we had spent all our money on moving here. I put it up in my son's bedroom with the two broken panels turned toward the wall, and he used it for five years. When I finally got around to buying a new lamp and was packing this one away, I saw the Tiffany mark. I had never seen it before. Do you think I can sell it? Are people really buying Tiffany lamps?" she asked.

The lamp sold six months later at Christie's for $2,800—broken panels and all.

Now, granted, this was not a $58,000 or a $250,000 Tiffany lamp, but it was a pretty good return on a $1 investment. If you think you have a Tiffany lamp, examine it closely on the base and on the shade for the Tiffany signature. If you find nothing, assume that the lamp is *not* by Tiffany. However, an expert in this area can positively identify your lamp, and, I repeat, even Tiffany-style lamps are selling for hundreds of dollars today.

When making your inventory be sure to include lamps. Even mass-produced, store-bought lamps are expensive today because of manufacturing costs. Yet these accessories are often overlooked in household inventories.

Looking Glasses

The earliest mirrors or looking glasses in America were imported. Historically, the first mirrors were only highly polished sheets of metal. Later, during the eighteenth century, cutting an even layer of hand-blown glass, which would not break in the cutting or which would not be terribly irregular once it was cut, was extremely difficult. Mirrors remained very expensive until the nineteenth century, and for this reason early mirrors are extraordinarily expensive.

In addition to the cost of the mirror itself, there is the frame to be considered. Because mirrors were so expensive they were found in only the wealthiest homes and then in the finest rooms as a status symbol. As a result, the frames of early mirrors are often outstanding examples of craftsmanship.

The most familiar style of mirror from the eighteenth century is the highly carved wooden frame in the Chippendale style with a bird motif—either a bird perched at the center of a broken-neck pediment or else a carved phoenix bird at the center of the fretwork crest. These eighteenth-century mirrors were reproduced in the nineteenth century, particularly during the Centennial period. Many of the modern European copies of both these and the Chippendale Rococo gilded mirrors are often mistakenly sold as period American mirrors.

It wasn't until much later in the nineteenth century, during the Hepplewhite period, that many mirrors were actually made in America. By the time of the Sheraton period, mirrors were found in more modest homes, and the typical Sheraton mirror with a gilt frame decorated with an eglomise panel (a decorative glass section usually depicting a landscape scene or a flower motif) became both common and popular.

For a mirror to have an investment value, all the parts must be original.

Unfortunately, I find many mirrors and clocks in which the eglomise panel is replaced by a Currier and Ives type nineteenth-century print, often cut out of a book or magazine. The picture usually replaces an eglomise panel that had been cracked or in which the paint was wearing off. Even a worn or cracked panel is considered acceptable as long as it is the same age as the rest of the mirror and frame.

Highly ornate Sheraton or Federal mirrors with gilded eagles and elaborate Corinthian columns flanking the mirror are expensive. However, simple mirrors with a molded cornice and rounded columns at the sides (often called tabernacle mirrors) can still be purchased for as little as $100. A manufacturer's label generally doubles the value of a nineteenth-century mirror.

Be sure to include your reproduction and new mirrors on your appraisal. Today a good-quality mirror with a simple frame generally ranges from $100 to $200, but fine mirrors bought from interior decorators' shops have now escalated in price and are often in the $500 to $1,000 range.

Oriental Rugs

The Oriental carpet market is one often spoken of as having investment possibilities, but not everyone agrees with this. An Oriental rug expert explained to me that the rugs of true investment quality are presently in Germany. Even Sotheby's and Christie's New York galleries are selling rugs that are primarily of interest only to American dealers. These dealers sell the rugs to other dealers and to interior decorators, who in turn sell the rugs to American collector-investors who mistakenly think that they are buying the finest investment-quality Oriental carpets. In reality, these "investors" are buying semi-antique and good-quality rugs, but not investment-quality rugs.

> You must understand that when an Oriental rug expert speaks of investment-quality carpets he is speaking in terms of hundreds of thousands of dollars.

The Oriental carpets usually found in American homes are Caucasian rugs or Persian floral motif rugs dating from the 1920s. The value of this type of 9 x 12 rug can vary—depending on the condition, repairs, color, design, quality, etc.—anywhere from a low range of $500 to a higher range of $5,000. The small scatter rugs found in halls and in front of fireplaces have an equally wide range, anywhere from $100 to $1,500 or more.

It takes an Oriental rug specialist who can identify the age and kind of rug to appraise these carpets. My experience has been that most people are disappointed to find that the value of their rugs is not as high as they had hoped. The disappointment comes, I believe, primarily from the publicity that has surrounded Oriental rugs and the headlines that lead the general public to believe that any Oriental rug is worth hundreds of thousands of dollars.

These short comments should help you to realistically assess the rugs you already have and serve as a warning to buy carefully and realize that when you buy an Oriental rug in America you are primarily making an investment in a decorative item and not buying a true investment-quality antique. But when you compare the cost of a semi-antique Oriental rug to newly manufactured carpeting, you will probably feel that the Oriental rug is worth the difference in price.

Incidentally, there is also a regional factor in the rug market. Southerners seem to love old, worn-out, faded, and torn Oriental rugs. The rest of the country prefers newer rugs in better condition. I know of one dealer who regularly travels to the North and Midwest, gathers up all the Oriental rug rejects, and brings them into the South, where he makes a grand profit.

Art

What better way to remember a foreign trip than to pick up a little souvenir painting? Why do all beaches have art galleries? Who doesn't love a beautiful mountain landscape hanging on his wall? Pictures and prints abound. But there is a tremendous difference in quality between a mass-produced etching or print, or an anonymous oil, and an oil or watercolor masterpiece.

No other aspect of the antiques world is as glamorous as the art market. Art sales are where the really big money changes hands today. Sotheby Parke Bernet sold "Juliet and Her Nurse," by J. M. W. Turner for almost $6.5 million. Christie's sold a Rubens painting, "Samson and Delilah," for $5,474,000. These are the paintings that people write about.

The reality of finding such a painting in a home is slim. But it can be done. A friend of mine found an original portrait of an American President hanging in an antiques shop, simply identified as "Portrait of an English Gentleman." Somewhere along the way, as the painting went from one owner to another, to an auction house, to a purchaser, passed on to an heir, back for sale again, the identity of the President was lost. But it wasn't by luck that the painting was identified. The man who discovered the lost painting was a student of American history, and he recognized the subject of the painting.

Great painters of a period are imitated and faked, even during their lifetimes. As James Craig of the well-known Craig and Tarlton Galleries, in North Carolina, explains, many artists were copied in their own time because they were so popular. While those paintings may have been sold as copies during the artist's lifetime, once the artist's work fades into obscurity, it is forgotten which is the real painting and which is the copy. Then once the artist and his work are rediscovered, it can be difficult to distinguish the original from the copy without an expert's examination.

Another problem is that artists who come back into vogue may have been copied during their lives, but the public and even the experts will not know that they were, and thus many pictures that have an artist's signature on them will be sold as his work, when in reality they were only copies.

Prints and Engravings

Pictures that are not hand-painted, and other than watercolors, acrylics, oils, etc., comprise an endless list. There are etchings, engravings, woodcuts, lithographs, mezzotints—the list goes on. And they can easily fool even the expert as to quality.

One nationally known dealer attended an auction where he was attracted to a small picture.

"Is it a watercolor?" he inquired of a friend, who was working at the auction house.

"Oh yes," the friend assured him.

The dealer knew that the auction assistant had trained under an expert who specialized in art, so he took his word and bought the picture.

Once he had the picture home and kept looking at it, the dealer became more and more concerned. Finally he took the picture out of the frame and underneath the mounting found clearly printed "New York Graphic Society." The watercolor was a print, of which hundreds had been struck.

To evaluate paintings and prints, they must first be authenticated and then appraised. Art is a very specialized area, and very few appraisers of artwork will be able to handle other personal property in your home. On the other hand, the general personal property appraiser is often totally unqualified to authenticate and appraise artwork. You may find, however, that an appraiser who has had a lot of experience in fine arts and antiques can guide you by suggesting that you should have your paintings appraised or telling you that, no, these are not of sufficient value to warrant an investment in an appraisal.

Clocks

I find the age of clocks to be greatly misunderstood. Quite regularly I am shown a 1920 mantel or shelf clock and told, "This clock is very old and very valuable. It probably dates from the eighteenth century."

Striking clocks, as we know them, date from thirteenth-century Europe. Of course, it is Galileo who is given credit for the stimulus for making pendulum clocks. But by the first part of the nineteenth century case clocks, either tall, imposing grandfather clocks or smaller mantel or shelf clocks, were frequently found in the wealthier American homes. By the end of the nineteenth century clocks were mass-produced and these abound. A walk through any flea market reveals numerous oak case clocks, some reproductions, some fake and some authentic. Even on television there are advertisements for clocks that "look as good as antiques" that can be purchased for only $29.95.

Because there are so many clocks from the nineteenth and particularly early part of the twentieth century, only those clocks which are unusual because of their fine cases or uniqueness, (such as calendar or regulator clocks) command great money.

But what money clocks can demand! Some regulator and calendar clocks have been valued at thousands of dollars, and the prices on even the most common shelf clocks at flea markets are always a little staggering to me.

Before investing in a clock be sure that you are truly buying what you are told you are getting. The clock should be in working condition, with all parts original, even the glass or eglomise panel (if a nineteenth-century shelf clock), and all the parts of the case, including the finials and the feet. Of course if you want to buy a chipped veneer mantel clock for the works to place inside a perfectly conditioned mantel clock that is missing its parts, then you have a different situation.

You should particularly beware of banjo clocks. These have been reproduced for years and are sometimes sold as being early nineteenth-century clocks, when in reality they are seventy-five years younger than that.

You can look for an increase in the value of Art Deco shelf clocks, particularly those with the statuary motifs characteristic of the Art Deco, and clocks from the 1930s made in combination with lamps.

❦ 14 ❧

Basements and Attics— Junk or Junque?

I am frequently asked: "What about all the things in my attic and basement? Are they really valuable, or should I just throw them away or have the Salvation Army come take everything for me?"

I have two answers.

First—*never* give or throw away a trunk or box without taking the time to go through it.

Second—people waste far too much time chasing after the value of a torn-up comic book, while they ignore the $2,000 china cupboard filled with their crystal and best china.

Yes, trunks in basements can hold wonderful treasures. My idea of complete and total absolute happiness is when I am turned loose in a grungy basement or attic filled with cobwebs, dust, and crawling things, and told, "Look to your heart's content."

Several years ago after our second child arrived, my father got tired of stumbling over toys scattered throughout my house.

One day when I was visiting my parents' home my father said, "I have a bunch of old trunks in my basement, I'm going to put them all out for trash, but if you can use one as a toy chest, you can have it."

Delighted at the offer, I went immediately to the basement.

Two hours later I reappeared.

"Do I get to keep the junk in the trunk?" I beamed.

In the trunk I had uncovered sterling silver button hooks, an envelope filled with hair jewelry dating from the 1860s, two charming 1830 silhouettes, an 1817 sampler, and an Art Deco inkwell—for starters.

Every day, treasures like these are thrown away because no one bothered to look. In the haste of cleaning up, anything can be carelessly discarded. In a few fortunate instances, Goodwill, the Salvation Army, or a secondhand shop will be the recipient of these "throwaways." But in far too many instances it all ends up on the dump pile.

But on the other hand, it greatly disturbs me when I see people chasing after rainbows in the dream of striking it rich.

Dirty Linen

I inadvertently got involved in just such an experience when a client brought in an "extremely rare" 1864 Lincoln and Johnson campaign banner. A museum in Kentucky had authenticated it several years before, I was told. But the owner had not wanted to sell it, even though the museum offered to purchase it. Then, someone in Kentucky told someone in Tennessee about it, and since Johnson had lived in Tennessee, a museum in Tennessee wanted it.

The banner just looked like an old faded piece of cloth to me, but who was I to dispute two museums' words?

Since refusing those offers, the owner had come on hard times and now wanted to sell the banner. But since he now lived in North Carolina and since Johnson was born in that fair state, a native son, no less, he wanted to sell it to the State Museum of Archives and History.

I knew nothing about political banners, but I called Archives and History, described the banner, and they said, yes, it sounds most interesting. At that point I called the Smithsonian and spoke to an expert in political memorabilia. Once again it sounded most interesting—even rare. Could I send photographs?

Even though the Smithsonian's interest was very appealing, my client said he'd rather the banner stay in North Carolina, and so I traipsed down to Archives and History with it. They were to examine it and get back to me.

A few days later I got a call from them.

"If you hadn't uncovered some great finds in the past," the curator began, "I'd tell you to throw your old dish towels in the hamper instead of bringing them to me."

The rare, museum-quality 1864 political banner turned out to be a Civil War *Centennial* souvenir dish towel, all of ten years old!

The Little Boat

For every story that discounts basement junk, there is another to make you spend hours hunting for that discarded treasure that is "worth a bundle."

David Redden of Sotheby Parke Bernet recalled with great glee the story of a German toy that was found in an estate.

"It was a nice little tin boat, about 34 inches long, made by the German toy company Maklin. It was a mass-produced industrial toy, but it had a wind-up clockwork motor and was still in perfect condition. We sold it for $21,000!"

In reality the tin toy was the battleship *Weissenberg*, rigged with four lifeboats, anchor, bridge, cannons, gun turrets, twin masts bearing banners, and the clockwork mechanism operated a four-bladed rear propeller.

A few points about its value are immediately obvious. First, the toy was in perfect condition. Second, its clockwork mechanism made it rare. Third, it was sold under the best possible circumstances—through a prestigious international auction house after being correctly identified. It was featured and advertised before the auction so toy collectors from around the world could compete for it.

Before You Throw It Away . . .

A rundown of potentially valuable items most frequently found stashed away in basements or stored in attics follows:

Photograph Albums—Pictures that show historical landmarks can be valuable, as are those that depict occupations that no longer exist. Of course, pictures of famous people or of historical events—Civil War, strikes, etc.—have value.

Books—Most books have minimal value, and family Bibles are valuable only to the family to whom the information is pertinent. However, some almanacs, children's books, cook books, and first editions have value. A. L. Burt and Grosset and Dunlap books are reprints, and their only value lies in the story or, in a few instances, the illustrations for decorative value.

Kitchen Ware—Almost all old kitchen utensils and furnishings have value. Ice boxes, wooden or metal, are being collected, as are old wash boards and hand-operated washing machines. While the values are limited, an entire collection or group of these nineteenth- and early twentieth-century goods can quickly add up to a few hundred dollars if you find the right buyer.

Maps, Charts, Aeronautical, Bicycling, Nautical, and Automobile Collectibles—There are collectors for all of these items; the most valuable are those generally associated with an historic event—a Civil War map, a tail insignia from a World War I bi-plane, a souvenir form the *Andrea Doria*, for example.

Cards—Old baseball or football cards, postcards, advertising cards, valentines, greeting cards, in fact, any kind of card can eventually find a collector. However, many of these paper items have been reproduced, and most have minimal value when compared to the cost of your sterling silver or crystal. If you come upon an entire collection of nineteenth-century baseball cards and give them to your six-year-old neighbor, you are giving money away. But most modern trading cards have a value of 50 cents or $1. If you want to keep them for another seventy-five years, the situation will be quite different, but you may not be around to cash in. If you plan to keep such items for their eventual potential value—tell someone.

Sporting Goods and Memorabilia—As sports-minded as we all are today, it goes without saying that these souvenirs and sporting equipment are avidly sought-after. Old tennis rackets, crewing oars, ticket stubs to famous sporting events, World Series and Super Bowl programs, all are collected. We should begin saving soccer accessories right now.

Architectural Accessories—Old door knobs, locks and brasses, even ceramic tiles are collected and often used in modern and restored homes.

Christmas Ornaments—nineteenth- and early twentieth-century glass, tin, and mirrored Christmas decorations are newly "hot" items. Some of the German and Japanese ornaments I remember buying for 5 and 10 cents as a child are now turning up in showcases for $12 to $35. However, many are also being reproduced. Choose carefully if you are buying. The truly hottest items among Christmas decorations are the sterling silver ornaments brought out in recent years by the American silver manufacturers—Towle, Gorham, Kirk, etc. These were limited editions, and now there are thousands more collectors than there are ornaments.

Smoking Items—Cigar molds, cutters, labels, tobacco figures, boxes, all have been collected for years. The resurgence of specialized smoking goods stores has led to more collectors—and to more reproductions. If you come upon any of the doll house rugs given away by Fatima cigarettes or the pictures of athletes and actors from the cigarettes at the turn of the century, you have items worth a few dollars each.

Campaign Collectibles—Banners (beware!), buttons, ribbons, and medals (the older and more obscure the candidate the better) are sellable. Several books have been written on campaign collectibles, but know that there are also many fakes and reproductions, especially ones used as advertising gimmicks.

Fire and Police Collectibles—Insurance company firemarks, firemen's parade trumpets, convention medals, firemen's and policemen's badges and insignia are collectible items with shops specializing in these goods. Local police and fire museums are always on the lookout for contributions of these mementoes and accessories. You might consider these as a tax write-off if you can't find a buyer, as some may have considerable value. Remember also that many police and fire chief badges of the nineteenth and early twentieth century are sterling silver and gold. Speaking of police collectibles, newspaper articles and artifacts dealing with the 1930s gangsters are of current interest, and one price guide even lists the values of "chain gang collectibles"— which is fine, I guess, as long as they didn't descend in your own family!

Legal Documents, Land Deeds, Letters and Diaries—Never discard a bunch of letters or deeds tied up in yellowing string without examining them closely. To begin with, if the envelopes are still present, the canceled stamps may be of value. But secondly, many letters relate to historic events—either of local or national interest. Guthman Americana recently assembled a collection of diaries and journals which were eyewitness reports of the 1781 surrender of Yorktown as told by a young Pennsylvania lieutenant. Their value is in the thousands of dollars, but just as amazing is the fact that the collection had been divided and Guthman purchased the papers from separate sources.

Pocket Knives, Fountain Pens, and Spectacles—Many small everyday items get packed away in old trunks. Often these were associated with family members and kept as reminders of Grandmother or a favorite uncle. But once a generation or so has passed, the sentimental value may have been forgotten and then items become just "old things." But there are collectors for old things, and the items in each of these categories have values ranging from a few dollars for the commonplace to hundreds of dollars for the rare example.

Sewing Box Goods—Knitting needles, sewing birds, thimbles, buttons, and darning eggs have long been high on the collectibles list. But remember, when going through old sewing boxes, that you may also find military buttons, Girl Scout insignia and badges, or any other kinds of accessory that would have gone onto clothing which may have additional value because of the organization it represents.

Clothing and Textiles—Clothing of the 1950s is now being bought out of secondhand stores and worn as "fashions." Christie's and Sotheby's have both featured designer clothing auction sales. Museums feature period costumes and fashions as part of both permanent and special exhibits. There is clearly more interest in clothing and textiles in general—table linens, bedspreads, etc.—than ever before. However, the condition is of utmost importance, as is design. The majority of old clothes and linens have little if any value, but look them over as wearables before casting them away.

Sheet Music, Old Records, and Piano Rolls—The return of the "old timey" ice cream parlor, beer parlor, pool room, and limelight restaurant have led to a search for period musical collectibles for use in these businesses. Once again, condition and rarity come into account. Many piano rolls are in unplayable condition, and even a John McCormick record that has a chunk out of it has no value. There is rekindled interest in the sheet music from the 1910s to 1930s for the cover artwork. You can still pick up a pile of sheet music at house sales for a couple of dollars, and if you try hard enough you can sell each item for $1, $5, or even $25 for an exceptional piece.

Office Equipment—The demand for typewriters, adding machines, and storage units obviously is not as great as the demand for antiques or collectible household items which can be used as accessories or conversation pieces. But, here again, the collector does exist. Certain furnishings, such as lawyers' bookcases, those glass-fronted units that can be stacked on one another, are now expensive and hard to find. The same is true for old post office mail boxes and dry goods display cases.

Toys—Every old toy in good condition has a value. Christie's and Sotheby's now regularly schedule toy sales, and every year new records are set for each category of toy. Until the middle part of the nineteenth century the majority of toys were made in Europe. The most valuable dolls are French and German, and even tea sets tend to be from England, Germany, or Japan, rather than America. Of course, later twentieth-century toys, are predominantly American-made. Original condition is of prime importance in toys and—like furniture—repairs and restoration, even of the paint on metal model toys and soldiers, can decrease the value. Early cartoon toys are in great demand, and today's superheroes and space toys are already becoming obsolete as this year's model outdates last year's model in sophistication and styling.

First Things First

But where does all of this lead? The objects in your attic and basement have value *if* they are in good condition, of sufficient quality, and if you can find a buyer.

I believe in the search and the dream. My own favorite possessions are ones I have come upon unexpectedly. But researching every old thing you find packed away is like looking for a needle in a haystack. My hard-and-fast rule is: *First, know the value of the property that you would have to account for if it were stolen, damaged, or destroyed.* Then, if you have the time, track down the value of your Lionel train set or your great-grandfather's Union Cavalry brass belt buckle. Who knows? It just might be very valuable.

🙚 15 🙚

P.S.—The Forgotten Essentials

Often when you make an appraisal or inventory you forget the most basic items—your refrigerator, stove, washer and dryer, even tools you use for hobbies or on the job. Sometimes you become so interested in insuring your antiques and expensive china and silver that you forget your basic household needs.

For those of you who wish to have a completely thorough listing of your personal property, here is a checklist for you to review.

All clothing
Uniforms and sports clothes
All sporting equipment, including bicycles, skates, etc.
Curtains and draperies
Blinds, shades, and interior shutters
Carpeting and rugs
Alarm and wall clocks
Kitchen utensils
Small kitchen appliances—irons, food processors, etc.
Large kitchen appliances—freezer, stove, etc.
Cleaning items—brooms, mops, pails, etc.
Painting items—ladders, brushes, etc.
Toys and hobby items
Tools—both hand and power tools, workbench, etc.
Luggage and storage trunks
Lawn and patio furniture
Garden and lawn tools—including trowels, rakes, etc.
Bathroom electrical appliances—shavers, toothbrushes, water pics, curling irons, etc.
Any health-related items—humidifier, hospital bed, etc.

All bed, bath, and kitchen linens
Home entertainment equipment—television, tape recorders, stereos, collections of records, muscial instruments, etc.
Expensive perfumes, wines and liquors.

It is wise to make a skeletal listing of these items—just in case. These necessities are so important that when a family has to relocate after a disaster, many adjusters make their advance payment on the basis of the listing of appliances, washer, dryer, stove, etc.

> Warning: When taking expensive linens, designer clothes, furs or leathers to be cleaned or repaired, have an accurate description and keep your receipt. Few laundries or repair shops carry insurance against loss or damage of *your* property. If anything happens *you* may have to file with your insurance agent.

An excellent suggestion from the Property Loss Research Bureau of Chicago is to sketch out the room arrangement of your dwelling with the placement of your furnishings on graph paper. Placing windows and closet doors in your drawing can also serve as a memory jogger for draperies, clothes, and stored items.

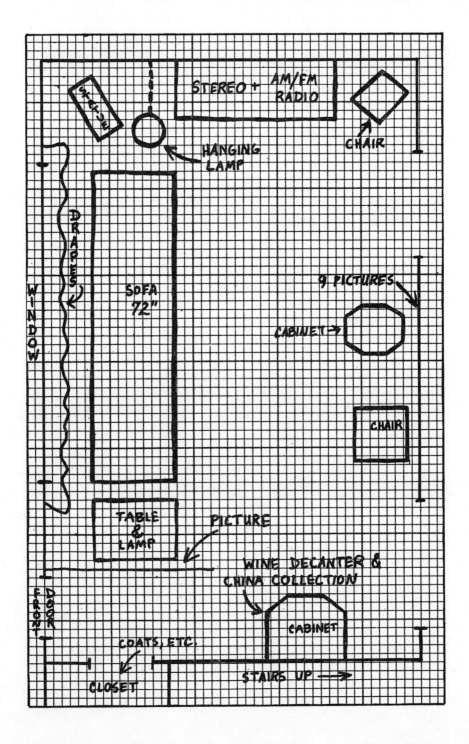

Reprinted from the *Personal Property Inventory Booklet,* copyright 1975, Property Research Bureau, Chicago, Ill.

16

Times When You Need
To Know What You Own
And What It Is Worth

There are three, and possibly four, times in your life when you will need to know what you own and what it is worth.

The first time is when you buy insurance to protect your personal property. Everyone needs some kind of household insurance for day-to-day protection, and if you move you will need additional coverage while your property is in transit. The information I share in Chapter 17 is not intended to be the last word in insurance advice. But it is designed to guide you toward knowing about possible options and to alert you as to why you must analyze your insurance needs.

The second time you need to know your property values is when you are faced with a catastrophe. Unfortunately, everyone seems prone to misfortune these days. A burglary is the most usual loss, but fire can be even more devastating. Chapter 18 alerts you to the problem that owners of personal property face and how they can prepare ahead of time for the problems these catastrophes bring.

The third time you need to know about your personal property is when you either wish to sell or donate property, or when property must be divided for estate purposes. In these instances, the Internal Revenue Service publishes guidelines. Chapter 19 deals with appraisals for tax purposes.

Finally, there is divorce. Personal property is often a bone of contention between couples. Knowing what you own and its value can be essential in divorce settlements. Chapter 20 deals with this problem.

🎜 17 🎜

Insurance—
Before It's Too Late

Home Is Where the Heart Is—and the "Money" Too

Stop for a minute and think of everything in your home. Clothing, furniture, tools, pictures, lawn equipment, jewelry, electronic and entertainment equipment, rugs and carpets, appliances, silver, bed and table linens, cooking utensils, crystal and glass, sporting equipment, books, musical instruments, photographic equipment, toys, perhaps office or work-related equipment—the list is endless.

Now, consider for a moment that if you are a homeowner, the total value of everything in your house may well *equal* or even *surpass* the value of your house itself.

This was not always true. Up until the recent spiraling of household and antiques values, the external dwelling was considered substantially more valuable than the contents of the house. So just what kind and how much personal property insurance do you need?

The 50 Percent Standard Policy—Is it Enough?

Today's standard homeowner policy covers all of your personal property—the items listed above, and all else—*except* automotive vehicles (cars, motorcycles, trucks, etc.) It gives you 50 percent coverage of the cost of your house (see limitations, later in this chapter). Simple mathematics shows that if your house is insured for $80,000, you have $40,000 coverage on all of your personal property. If your house is insured for $150,000 your personal property coverage is for $75,000. Do you honestly think that your personal property is worth only half the value of your dwelling? None of my clients' is—why should yours be?

Packed and Ready to Go

Consider, too, that your house is where you keep *all* of your personal property—probably worth more than your cash wealth—in a very small, concentrated area. A thief moves quickly from dining room to living room and on to the bedroom, gathering silver, jewelry, and other objects as he goes. Fire jumps from curtains to sofas to rugs, and spreads rapidly across a roof or along wiring. Tornadoes flatten an entire city block in a matter of seconds.

To ensure replacing the possessions in your home there are two major types of coverage you and your insurance agent should consider.

The Floater Policy

The first type is the "floater" policy in which you specify certain antiques and valuable items that you wish to insure separately from your general household property. You have these items appraised and use the appraised figure for their insurance value. This figure can "lock you in" to a specific amount of insurance compensation, but it is better to receive a specific amount for an antique or heirloom which you value highly than to find out that after you have spent all of your insurance money replacing the necessities you haven't a penny left to apply to replacing these items.

Should you decide to carry a floater policy, it will be your responsibility to remember to review these figures periodically to keep up with inflation. If you want to have guaranteed replacement on your floater policy to cover fragile collections or even breakage of a particular individual piece, inquire about the all-risk floater and specifically request breakage coverage.

Always remember that insurance laws and policies vary from company to company and from state to state.

The Replacement Value Policy—A Major Breakthrough

The other major way to assure replacement of your personal property after a loss is the new replacement value endorsement on the homeowner's policy. In most states, under this endorsement you increase the coverage on your household contents from the standard 50 percent to 70 percent of the value of your home dwelling. This is the coverage most agents are advising their clients to buy today, and the additional protection is well worth the comparably small additional premium.

This endorsement reflects a major breakthrough in insurance. Here, at last, is a realistic approach to the *real* value of today's personal property. Insurance companies are finally beginning to realize that in light of inflation *depreciation* on personal property is not as great as it once was.

In fact, many items of personal property—furniture, china, silver, etc., are *appreciating*, not *depreciating*. This new thinking gives you, the consumer, the advantage of being able to replace your property in kind, an advantage you did not always have. Furthermore, the courts have recently been ruling that *the replacement value of personal property in insurance cases is the cost of replacing the specific item lost with another item equal in kind and quality at the time of the loss.*

To see how this endorsement works to your advantage, take the example of the bedside table I mentioned in Chapter 3. When you bought it in 1963 it cost $50. If you lose the table in 1982 and have the replacement endorsement on your homeowner's policy, you can have your table replaced with one of comparable quality (which now is about $300).

Thus, the language on the new personal property replacement cost endorsement reads like this:

> "Replacement Cost" means the cost, at the time of the loss, of a new article identical to the one damaged, destroyed, or stolen. When the identical article is no longer manufactured or is not available, replacement cost shall mean the cost of a new article similar to that damaged or destroyed and which is of comparable quality and usefulness.

When You Overpay for Your Coverage

As always, there are limitations and loopholes on the amount the insurance company is going to pay in replacing your possession. Insurance companies still have the option to repair or replace items lost rather than make a cash settlement. I am finding that more and more insurance companies are choosing to replace possessions for the clients in lieu of a cash settlement, especially when the possessions lost are still manufactured today.

One insurance agent told me that when his clients lose expensive camera equipment it is usually replaced by mail, within a few days' time. The adjustor calls in an order to a discount house and the camera, lens, etc., are shipped to the owner. Thus, if you entered your camera equipment for $3,000 but the insurance company only paid $2,500 to replace it, you may feel you were cheated.

This replacement value policy can create a problem for the policy owner when prices decline, as in the recent case of silver. If your silver was appraised when silver prices were at their highest—$200 and more for a single fork, but your silver was stolen after silver prices fell, and the insurance company replaces your forks for only $75 each, you may feel doubly robbed.

"I was paying the premium for a $200 fork, not a $75 fork," you complain.

To avoid such problems you should consult your agent whenever a large price change occurs—either up or down—on items you have insured.

Depreciation Is Still a Factor

Another limitation on the replacement value policy states that the company's liability will not exceed four times the actual cash value of the depreciated cost of the item. In other words, let's say you lost an expensive television which is now several years old, but would cost $850 to replace. However, the actual cash value of the TV, due to the depreciation applied to *limited-life terms,* is only $100. In keeping with the replacement value policy language, the total amount you can expect from your insurance is four times the cash value, or $400, leaving you $450 short of its true replacement value for an identical new product.

I personally think that, for the money, the replacement value endorsement offers the best coverage for your personal property. It is certainly better than the standard policy. If you have valuable antiques or extensive collections or feel that your belongings are particularly susceptible to loss, you will want to consider combining the replacement policy with an all-risk floater policy for maximum protection.

Limitations You Must Know About

Regardless of what kind of policy you decide on, there are five limitations you need to know about. These vary from state to state and the maximum compensation allowed also varies, so ask your agent for the specifics about:

- Limitations on coins and currency, both circulated and collections of rare coins and currency. ($100 maximum compensation)
- Limitation on deeds and securities, purchases of travel tickets, passports, stamps—both new and old collections. ($500 maximum compensation)
- Limitation on certain recreational property, boats and outboard motors, boat trailers, etc. ($500 maximum compensation)
- Limitation on jewelry, gems, watches and furs. ($500 maximum compensation)
- Limitation on metals, silver, gold, pewter, guns and gun collections. ($1,000 maximum compensation)

Getting Your Personal Property Insurance

Until the insurance industry becomes more aware of the value of personal property, seeing that you have adequate personal property insurance is going to be *your* responsibility. As one person put it, "Every insurance agent in town called me about my life insurance. They all wanted to come out to the house and see me. But when I tried to get insurance on my antiques and personal property a secretary asked me *over the phone* how much I wanted to write the policy for!"

However, I see changes taking place in the insurance industry that will soon, I hope, lead to better-informed agents and adjustors who are experts in personal property. Insurance companies are losing so much money in personal property claims that they are beginning to learn about furnishings just to be able to protect themselves. Eventually they will be able to protect you, too.

Burglary and Values—Both Are on the Rise

Obviously, when lists of stolen silver, jewelry, rugs, antiques, and electronic equipment come in on a daily basis, often totaling $50,000 to $75,000 per claim, insurance adjustors are going to learn about personal property values. These large losses are also the reason why the adjusters are putting the burden of proof of ownership on the insured when a loss is filed. And well they should, to keep the rest of our premiums from going up to cover the paying off of false claims!

Insurance Companies Have Problems Too

In my years of appraising I have been involved in more false and errone-ous claims than I wish to remember. The astute adjuster watches for "red flags" that suggest errors in the claim. In fire claims, for example, are there more pieces of furniture listed than could possibly have fitted into the dwelling? In cases of robbery, do the items listed far exceed the value of insurance the insured was carrying? Is there clear evidence of a robbery, and was it reported to the police immediately? And then there are the times when the adjuster has that "gut" feeling that the claim is in error but can't put his finger on why.

An adjuster called me in just such an instance. Would I go with him to question the insured about the property that had been lost in a fire. There were a couple of listings that really disturbed him. One was the claim for a wicker rocking chair for $1,000, and the other was for a quilt for $2,500. Once I had the list in hand, I also picked up several other discrepancies in values and so I agreed to work on the case. We drove out into the country and met with the insured, her attorney, and her son.

"How do you know your wicker rocker was worth $1,000?" I asked. The insured had seen one, not as good, for sale in an antiques shop for $400, so she figured hers was worth $1,000.

"And what about the quilt?" I inquired. Well, one night she was listen-ing to a call-in radio program. Someone had called in and described a quilt. The guest appraiser had said that the caller's quilt would be worth at least

$1,000, so the insured looked at hers and decided it would be worth $2,500. (Incidentally, that taught me the danger of appraising over the radio!)

Throughout this dialogue two people said nothing, the attorney and the son. Close to the end of our session, however, I came to this listing:

Leather-bound books. *One Hundred Greatest Masterpieces of American Literature.* Franklin Mint. $50 each. Total loss: $5,000

"Whose books were these?" I inquired.

"Oh, those were Clinton's [not the son's real name]," the mother replied. "He just loves to read great literature."

At this point I directed my questions to Clinton. Clinton, it seems, was unemployed. He had managed to graduate from high school, and had held a variety of jobs, but none of them had lasted long.

"What were some of the titles of the masterworks?" I asked.

When Clinton couldn't recall any of the titles, his mother tried—also without much luck.

"Do you mean to tell me that you don't remember the names of books for which you paid $35 apiece, and that you say are now worth $50 each?"

"Ah, well, ah . . . we didn't buy the whole set. We started buying them, but then dropped them," was the stammered reply. That dialogue set off a full investigation. The total loss was eventually disclaimed and the insurance company did not have to pay a single penny.

But for every false claim that is filed, there are one hundred claims filed where the *victim is being false to himself because he did not know what he lost or how valuable it was.*

When You Need to File a Claim

In light of the justified cautious attitude of insurance adjusters today, what should *you* do if you have to file a claim? Briefly, you need to take the same steps you would were you to be audited by the IRS.

My advice is—*do your homework, be prepared,* and *tell the truth.*

The two major points you will have to establish are: (1) what you lost and (2) proof that you owned it. To make it easier, here is what you need to know:

- What you lost—give the item a proper name.
- How many of each item listed you lost.
- A description of each item—size, material, age, and condition.
- Purchase value and date, if known.
- What you consider a fair value for the item today.

For example:

Item & Value	Description	Purchase Date and Value	Current Value
1 Chair	Mahogany sidechair with needlepoint seat.	Inherited from family.	$295
7 Forks	Sterling silver, fancy pattern by Gorham. Monogrammed "B."	Mother's wedding present.	$50 each $350
Set of crystal (24 pieces)	Round bases, deep bowls, 8 water, tea and juice glasses. Silver rims.	Wedding crystal 1962. $4 ea. $96	$22 each $528
Painting	Scene of Venice. Watercolor. Framed in gold & black frame.	Present from sister-in-law in 1972. Framing cost: $48	$250 estimate

Do Your Homework

One reason why insurance companies take so long to settle personal property claims is because they themselves do not know the value of personal property. I can promise you that if you will present a well-documented and prepared claim, in addition to the skeleton list required by the company, your claim will more likely be settled quickly and you will probably be satisfied with the settlement.

To avoid disappointment, be sure that the source you use in establishing your values is knowledgeable in the field. In Chapter 22, you will learn who appraisers are and how to find them. But let me warn you now that there are scores of people claiming to be experts whose advice is not worth your time of day. Just because you have a piece of paper with a value on it signed by an appraiser does not mean that this value will be accepted by the insurance company.

Establishing Proof of Ownership

Once you have your list compiled, you next need to establish proof of ownership. Of course if you had made your list up ahead of time, the proof of ownership would have been established. But since you did not, now you must gather the information the best way you can.

- Collect all bills of sale, canceled checks, any sort of receipt that can establish proof of ownership and at the same time jar your memory. For example, finding the receipt for one item will often help you remember that you bought another item from the same store.
- Gather together prints of all interior photographs that you, relatives, or friends have taken of your family. Backgrounds in family pictures often contain many material objects you can identify as lost.

- Ask others—family members, neighbors, visitors, anyone who can help recall objects they remember in your home. They can also serve as witnesses to the fact that you owned specific objects, if necessary.
- Contact store clerks who sold you items to help arrive at a fair replacement price to accompany the claim. This also establishes the fact that you actually owned the items involved.
- As an alternative to photographs, especially in the case of fire or other destruction of property where photographs would also have been destroyed, find pictures in magazines and books as similar as possible to the items you have lost. You can even draw rough sketches which will help the adjuster or appraiser assist you in arriving at a fair dollar settlement.

Remember the couple in the second chapter who didn't even remember how many chairs they had, much less what they looked like? I repeat, do your homework before submitting your claim.

The Double-Check

But at the same time, expect the insurance adjuster or investigator to double-check your sources and claims. I recall one case, in particular, when the owners voluntarily told me where they had purchased their furniture and how much they had paid for it at the time. Just as routine procedure I called the furniture store and asked for verification.

"Did the Joneses buy an oak bedroom suite from you in 1976?" I inquired.

The records showed that they had.

"And would you remember the general price range of the suite? Would it have cost $1,200 or more like $5,000 at the time?" I asked.

"Oh, they couldn't have bought anything that expensive," the salesman replied. "They paid their bills on time, but they did not buy expensive furniture."

I looked back to double-check the figure that the Joneses had submitted on their insurance claim for replacing the suite. It was $5,000. Whether the figure was arrived at out of ignorance or intent to deceive, or whether it was just a mistake, had a more accurate figure of $1,800 or $2,000 for a 1981 replacement value been given, the embarrassment that followed could have been avoided. Do your homework.

So You're Going to Move

When a family moves, it's a high-stress time. As moving costs go up, more people are trying to save money by doing it themselves, an exhausting process.

Obviously, the way to get around all of this, is to hire professional packers to come in and take care of everything. The problems that result are also obvious. You have complained about them yourself. The packing wasn't properly done. Your most prized possessions were thrown into a truck. The box of crystal had a heavy brass ashtray on the top and arrived with only the ashtray intact.

Then there is always the possibility of the boxes and crates never arriving. Remember the horror stories about the box that was left behind and the time you received someone else's china instead of your own. Anyway, all boxes and crates look alike.

Which Box?

Everyone knows the case where the owners had packed one group of boxes to be picked up by a charity and another group of boxes to be moved to their new home. You know what happened. The charity ended up with the family's good china and when the family unpacked what they thought was going to be their best china, they found their second set of china, which had been intended for the charity. The question is, "Can you afford the high risk of moving without knowing what you own?"

Packed, But Not Unpacked

Moving losses are much like robbery or fire losses. It is those objects you do not use on a day-to-day basis but often treasure most, and want to pass on to the next generation, that you may not miss for a long time (one reason why you do not use them is because they're antiques and you're trying to keep them in pristine condition for your children).

That's Mine

One of my clients did not miss her mother's cut glass lemonade pitcher until several months after she was finally settled in her home and decided to go antiquing. While browsing in an antiques shop she saw a cut glass lemonade pitcher identical to hers. Naturally she began wondering where she had put hers when she unpacked. Next she realized that she did not remember unpacking the pitcher at all. A thorough search of all the cabinets and closets revealed nothing. Then, she realized there were other pieces she hadn't seen since she'd unpacked.

She began looking for the things she remembered packing in the same box with the pitcher. None of these appeared. By now, my client was distraught. She went back to the antiques shop where she had seen the pitcher. There she began finding other heirlooms which she recognized as her own—including her grandfather's baby cup with his name and birthdate engraved on it!

Yes, she got them back. She bought them back.

Why One Moving Company Paid Over $16 Million in Claims Last Year

Breakage is, of course, a high-risk chance in moving. Scratches and dents are facts of life, and so are splintered chair legs, and even totally demolished chests and secretaries.

I have been involved in moving claims where vans have been wrecked, and even one in which a van was "lost" for almost a month. (Who pays for furniture rental while you wait for yours to be found?) But a particularly harrowing sight met my eyes just as I began writing this book.

I was driving down Interstate 85 early one spring morning when suddenly, in the opposite lane, I saw a charred and burned moving van abandoned along the side of the road. Who would have anticipated that a moving van on an interstate highway would catch on fire?

I did not know when the fire had occurred, but I could see that the truck was deserted with only orange cones and some burned-out flares to mark it off. Had the contents of the truck also been burned, or, if they survived, how long had they been left on the truck, unattended, unguarded, and unprotected, I wondered. Later that afternoon, as I returned along the same highway, there was another moving van and the objects from the burned van were being loaded onto a second truck.

If you are anticipating a move, you have an urgent reason for making an inventory of your personal property. Accidental loss, breakage, theft, depreciating damage—these are only some of the risks involved in moving today.

🐚 18 🐚

Disasters—
Theft and Fire

Theft—Or What You Saw Is What They Got:
What You Need to Know About Burglaries

In approximately a third of the break-ins in America the burglar gains unlawful entry *without using force.*

Personal property and art crime is second *only* to narcotics crimes.

These are typical headlines that appear in every newspaper across the country daily:

THREE FBI IMPOSTERS SOUGHT IN JEWEL THEFT

SERVICE TRUCK YIELDS LOOT

THIEVES FIND CHURCH ITEMS IRRESISTIBLE

STOLEN GOODS ARE VALUED AT $4 MILLION

Chances are, a family member or neighbor of yours has been robbed recently. But both you and I know it's not going to happen to you or me. Or do we?

The chances are roughly 1 in 100 that you will be the victim of a personal property burglary. But until theft hits close to home, most of us are going to ignore the possibility. I can best illustrate this point by telling you what happened to my friend the insurance agent. Mind you, he is an insurance agent who tells *other* people to have appraisals made. In fact, he often called me asking me to make appraisals for clients.

But he never asked me to make one of his property.

Furthermore, this insurance agent *invested* in antiques. Every time he bought a new piece his dealer would warn, "Have your collection appraised. It has greatly increased in value over the years."

Then, last Christmas his brother's house was broken into and robbed. When his brother could not collect his insurance because he couldn't remember everything he owned, had no proof of ownership for many of the stolen items, and had no idea of the current value of his lost possessions, the insurance agent panicked. He called me to appraise his collection.

"I just never thought it could happen to me. Now I know it can," he said.

That's Incredible

The tales of robberies are as unbelievable as fiction, yet they happen every day. One of the most startling happened in a quiet community where a van, disguised as a Salvation Army truck, pulled into a driveway. The crew quickly loaded Oriental rugs, furniture, china, cut glass, silver, and art works, even crystal chandeliers and a piano, into the van and drove away. No clues were left. No recovery was ever made.

Repeat Performances

Repeat robberies have also increased at an alarming rate. Once the robbers learn how to gain entry into a home and discover where things are kept, they return, knowing the job will be easier the second time.

One woman who was robbed decided that since she lived alone she did not want the responsibility of worrying about her antiques—the ones the robbers had left—anymore. She packed up a couple of boxes of china and drove to a reputable shop where she had bought antiques in the past. She explained her situation and offered her china for sale. The shop owner was happy to purchase it. Excited over her good fortune, she told him about some brass candlesticks and sterling silver she had at home which she would also sell. Yes, he'd buy those too. She drove straight home to get them. A while later the dealer received a call from her. She was sorry she couldn't sell him the other pieces. While she was at his shop her home had been robbed—again.

Gone, But Not Returned

This raises the question of what happens to stolen property? Usually it is sold almost immediately at flea markets, or to antiques dealers, at auctions, to scrap metal dealers, to fences, to receivers. It is hawked on street corners, sold at fine uptown galleries, shipped out of state, across the county, and out of the country. But very seldom does it find its way back to the original owner.

Why can't people recover their stolen property? There are two major reasons. The first will make you indignant. The second should make you get on with an inventory.

Identity Crisis—Theirs

The first reason is that the police usually do not know enough about the *nature* of stolen property to effectively recover it. How can a policeman trained in law enforcement know how to identify a Tiffany lamp, a Paul Storr tea urn, or a set of Belter furniture? These are the high rollers, the items worth $10,000, $15,000, or $25,000 each. But the same problem—identifying an Imari bowl worth $250, or a Georg Jensen fork worth $185, or a set of Lenox china worth $1,200—hinders the recovery of personal property taken from your home and mine.

One detective, an expert on art property, told me, "When someone reports the loss of a rug, the police may be thinking $19.95 a yard, not $6,000 for a rare Oriental . . . when someone reports a stolen lamp, the police may be thinking $29.95, but if it is a Tiffany it is worth $15,000 . . ."

Raymond Kendall, of the famous international police organization, IN-TERPOL, admits, "We know that 99 percent of police officers have absolutely no special knowledge of 'cultural property' at all."

The second reason why people cannot recover their stolen property is lack of sufficient proof of ownership and inability to adequately describe personal property to identify it for retrieval.

The following story told by Robert Volpe, the art and antiquities expert on the New York City police force, illustrates the problem better than any other I could tell.

Crime But No Punishment

According to Volpe, a fence who specialized in toasters, TVs, tape decks, etc., was offered a statue by a thief. At first the fence was going to turn it away, but the fence's girl friend saw it, liked it, and so the fence bought it for her. Word got out that the fence's girl friend liked antiques and art. Soon thieves began bringing the fence pictures and silver and the like. Naturally the fence found where he could sell these antiques, but he also found that he liked these things too. *He* became a collector. Eventually the fence was caught, and when the police went in to arrest him they found a house laden with antiques—Tiffany lamps in every room, including the bathroom, Oriental rugs on the floor, Georgian silver in the kitchen cabinets! It was a fine display.

Now, the amazing thing is that at this point the fence admitted to the police that he was almost relieved that he had been caught. He had come to love and treasure his collection so much that he worried that some dumb thief would come in and steal all his precious pieces and not know what he was stealing!

The police put the stolen items on display and thousands of people viewed the property in hopes of finding their missing goods.

But, Volpe says, few people could positively identify pieces and reclaim them. Either they didn't have police reports to back up their claims or several individuals claimed the same piece. Others just couldn't be sure that the pieces were really theirs.

At this point the fence himself showed up and claimed everything in the room.

"It's mine," he declared. "You, the police, are my witness that I was in possession of these things because you were there . . . you saw all this in my house," the fence stated.

Furthermore, the fence could properly identify the pieces. He had catalogued and photographed all of them. (Incidentally, thieves and fences photograph pieces so they can show what they have to offer.) In short, he had the proof that the stolen goods were his.

Checklist

Local community watches have been established in many areas. Checklists are distributed by police and sheriff's offices. But if you do not follow their guidelines, you are not doing the most you can to protect yourself. Turn to Appendix A and take the Checklist for Homes right now.

Our Life-Style

I do all these things, you think. But do you?

"I can walk around my local area in Paris and see shutters down, mail left out, and all the visible signs that people are away," says Raymond Kendall of INTERPOL. "You can find out who is away just by driving through a neighborhood. Or you can do as one burglar I know did. He read names and addresses off luggage tags at the airport to compile a list of victims."

"It is our *everyday* contacts with life that expose us to the criminal element," says Robert Volpe. "We allow everyone into our homes today—repair people, service people of all kinds. Sometimes a person who has been in your home innocently talks to the wrong person. He'll say, 'Wow, you gotta see the house I went into to pick up the diapers today!' in the hearing of the wrong person."

Thieves Go Shopping

"You can see thieves shopping along Madison Avenue," Volpe says. "And they go shopping in neighborhoods too. There are some individuals who are only spotters. They're the ones who haven't the courage to go into someone's home. But they spot a victim and sell the information. The problem is, a lot of individuals do not think of themselves as collectors. They have things in their homes that they do not even realize are valuable collectibles or antiques. But the thief is aware of it. And to make matters worse, these are the individuals who are not properly insured and whose homes often are not properly secured."

Fire—Ashes Blacken Your Memory

Any loss of personal property is devastating. But fire is perhaps the most traumatic of all experiences. You may have barely escaped with your life. Among your losses from a fire may be not only your home, but records of your personal property, even your inventory or appraisal and photographs which could have served as proof of ownership. A thief seldom takes such items.

Yet the problems that result from fire losses are the same as those that occur after a theft. You must know what you lost.

Generally, I have found adjustors a little more lenient when working with fire victims in demanding proof of ownership on each item. Usually, so much has been lost in a total fire that the victim can never be compensated for his entire loss because he is underinsured and bound by the coverage he had.

One fire in a wealthy suburban neighborhood was concentrated in the kitchen and dining and living rooms. But the damage in these three rooms almost equaled the value of the insurance written on the entire house. Other than jewelry, *the greatest concentration of your valuable personal property is usually housed in those three rooms.* This is where you keep your silver, china, crystal, linens, best furniture, and finest accessories.

While you can only try to protect yourself against fire and other disasters of nature and society, you can be prepared to cope with the aftermath by making an inventory or appraisal first.

Where to Keep Your List

"I had a list and photographs, but they were lost in the fire," I have been told.

Always have a second copy of your inventory. Keep one copy and give the other to a trusted relative, attorney or friend. You may want to keep the appraisal in the most obvious place—your safe deposit box, but you should be aware of some potential problems if you do.

In case of a fire, you might not have easy access to your safe deposit box if you cannot locate your key in the rubble.

As the next chapter reveals, there can be a significant difference between an insurance and an estate appraisal. An insurance appraisal left in a safe deposit box can be used in an estate inventory when the contents of the box are inventoried by the Clerk of Court in beginning the probate process.

Consider, therefore, alternative places to keep your appraisal—a lock box or safe in your office, if you have one, or in a trusted person's safe deposit box, carefully labeled as your property, of course. Most of all, be sure that a second copy is in safekeeping. Most appraisers retain a copy of your appraisal if you have a professional appraisal made.

Hopefully, you will never be the victim of a robbery or fire. But why not use the principle of preventive medicine—take the time now and make an inventory and hope you'll never need it.

❧ 19 ❧

Estates and Donations—
You May Have Been Richer
Than You Thought

Mention IRS and hearts stop beating. Domineering men become timid pussycats and Milquetoast types turn into raging lions. This chapter is written to alert you to the fact that the Internal Revenue Service has provided specific guidelines that you need to be aware of if you are responsible for the administration of an estate.

When an Estate Does and Does not Need
an Appraiser's Services

Basically an appraisal is needed if the property in the estate must be equally divided among several heirs, or if the estate's fair market value is large enough that a federal estate tax report must be filed. (Each state has its own laws for state death tax reports and the new tax law passed in 1981 will increase the exemption to $600,000 in 1985.)

On the other hand, if the value is under the estate tax threshold, if there is only one beneficiary, or all items are specifically bequeathed, then there is *no* reason for an appraisal to be made for the heir's benefit. An appraisal is most useful when several heirs are named but there are no specific bequests in the will, and the property is to be divided equally among them. Usually, in such circumstances, no one can agree on what equals what.

In such instances an appraiser who has no sentimental attachment or monetary interest in any of the property can prepare an unbiased appraisal from which the heirs can then work.

When I make such an estate division appraisal, I use the same format I use when preparing an appraisal for estate tax purposes; "fair market values." I tell the heirs that if I sign my name to the appraisal for scrutiny by IRS then they can be assured that my values are fair to all involved. If an estate's property is going to be sold, either through an auction or house sale shortly after a death, there is no reason to have the estate appraised for tax purposes. As long as the sale of the property is legitimately transacted (at arm's length and with all parties knowing all relevant facts, according to IRS) the sale prices will stand as the "fair market value" of the estate.

But what if nothing is to be sold? My experience has shown me that tax attorneys are now looking more closely at the total value of an estate to see if the property is indeed valuable.

"I used to just pass on estates that had the usual amount of silver flatware, good china and crystal, some nice antiques and furniture, but no fine art collections or jewelry, stamp or coin collections," one tax attorney told me. "But now that all values have jumped so high, I'm taking a second look at personal property in estates. I'd say I'm taking a more cautious approach."

In other words, gone are the days when a man could die leaving hundreds of thousands of dollars in real estate, stocks, and bonds, and the attorney would list the value of his personal property at $500 or $1,000.

Another reason for the tax attorney to be cautious is the IRS Regulation §20.2031-6 (b) which states that if personal effects articles having a total value in excess of $3,000 exist in an estate (jewels, furs, art works, coin and stamp collections, silver, etc., are cited as possible examples), then an appraisal shall be submitted with the return.

Thus, to learn the value of estate property, many attorneys are now advising executors of sizable estates to have professional appraisals made.

Choosing an Appraiser for Estate Purposes

If an estate appraisal is needed, be extremely cautious in your choice of an appraiser. There are appraisers with self-serving interests who will offer to make an estate appraisal contingent upon the amount of taxes they save the estate. Equally as bad are those appraisers who charge a percentage of the total amount of the estate's value. They may be tempted to appraise used furniture at full retail prices just to increase their pay checks.

Swan Song

My favorite story concerning estate appraisal is the "pink swan story." It points up the problems that can beset estate appraisals when the heirs know nothing about the deceased's property.

Many years ago a very popular hostess who was noted for her passion for pink was given a large pink swan vase as a gift. Two of her friends had bought the swan at a local estate auction for $10. The friends often joked about how happy the auctioneer must have been to have more than one bidder run this obviously 10-cent-store item up to an exorbitant $10. But they were determined to buy the swan to give as a "joke" to their favorite hostess.

The swan became the focal point of every party. Sometimes it was used as a centerpiece with flowers floating in it. Other times it was filled with greenery and pink-and-silver Christmas balls. Over the years one wing became chipped and one foot got cracked, but no party was held without the ever present pink swan.

Some twenty years later the hostess died, and only six weeks later her husband died unexpectedly. No provision had been made for such a quick succession of deaths and the only heir, a daughter, had to pay double tax on all of the jointly owned property—even the cracked and chipped swan. When the appraiser valued the swan he knew nothing of the story. The $10 swan was valued at $125, or $250 for the double taxation.

Three years later the daughter began disposing of part of the personal property left by her parents. She looked over the appraisal, saw the swan listed at $125, and packed it into the "sell" box.

The dealer who took the estate items on consignment really didn't want the swan, but he took it as part of a total lot. Everything sold. Everything but the pink swan.

Eighteen months later, in desperation, the dealer sold the chipped and cracked swan for $15 just to get rid of it. He advised the daughter of his action and handed her a check for the swan, minus his commission of 33 1/3 percent. Her check was for $10—the same amount the swan had brought some twenty-two years earlier.

What Are Estate Values Anyway?

IRS actually tries to keep such outrageous errors from occurring in estate evaluations by stating guidelines for estate appraisal valuation. This is the wording used by IRS, which all good appraisers can quote in their sleep (even gagged) if necessary.

> The fair market value of the decedent's household and personal effects is the price which a willing buyer would pay to a willing seller, neither being under any compulsion to buy or to sell and both having reasonable knowledge of relevant facts.

The appraiser should know what a willing buyer and seller would pay, and know what she is looking at.

If the appraiser had correctly identified the pink swan as a decorative item of questionable quality, there is no way that she would have set a fair market price for the object as $125.

Many heirs worry about the value of used or secondhand property in estates. "You're going to put those in low aren't you?" they ask, almost pleadingly. There is *no other way* that an honest appraiser can appraise a piece of used furniture which has no value as an antique.

For example, take an undistinguished upholstered lounge chair which has not been recovered in fifteen years. Even at full retail price, its value would be modest, for you would find such a chair for sale *only* at a garage sale or in a flea market or at a Salvation Army store. Its top retail price would be $25 to $35.

"But I couldn't go out and buy a new chair like that for $35," you say.

No, but you are *not* buying a new chair. You are buying a used piece and paying its retail value—$25 to $35. Once you own the chair and have spent $250 to have it reupholstered, then if you wish to insure it for its replacement value—say, $300, that is a different matter.

But what about the twenty-five-year-old mahogany secretary in perfect condition? This piece would be suitable for sale in a decorator's shop or antiques store which also sells reproductions. Its value would not be that of a new piece today because those shops must sell these "old reproduction" pieces below the cost of a new piece in order to move them.

The secretary could easily be sold for anywhere from $800 in a house sale to $2,400 in an interior decorator's shop. Once again then, the estate value of the secretary could reasonably be stated to be $800, but its replacement value for insurance purposes could be placed at $2,400, or three times its estate value.

A true antique, however, would be even closer to its full and ultimate value because it would sell for what it is—an antique—under all circumstances. Thus an eighteenth-century walnut chest of drawers, which would sell locally for $3,000 to any one of several buyers, whether at auction or in a private sale, would be stated as having an estate value of $3,000.

What Needs to Be Appraised in an Estate

No one, IRS least of all, expects every kitchen and bathroom article to be counted and valued in an estate. Obviously furniture, silver, collections, and large vehicles—cars, boats, etc.—are included in an appraisal.

What happens, however, when there is an estate where one classification of an item is much more significant than the rest of the property? In other words, what do you do when the deceased had a library of first editions, but everything else was the usual household contents? At this point you will want to call in a book specialist to work along with the general household appraiser both for tax purposes and for the fair division of the estate.

What you want to guard against, however, is hiring two or more appraisers who are not coordinated in their value structure. I was once involved in an estate appraisal where one appraiser in an entire "team" of appraisers assigned values totally out of line with the rest of our figures. This created a discrepancy in the appraisal, the value of the estate, and the tax basis. *Consistency is important in estate appraisals where more than one appraiser is hired.*

Gathering More Information About
Personal Property Estate Tax Laws

You can find thousands of attorneys and CPAs who specialize in tax laws and who understand and interpret the federal regulations dealing with estate taxes. You may also want to write to the Department of the Treasury, Superintendent of Documents, U.S. Government Printing Office, Washington, D.C. 20402 and ask for Publication 561, Valuation of Donated Property. The guidelines set forth in this publication are equally applicable to *gift and estate property.*

Personal Property Donations

The rules of "fair market value" also apply when an appraiser evaluates property to be donated for tax purposes.

This rule prevents the donor from falsely declaring that a ten-year-old color TV worth $50, and donated to a local charity, has a "fair market price" of a brand-new color TV costing $595. To determine the value of an *antique,* an appraiser must establish what prices other items similar in age, style, quality, and condition to the one in question have sold for recently.

Those prices are then used as a basis for the current fair market value of the items to be donated.

Death and Taxes

No longer can the value of personal property be carelessly dismissed. As it increases in value, the gross value of your estate will reflect this increase.

You may want to consult a tax attorney or CPA and find out how your personal property will affect the value of your estate *now,* while you can still have some control over its eventual dispensation.

20

Divorce—What
You May Leave Behind

Feuding, Fussing, and Fighting

I know from experience that the division of personal property in divorce cases can be the most unpleasant of all settlements.

My husband (who is an attorney and from whom I've never been divorced) was casually walking through the court house one day when he saw a judge who looked even more distraught and harried than usual.

"A tough one, eh?" my husband said.

"They're fighting over who's going to get the Tupperware!" the judge exclaimed incredulously.

Tea for One

In one instance, both parties agreed to divide the property according to my values—they just couldn't decide who was going to get what. After days of squabbling in the wife's attorney's office, they came to the last item—a group of six tea cups and saucers. The couple fussed over these cups and saucers for a full half-hour. Finally, the exasperated attorney called in the husband's attorney to complete the negotiations. Later, when the attorneys told me the story, I vividly recalled the cups and saucers. Not only were they not valuable—they were ugly as well.

What You Leave Behind

Because women generally know more about the objects in their homes, husbands can unwittingly surrender large sums of money by giving up all the personal property in the house. And a wife can be just as profligate if she carelessly leaves property behind, without finding out its true value.

A lawyer friend who specializes in divorce cases says most men will settle for the stereo (to use while courting the new girl friend) until they find out how much plates and glasses and towels cost. Then they want to renegotiate the entire property settlement.

Each state has its own laws governing division of property in divorce. However, for both parties' protection, when valuable personal property is involved, an objective appraiser's services can be priceless.

❦ 21 ❧

Hints on How to Make A Photographic Inventory—What It Can and Cannot Do

When a Picture Is Worth a Thousand Words

I am often asked about making a photographic inventory. "Can't I just take some snapshots of my property?" Or, "Should I call in professional photographers and have them photograph or videotape my pieces?"

Certainly, photographs and videotapes are much better than no record at all, and if this is what you wish to do, I encourage you. But the major drawback is that photographs do not tell you the value of pieces.

Unless you are going to the trouble or expense of having close-up pictures made of the marks on your silver, china, and accessories, you are no closer to knowing what you have than you were before the pictures were made. However, you will have a record that the property existed in case it is damaged or destroyed, and such proof is very important in itself.

Having photographs of possessions without a record of their value will not help you know how much insurance coverage you need. It is important to realize this, especially if you consider the fact that most states now impose a $1,000 limitation on silver that has not been listed and evaluated for your insurance.

To understand the handicap of working from a photograph without any other written information, compare a photograph of an 8-inch sterling silver Revere bowl that retails for $1,200 with a silverplate one that costs $45. Compare a photograph of a good reproduction sideboard valued at $2,800 with an almost identical eighteenth-century American one worth $6,500. In photographs they may not be distinguishable. In fact, looking at photographs of the bowl one often cannot determine whether it is sterling silver, silverplated, stainless steel, or pewter.

An appraisal that is carefully or professionally prepared tells you which is sterling, which plated, which antique, which a reproduction, and what the value of each is. Often a written professional appraisal costs no more than a professional photographer's inventory. A quick check shows that the price of a photographic inventory of a seven-room house could cost between $250 and $500. This same collection could be professionally appraised for $400 to $600. (Appraiser's fees are discussed in the next chapter.)

Begin with Four Corners

If you wish to make a household photographic inventory yourself, follow this procedure.

1. Begin by making four corner shots in each room. Stand in one corner and photograph the corner diagonally opposite. Proceed until all four parts of the room are photographed.
2. Open all closets and cabinets and take interior photographs.
3. Include individual interior shots of cupboards and cabinets where silver, china, crystal, etc., are stored.
4. Photograph collections such as coins, dolls, etc., both as a group and individually.
5. Photograph all items of antique value individually.
6. Take a close-up picture of your silver, china, and crystal patterns, featuring one of each type of item—example, one dinner plate, one salad plate, one bread and butter plate, and one cup and saucer could be photographed together in one frame. Then take a picture of the entire pattern assembled together.
7. Do not forget chandeliers and rugs. Make sure these show up in your four corner pictures.
8. When photographing individual pieces—a vase or figurine, for example—place a ruler in the front left corner to give dimensional proportion.
9. Include pictures of attics, basements, storage rooms, lawn, porch, and patio furniture, as well as tools, appliances, and home entertainment equipment.

Basic Equipment and What It Can Do

A simple Instamatic type camera with flashbulb attachment can furnish you with adequate pictures for a household inventory to supplement a written appraisal, or as a simple accounting of what you own. Of course, it is best to use color film. However, this type of simple camera can only close-focus at about 3½ to 4 feet, so you may not get the detail on individual pieces that you desire.

If you have a Polaroid SX-70 type camera, you can get up to a 10-inch focus, which will give much clearer detail. The best pictures (without spending hundreds of dollars on lens and equipment) are taken with a normal SLR (single lens reflex) 35 millimeter camera using slide film. These cameras can generally focus up to 18 inches and once you have the slide you can enlarge it on a screen for closer detail.

Ultimately, the best record of your personal property is one that supplements a written evaluation with photographs. While photographs alone may not be sufficient, they are better than nothing. Just be sure to have two sets made and keep one somewhere other than your home, in case of fire or storm which could destroy your house—and your photographs.

22

Finding an Appraiser

Finding a qualified, competent, and knowledgeable appraiser can be difficult. There are an estimated 125,000 appraisers in the United States, according to *The New York Times,* but because there is no state certification, registration, or licensing program for appraisers (as there is for doctors, lawyers and CPAs, for example), literally anyone can call himself or herself an appraiser.

The Certified Appraiser

A question commonly asked is, "Are you a certified appraiser?" Since there is no one to do the certifying, there are no certified appraisers. Granted, some appraisal forms include a phrase such as, "I hereby *certify* that the following appraisal . . ." Here the appraiser is the *certifier,* but she or he is not certified.

Conflict of Interest

Appraisers often wear a variety of hats—appraiser, antiques dealer, interior decorator, used-furniture dealer, jeweler, auctioneer, pawn-shop owner, art consultant, to name a few.

The occasional conflict of interest is obvious. When does a dealer stop dealing and begin appraising? Can he or she keep from being influenced by the fact that one day, if not today, he or she might be able to return to your home and buy the items appraised? This is a much-debated question. Dealers who are appraisers maintain that, because they are active in the marketplace and know what a piece will sell for, they are more capable of knowing the true value of a piece than an appraiser who is not a dealer.

The American Society of Appraisers recognizes that some dealers are going to be appraisers, and states:

> ... it is unethical and unprofessional for an appraiser to accept an assignment to appraise a property *in which he has an interest or a contemplated future interest.*
>
> However, if a prospective client, after full disclosure by the appraiser of his present or contemplated future interest in the subject property, still desires to have that appraiser do the work, the latter may properly accept the engagement, provided he discloses the nature and extent of his interest *in his appraisal report.* [*Italics added.*]

Until the growing demand for appraisers *who only appraise* can be met, the public will be forced to use appraisers who are also dealers. However, you may ask for a signed statement of disinterest in the property if the appraiser does not already include such a clause in his or her final appraisal report.

Ivory Tower Appraisals

Most museums decree that their staff members cannot quote values in their official capacities. Even museums that feature "heirloom" or "discovery" days, when the public may bring in items to be *identified* and *dated,* do not *appraise* or value these items.

Some museum staff members do "moonlight" by doing appraisals after hours and on their days off. There is no doubt that many trained museum employees are extremely knowledgeable. When I have questions, I often call on them for information. They have access to books, research materials, and often esoteric information unavailable to many appraisers.

However, I have run into some problems when working with museum personnel in making appraisals—problems they themselves recognize.

- It is difficult for museum workers to keep up with the rapidly changing marketplace. In other words, they can identify a piece quickly and correctly and still not know its current market value.

- Museum personnel can become so accustomed to dealing with "museum-quality" pieces that antiques and personal property of substantial value may pale when compared to the museum masterpieces that are the museum person's basis of comparison. "How can I look at a nineteenth-century English oil landscape that might have a value of $2,000, and treat it seriously, when I've been surrounded by Gainsboroughs, Constables, and Turners?" one curator asked me.

If you do hire a museum staff member to make your appraisal, ask the same questions that I suggest you ask of any appraiser. Also realize that the appraisal he or she is making is made in that person's own name and not that of the museum.

Appraisal Associations

Because the demand for appraisers is greater than the number of existing appraisers, both unqualified appraisers and questionable appraisal societies have sprung up overnight. In fact, one way an appraiser can achieve instant "respectability" is by joining an appraisal association or organization. These organizations exist everywhere and membership is often obtained by simply filling in an entry form and returning it with an accompanying check to "headquarters." Fees can range from $10 to over $5,000. Many of these appraisal organizations can be compared to mail-order colleges where you send your money and receive a worthless "diploma."

There are exceptions, of course; one is the American Society of Appraisers, which is recognized as America's only multi-disciplinary appraisal testing/designation society. Its personal property and fine arts appraisers number around 500—a handful of the total needed to meet the public's request for qualified appraisers. Dexter MacBride, the executive vice-president of the American Society of Appraisers, reports that his office receives as many as 1,000 letters a month asking for information about appraisals and for help in finding qualified appraisers.

Membership in the ASA is not prerequisite to being a good appraiser. It does mean, however, that the ASA appraiser has submitted his appraisals for examination by his peers, has taken and passed a multi-section examination on ethics, appraisal principles, and his specialized area, and is experienced.

Because of the rigid requirements imposed on its members, the American Society of Appraisers is often referred to as the most prestigious of the appraisal organizations. But the Appraisers Association of America is also widely recognized and its prospective members must also submit appraisals and meet AAA requirements before they are accepted as members. Neither the Appraisers Association of America nor the newly formed International Society of Appraisers tests its members. These three associations, the ASA, AAA, and ISA, have nationally noted and recognized members. The addresses of these and other appraisal groups that I know of are listed at the end of this chapter. Most groups will furnish a membership roster upon request or will supply the name of a member in your area.

Locally, you may find personal property appraisers listed in the Yellow Pages, but if not, call your insurance agent, bank, attorney, or museum. A call to a college or university art department may be worthwhile. You can also call antiques shops, interior decorators, or auction houses. They may offer appraisal services or refer you to an independent appraiser.

Appraisers are plentiful in metropolitan centers, but are often scarce in less populous areas. Many appraisers will travel to accommodate clients who live in areas without an appraiser.

But if *finding* an appraiser is difficult, getting *the right* appraiser is even more complicated.

"If there is no such thing as a certified appraiser and I can't really trust some of the appraisal societies, how can I tell if I'm getting a qualified appraiser?" you may ask.

Unfortunately, the ultimate responsibility does rest with you, but you can help yourself by asking the appraiser some specific questions.

Start by asking:

- How long have you been an appraiser?
- What is your area of expertise?
- What is your educational background?
- For whom have you worked and what are your references? (Look for business references, names of banks, insurance companies, museums, etc., and check these out.)
- Do you belong to a professional appraisal group? (Even though this may be meaningless, it does tell you something about the appraiser's basic approach to his or her business.)
- How do you arrive at your values? (She or he should attend auctions, have an extensive library, attend conferences and lectures on antiques, subscribe to national publications and auction catalogues, and have extensive "current price" indexes at hand as well.)

Next, *tell* the appraiser your specific needs:

- What you need to have appraised.
   (One piece or a household—only furniture, or several different categories, Oriental porcelain, English silver, Depression glass, etc.)
- What the purpose of the appraisal is.
   (Insurance coverage, moving damage, estate division, etc.)

Once you are satisfied that you and the appraiser can work together, learn what charges are involved.

Appraiser's Fees

There are still appraisers who charge a percentage of the value of the items they appraise. As mentioned, this practice is questionable, at best, since the result is appraise high, fee high.

Another questionable practice is charging contingent fees. This is so blatently suspicious that the American Society of Appraisers, in its Code of Ethics, calls it unethical, unprofessional, and self-serving. Contingent fees come up when an appraiser tells you she or he will appraise "high" an item that you want to sell or take as a tax donation, in return for a share of the tax benefit. Or the reverse, she or he will appraise an item "low" for estate or tax purposes for a cut of the taxes saved.

Hourly Fees

The majority of good appraisers today charge on an hourly or daily basis, usually ranging from $35 to $150 an hour, or $350 to $1,500 a day—plus expenses. Do not expect an appraiser who charges $50 an hour to walk into your home, spend an hour, leave, send you an appraisal and a bill for $50. Appraisers also charge for research time and the preparation of the appraisal. Many appraisers send a contract to their clients explaining the exact expenses involved. A sample contract is included in Appendix B. If you do not receive such a contract, ask the appraiser to spell out the exact working terms before she or he comes to your house.

You may certainly ask the appraiser for an estimate of what your appraisal will cost. For large jobs, appraisers often make a preliminary visit to your home and, for a fee, give you an estimate of the total cost. For smaller jobs, if you will honestly tell the appraiser what needs to be appraised, she can probably give you a fee range over the phone.

I have found that most people are extremely modest about the scope of their possessions when speaking to an appraiser for the first time. Don't be. Tell the appraiser what to expect.

"I have a seven-room house, approximately 3,000 square feet, and a combination of antiques and reproductions that need appraising for insurance purposes. There will be approximately twenty-five pieces of furniture and numerous accessories around—probably about fifty or sixty, not including the silver. I have two sets of silver flatware, a cupboard full of silver hollow ware, three sets of good china, and a collection of antique dolls."

This information tells the appraiser that she should plan to devote the better part of the day to making your appraisal. Based on $60 an hour, she then roughly calculates that your bill may be expected to run around $450 to $550 (higher or lower, depending on the appraiser's base rate). You now have a ball-park figure and can decide whether or not you want to hire an appraiser.

What Do I Get for My Money?

Now, what can you expect in return for your $450 to $550?

You should receive two copies of a professionally presented appraisal, listing each item you asked to have appraised. A full description of each piece will tell you, to the best of the appraiser's ability, the age, characteristics, physical condition and, if possible or significant, the national origin of the piece. When the maker is known—whether company, craftsman, or artist—this will be included. Where pertinent, dimensions and silver weight will be stated. Numbers or sets will be included. Finally, each item or group will be assigned a value appropriate to the purpose of the appraisal—insurance, private sale, estate taxes, etc. The date of the appraisal, purpose of the appraisal, and the appraiser's signature must always be present.

You should *not* accept a scribbled handwritten appraisal with incorrect spellings, scant listings, and inaccurate numbers. A professionally prepared appraisal that states "6 dining room chairs—$1,200" is meaningless.

The purpose of an appraisal is to establish rightful ownership of personal property, to identify the objects by describing their inherent characteristics, and to value the items based on known comparable objects in the marketplace. Getting a sloppy or half-prepared appraisal can be likened to having a leaking fuel tank patched with sealing wax and string. You're throwing money away. An example of a professionally prepared appraisal is included in Appendix D. Do not settle for less. Feel free to ask to see a sample appraisal before you hire an appraiser.

What You Cannot Get for Your Money

For $400 or $500 you cannot expect to have every single piece in your house researched and authenticated. If you have a piece you consider extremely rare or valuable, advise the appraiser of this beforehand. Tell her you want it authenticated. Ask her if she has the expertise to do this. A good appraiser knows what she does *not* know. At this point she can either accept the job or refer you to someone more knowledgeable in this area.

There are generalists and specialists in the appraisal world just as there are in the legal and medical worlds. Do not expect one person to know everything about everything.

Saving Yourself Money and the Appraiser Time

When you are satisfied that you have located an appraiser with good references, who is knowledgeable about your pieces and will be able to make an appraisal suitable for your purposes, you are ready to have the appraisal made. Appointments are usually made for a future date. This gives you time to organize your thoughts and your property.

You should now do the same thing I advised you to do if you make your own inventory. Take an overview of your property. Separate what you know about from that which you do not know about. Set up a system so that you are ready before the appraiser comes to your house. Countless hours can be wasted looking for Aunt Suzy's water pitcher—on your time.

- Gather together any earlier appraisals and all bills of sale or receipts. Place these on the appropriate item. (They may or may not help the appraiser, but make them available.)
- Arrange your silver in appropriate groupings. Put all of one silver pattern together and count each specific piece—15 forks, 7 soup spoons,

- etc. Either label each grouping or make a list on a piece of paper. Example: "Chantilly, 15 forks, 7 soup spoons, etc."

    Do not mix patterns by placing all like pieces (forks, spoons, etc.) together. Put all pieces of the same pattern together.

- Separate sterling silver hollow ware and silverplated objects into two distinct groups.

- Finally, arrange each of these two groups, sterling and silverplate, by like pieces—all water pitchers together, all meat platters together, all Revere bowls together, etc.

- Match and count all china and crystal patterns. If sets are stored in boxes, closets, or cabinets, take one of each piece out and count the other pieces. The appraiser needs to see the items in your possession to establish their existence and condition, but you can save her time by counting these pieces in advance. China serving pieces are often stored separately, so remember these before the appraiser rings your doorbell.

- If you are having your linen appraised, organize this in clear sight as you have your china—a sample of each item set out with the quantity already counted.

Can I Help the Appraiser?

I find many of my clients just do not know what to do while I am working. Certainly, someone who knows about the personal property, either you or a housekeeper, should be within calling distance if the appraiser has questions. Unless you as a client want to spend your money talking to the appraiser, it is better if you make yourself available and remain silent—except when you can add pertinent information.

So, What's It Worth?

Since I use a tape recorder, it is natural that clients want to listen to my descriptions of their pieces. They also often have questions I am more than happy to answer. Other people's presence does not bother me, and I think most appraisers feel the same way. However, the constant query, "What's this piece worth?" is worrisome. Appraisers seldom know the exact value of every item they are appraising on the spot.

Most appraisers assign prices to the pieces they are sure of at the time of the appraisal. On pieces where there is a price range that needs narrowing, the appraiser notes the price range. Finally, on those pieces that need more research or investigation before a value is given, the appraiser will fill in the description and may note where to find more information on the piece, but will omit the price.

This procedure is no different from that in any business or profession. An attorney tells you he will look up a case and then give you his opinion on your situation. A consultant tells you he will study the situation and determine which system is best suited to your business. You must realize that the appraiser is working to give you the best results in just the same way the attorney or other consultant is, and sometimes the right answer is not immediately obvious.

If you feel that the appraiser's figures or facts are inaccurate, ask her or him how she or he arrived at these conclusions. You may wish to get a second opinion. Or the appraiser may ask to bring another expert in to look at the piece.

Choose your appraiser carefully and go over the appraisal carefully once it is in your hands.

APPRAISAL SOCIETIES AND ASSOCIATIONS
(*Listed in alphabetical order*)

American Society of Appraisers
Dulles International Airport
P.O. Box 17265
Washington, D.C.   20041

Antique Appraisal Association of America
11361 Garden Grove Boulevard
Garden Grove, California   92543

Appraisers Association of America
60 E. 42nd Street
New York, New York   10165

International Society of Appraisers
724 W. Washington
Chicago, Illinois   60600

International Society of Fine Arts Appraisers, Ltd.
P.O. Box 280
River Forest, Illinois   60305

Mid-Am Antique Appraisers Association
P.O. Box 981 C.S.S.
Springfield, Missouri   65803

Registered Appraisers of Florida, Inc.
P.O. Box 15797
Sarasota, Florida   33579

❦ 23 ❧

Price Guides—
Bibles or Boondoggles?

An expert may not need a price guide in his field of expertise. But almost every dealer, appraiser, and auctioneer uses some form of price guide at one time or another (which translates into pretty frequently) in his work.

The price guide may be a book written by the Kovels, P. S. Warman, Dorothy Hammond (see Appendix), or any of several authors whose price guides appear as regularly as the New Year. Or, the price guide may be an auction house catalogue with estimated pre-sale prices given for the items to be auctioned. After the auction, the houses send a printed follow-up sale price list. Or the price guide may be an actual retail price list provided by the manufacturer, listing specific prices of currently manufactured goods.

What do all three have in common? *The prices stated in any of these three price guides or lists, even the retail list, can and do fluctuate and can only be used as guides to prices.*

For example, let's look at three objects and their prices as stated in the appropriate price guide or list.

Price Guide:
An 11½-inch Rose Medallion punch bowl is quoted in one price guide as having a value of $775 and in another a value of $1,200.

Auction Catalogue:
Two years ago I bought two *identical* celestial globes at a Christie's sale. The first one sold for $480. The second one sold twenty seconds later for $380. These prices are now stated in the Christie's sale price list.

Manufacturer's List:
A wing chair, which retails on the manufacturer's price list for $650, has a discounted sale ticket of $575 and the furniture dealer tells you that price is negotiable. He'll take $500.

The actual prices for all three examples—the bowls, globes, and chair—have an obvious range: $775—1,200, $380—480, $500—$650. But the printed prices create a base from which the final price or value can be established.

No, price lists are not the final word. They are guides which either support or contradict your thinking. The mistake comes when a value is taken from one source or price guide and considered the final word. There are just too many unknown facts about each individual item entered in a price guide to make *one price* taken from *one price guide* absolute.

But by taking the *price ranges* from several price guides you get a base from which you can work. Add to this base an understanding of all of the unknown factors that affect specific prices, and you will know why price guides are what they say they are—price *guides*.

Take the 11½-inch Rose Medallion bowls, for example. Why is one $775 and the other $1,200? They are both the same size. Perhaps one bowl is more fully decorated in the interior than the other. One bowl may have some minor chips or a hairline crack which has lowered its value. Where is each being sold? Rose Medallion generally brings higher prices in the southern states than in the New England states. Is one bowl being sold in a more expensive shop than the other? What are the dates of each bowl? A Rose Medallion bowl dating from 1860 will bring more money than one dating from 1900. A price guide does not tell you any of these variables.

What about my globes, which, incidentally, had pre-sale price estimates in the Christie's catalogue of $300 to $400 each? Why was one $100 more expensive to buy than the other? Who was in the audience that day? How much money had the other bidder already spent on other purchases that day? How much money was I willing to spend to get the globes? (I was willing to spend more than I did, in fact.) Even after the globes were sold to me, what are they really worth? Are auction prices wholesale or retail prices? (See Chapter 24 on auction houses.)

And, finally, what about that newly manufactured chair? The manufacturer suggests on his price list that the chair be sold for $650, but if it goes from an eastern furniture manufacturer all the way to the West Coast, its quoted price will be even higher than the $650. On the other hand, if the chair is sold at a furniture discount house, its price can be substantially lower. And when inventory sale time comes around, a customer may even be able to buy the chair for its wholesale price.

The point is, once a *price range* is established through comparing two or more price guides you can get a general concept of value. Price guides tell you that you probably cannot sell your 11½-inch Rose Medallion bowl for $5,000, but that if you find one for $200 you'll be getting a super buy.

The auction house prices of my globes tell me that I would be foolish to sell them for $100 each, but I should not expect to sell them for $1,000 each (unless I luck out and find somebody who wants them even worse than I do).

Once you know that a wing chair made by a good middle-line furniture manufacturer is going to retail for $650, you know that you have a "steal" if you find a similar one in excellent condition in a house sale for only $150.

When you know what you are looking at (make sure the bowl really is "antique" Rose Medallion and not a five-year-old Japanese reproduction of Rose Medallion) and you understand that price guides have limitations, you can use them as general reference guides for compiling *a range* of value for some of your personal property.

However, the mass-market price guide, even the *Official Sotheby Parke Bernet Price Guide to Antiques and Decorative Arts,* is going to be pretty useless in providing a value for a rarity such as a Paul Revere teapot, a Townsend-Goddard chest of drawers, or a Rembrandt portrait.

> The exceptionally fine, rare, and valuable piece always needs to be authenticated and evaluated by an expert.

❦ 24 ❧

Auction Houses—
The Best Show in Town

Educational Background

There really is no better place to learn about antiques than an auction house. Visitors at pre-auction viewings (usually held the week preceding the actual auction) are free to take out drawers, examine chair bottoms, scrutinize English silver hallmarks. In fact, there are even people there to help you by answering questions.

If you are only accustomed to the Friday night country auction held in the back room of a roadside store, you may be overwhelmed at both the sophistication and the swiftness of a New York auction. The two most famous auction houses there, and in the world, are Sotheby Parke Bernet, called Sotheby's, and Christie, Mason, Wood, called Christie's. There seldom is shouting or yelling from either the auctioneer or the audience, and often an item can be bid upon and sold without your ever knowing who was doing the bidding.

Bidding—Not for the Uninitiated

Be forewarned, if you're going to bid at a New York auction: you won't have time to think about what you are doing. You must know how much you are going to bid ahead of time and act immediately. This is not the place for the timid, shy, or hesitant bidder. But while you may get passed by, you can also get caught up in the auction fever and overspend.

Several dealer friends of mine never attend a sale. They visit pre-sale viewings where they carefully scrutinize each piece. They leave their bids with the department head or the bidding service provided by each house. Then they take their chances on whether they will get what they want or not. These are wise and astute buyers who do not want to be caught up in the auction fever.

Buying from an Auction House

The message of the auction buyer is *"Caveat emptor"*—"Let the buyer beware." Even though the major auction houses do all they can to guarantee that the item is authentically sold, they, too, can make mistakes, and they protect themselves by publishing their buy-back policy at the beginning of each catalogue.

To correctly identify each piece they sell, the auction houses carefully explain the terminology they use to specifically identify the period, style, origin, date, and condition of each piece. For example, let's take a Chippendale chest of drawers and see how it is catalogued. Because you've read *Why You're Richer Than You Think,* you know that the Chippendale chest of drawers can either be a period chest of drawers from the eighteenth century, an old chest of drawers in the Chippendale style, or a recent reproduction. (Needless to say, the auction houses generally are not going to sell the new reproductions unless they are included in a house sale, in which case reproductions are clearly identified as such.) But to make the distinction between the period piece and the old reproduction in the Chippendale style, the catalogue carefully describes the piece in bold type heading.

An entry that reads "**Chippendale Mahogany Chest of Drawers, Philadelphia, Circa 1760-80**" designates that the chest is guaranteed by the auction house to be of the period.

However, if the heading for the chest of drawers reads, "**Chippendale Mahogany Chest of Drawers,**" *without any mention of the origin or the date,* the experts at the auction house consider the chest to date from the eighteenth century, but with too many later changes or restorations for the chest to be considered a period Chippendale chest.

And in the case of the old reproduction, the heading reads like this: **Chippendale Style Mahogany Chest of Drawers.** Notice there are no dates or origin given. The further presence of the word "style" indicates that the chest of drawers is not of the period but is rather in the style of the Chippendale period.

Warning: Condition—Delicate

You must be particularly careful when buying at auction antiques that you have not personally inspected. Not all pieces are in good condition.

Sotheby Parke Bernet notes that because the majority of the items they sell have been used for an extended length of time, it will not assume responsibility for mentioning scratches, minor damage, age cracks, chips, etc.

Brian Cole, of Christie's East, once remarked that the biggest shock the newcomer to the auction scene has is when he walks into a pre-auction showing and sees the condition of many of the items being sold. Veneer may be chipped, a desk leg may be gone, upholstery is often old and worn, and the silver may be unpolished. While this scene is a far cry from the glamorous concept of the auction house, it also means that the astute buyer can pick up excellent bargains if he has the ways and means to bring the pieces up to pristine condition.

Auction Sale Prices—Retail or Wholesale?

A much debated question in the antiques world is, when you buy at auction are you paying full retail value or are you paying wholesale value? A few years ago the answer was simpler than it is today. In the past, the auction audience consisted almost totally of antiques dealers and interior decorators who were buying to stock their shops and furnish their clients' homes.

Naturally, the dealers marked up the retail price of their auction purchases to cover their expenses in attending the auction, taking a day out of the shop for a buying trip, shipping the goods from the auction house to their shops, and the necessary cleaning and repairing of the pieces. (Overhead can be hefty when you buy at auction.) In addition to covering these expenses, the dealer would, of course, also add enough to make a profit.

But now auction houses have become popular hunting grounds for young families who are furnishing their homes. Needless to say, when the private individual bids against a dealer, he is willing to pay more for an item than the dealer is. Even if he pays more, the collector figures it's still cheaper than if he bought the same piece from a dealer. Thus, when a dealer and a collector compete, if the collector has the last bid, he still feels that he has made a good buy.

Insuring the Auction Purchase

In light of this change, with more private individuals buying at auctions, I asked experts at both Sotheby's and Christie's how *they* would insure a mid-value item purchased at an auction. I used as my examples a $500 chair or an $800 table. In both instances the experts replied that they would insure these items for at least two or three times what they had paid for them at the auction house. Thus the wholesale concept still partly holds true at the auction houses, even though the private collector is now an important bidder.

However, as the price paid for an item increases, the insurance mark-up decreases. In other words, if you pay $20,000 for a table at auction, a retail value of $40,000 or $60,000 may be unrealistically high. You see, it is not uncommon for a prestigious dealer to buy an exceptionally fine antique at auction for a specific customer. In these instances the dealer does not add a full 100 percent mark-up, but rather charges the client a percentage to cover his services.

At other times dealers will pay top dollar for a specific piece which they know they can turn over quickly, even though they know that a 30 or 40 percent mark-up is the most the piece can bear. These last two examples are relevant only to expensive items; I would stick with the two- to threefold increase on the usual modest auction purchase.

Auction Houses as Appraisers

Sometimes an appraiser or dealer who is unable to identify a particular antique will suggest that you contact either Sotheby's, Christie's, or another of the auction houses to identify it. This is fine for one item, but you can't handle a household that way. If you are genuinely interested in selling a particular piece, have investigated its origin or value as thoroughly as you can locally, and wish to have a New York expert's opinion, you can write to the department at Sotheby's or Christie's that would handle your property, sending a photograph and all the information known about the particular piece. In your letter inquire if the auction house would be interested in selling the item and request a pre-sale estimate of the piece. Don't expect a reply by return mail. When you do hear from the auction house, if you disagree with the opinion, seek another.

I recall taking an interesting glass decanter to New York for possible sale at one of the auction houses. I did not know its exact origin, but from what the owner could tell me, I felt it could have potential auction sale value, and the owner needed money. One auction house said, *"Olé,"* meaning the decanter was from Mexico and worth about $10. The other stated the decanter was American and was willing to sell it. In this instance, of course, a third opinion was needed. The majority opinion concluded the glass was Mexican.

Selling Through an Auction House

If you plan to sell property at an auction house, inquire about two major points:

- The commission or percentage the house takes to cover the expense of selling the item. The figure will generally run between 10 and 25 percent, according to the value of the piece (the higher the sale price the lower the percentage commission charged) and the individual auction house's commission policy.
- The "reserve" or the confidential minimum price agreed upon by the auction house and the seller, below which the item will not be sold. A reserve protects the owner from having property sold below its true value. For example, if you have a fine eighteenth-century needlework sampler which you wish to sell, the experts may tell you that a pre-auction estimate for the sampler is between $900 and $1,200. Discuss this estimate with the auction house expert, who may advise you not to sell

the piece below $750. If the sampler does not sell for above $750, either it is returned to you or it can be held and reentered in a later auction. Some houses charge a commission on unsold lots; others do not. Hopefully the sampler will exceed the $1,200 top estimate—many items do.

My Things Aren't Good Enough for a Fancy Auction House

"My mother just died and left a house full of antiques, good reproductions, and fine-quality furnishings. I don't have time to sell the items to different dealers piecemeal, but I want to dispose of all of her property. Would any of the major auction houses be interested in coming in and having a house sale and getting it all over with?" This is a question I am often asked.

Brian Cole recently told me of several house sales that Christie's East has conducted, ranging from a five-room apartment on Park Avenue to a three-room apartment in Greenwich Village, and from a mansion in the midwest to a six-room house in Atlanta. You don't have to live in a palatial home to have property of value these days, and the larger auction houses are often anxious to conduct house sales. A letter of inquiry and some photographs will draw a response from any auction house. They have to hold auctions to stay in business.

In Appendix C are listed some of the larger auction houses located throughout the United States. You can buy their catalogues, sell your things through them, or enjoy attending their sales.

25

Collecting
for Investment Purposes

No book on antiques and personal property can be considered complete without a few words on investing and collecting. All along I have talked about the investments your parents, grandparents, or great-grandparents made when they bought their china, furniture, silver, or even your toys!

What then should today's young collector who wishes to make the same kind of good investment do? There are three basic rules. Remembering that your grandparents probably did not *consciously* go out and *invest* in personal property for investment sake, I would advise you to do exactly what they did:

Buy what you like.
Buy what you can afford.
Buy the best you can afford.

If you (or a later generation) discover that you have made a good investment, that is your bonus. However, while you are buying what you *like* and can *afford*—be it Victorian furniture, Georgian silver, brand-new Waterford crystal, or 1950 movie posters, always buy the best examples of your choice that you can afford. In other words, buy the best quality that your pocketbook can stand. Do not buy damaged or broken pieces for investment.

The collector who wishes to make a conscious study of antiques or art or jewelry, or any specific area of personal property, should follow these rules:

Narrow your collection to as small an area as possible.

Buy your first pieces from a fully established and reputable dealer who will help educate you in your chosen area.

Study this one area until you become an expert yourself.

Let's say you like Victorian furniture and want to collect it. Victorian furniture dates from 1840 to 1900 and includes everything from whatnots to wardrobes. You will only become frustrated if you choose too large a field. Narrow your sights, choose a particular style of Victorian furniture—Eastlake or Renaissance, for example—and buy the best quality you can afford.

The same rule applies to each area. Rather than collecting "china," decide on one type of china—Satsuma, Minton, Homer Laughlin; or try a specific item—demitasse cups and saucers, or compotes. If you end up making an investment that pays off in a cash return, that's a bonus. But taste is so quixotic today that no one can positively guarantee what the next generation, or the next, will consider desirable.

Limited Editions

What about today's mass-produced "collector's items" or "limited editions"? Franklin Mint editions, Royal Copenhagen Christmas plates, and Boehm birds are three obvious examples that quickly come to mind. What is their investment potential?

Who knows?

They are advertised as "good investments," but connoisseurs turn up their noses at them. "You *know* collector's plates will never go up in value," I am sometimes told.

"I don't know that," I honestly reply. "Whoever thought that pressed glass, which cost a few pennies and was bought from Woolworth's by the barrel, would be displayed in museums and be the subject of $25 books? Or who would have thought that the Battersea or enamel boxes sold as travel souvenirs in eighteenth-century England would bring hundreds, even thousands of dollars some 175 to 200 years later?"

The Hard Sell

Just remember that investment is part of the sales pitch and the hard sell exists in the antiques and collecting world just as in any other business.

Wall Street Views

There is little question that personal property is a good investment today, and I encourage my clients to consider antiques and silver as possible investments. The evidence is there. "Antiques and old houses have been among my best investments," Richard Jenrette, chairman of the board and chief executive officer of Donaldson, Lufkin and Jenrette, the Wall Street brokerage firm, has said repeatedly.

Glance at almost any investment book written today and you will find a chapter on art, antiques, and collectibles. However, if you read stories about collectors who have turned their collections into profit, you quickly realize they are no different from successful investors in the stock, commodities, real estate, or any other market. They all devote a great deal of *time* to *learning* about their investments.

Why You're Richer Than You Think

My ultimate message at the end of the book is the same as at the beginning. Look around you. You are already surrounded by valuable, and, in some instances, rare antiques and personal property. I wrote *Why You're Richer Than You Think* to help you protect your belongings while learning more about them. There may be some fakes, but there are also hidden treasures waiting to be discovered. Recognize both, and you will be doubly richer than you think!

Twenty-One Questions

These questions are representative of those I am constantly asked both in private homes and at public talks. They cover specific and general areas of personal property and antiques.

1. *Q. I have just inherited a house full of personal property. What can I do to find out what I've got?*

   A. Consult an outside person who has no sentimental attachment to the property and who also is knowledgeable about personal property values today. A good personal property appraiser should be able to tell you about the majority of items in a household and refer you to other experts for those pieces she does not know about. Most appraisers can also give you guidelines as to how to dispose of pieces you no longer wish to keep. Tax benefits are available to donors of personal property whether they go to the Salvation Army, to a church bazaar, or to a restoration or museum. However, do not expect the appraiser to purchase pieces being appraised, as this is a direct conflict of interest.

   The alternative is to call in an antique dealer who can both tell you about the items and their value and offer to purchase pieces or take them on consignment to sell in his or her shop. An auctioneer performs a role similar to the dealer.

   If you already know which items you wish to keep and which ones you wish to dispose of, then an antiques dealer or auctioneer can handle the job for you. However, if you are baffled about values, the best course is to hire an appraiser.

2. *Q. I bought a chair from a reputable antiques dealer twenty years ago. Now I want to sell it. Should I ask the dealer to buy it back?*

   A. Yes. Many dealers are extremely anxious to buy back pieces they sold in the past. Dealers complain that every year it is getting harder to find quality pieces. Therefore, if your chair is of fine quality, the dealer will almost always be pleased to put it back into stock. In fact, advertisements in antiques journals and magazines boast, "We have just repurchased these items and are happy to offer them once again." Sometimes owners worry about whether the dealer will pay enough if he buys the chair back. Remember that the dealer must make a profit, thus he cannot pay you full retail value for your chair. However, because the dealer did sell you the chair in the past, he cannot come in and tell you the chair is not what you think it is since *he* sold it to *you* as a specific piece and charged you according to its quality, condition, age, etc. Some dealers offer to buy back pieces for the same prices you paid for them. Other dealers are willing to make allowances for inflation and increased values.

3. *Q. How do I find a certified appraiser?*

A. First, there is no such thing as a certified appraiser. Granted, some appraisers belong to professional organizations and societies, which shows their professional approach to the appraisal profession. However, appraisers are not "certified" or "licensed" by any national group. And unfortunately, many insurance agencies will accept almost any appraiser's figures. But, as personal property becomes more valuable and the insurance companies become more knowledgeable, good insurance companies are looking at the merit of each appraiser and his or her credentials. You, too, should ask for an appraiser's credentials and references. And if an appraiser tells you he or she *is* certified, watch out.

4. *Q. My silver is monogrammed. Does that make it less valuable?*

A. For insurance purposes, silver has a specific value determined by the pattern and condition. If you have to replace silver with a monogram on it, getting the new silver monogrammed will add to its expense. On the other hand, it is easier to sell silver that does not have a monogram on it because the new owner may wish to add his own monogram or leave it unmonogrammed. However, you will not find that a monogram will affect the price of estate silver as a rule.

5. *Q. I want to donate some things to a museum. Will they give me an appraisal I can use for my taxes?*

A. When donating items to museums you must first be sure that the pieces are appropriate for the museum's collection. Often, acquisition committees will not accept donations because they are inappropriate (not the right age, not of adequate quality, in poor condition, etc.). At other times museums are happy to accept almost any item that a person wishes to donate, *if* the donation is made *without any strings attached.* This means that the museum can exhibit the piece, put it into a study collection, which means it may never be seen in an exhibit but is important to the research of the museum staff, or keep the property only until the museum decides to sell it. (Incidentally, pieces sold by museums usually bring more money than sales of comparable pieces from private estates because of the museum "provenance.") The sale money is then put toward purchasing an item needed or deemed more important by the museum's acquisition committee.

If the museum does accept your gift, generally they will not give you an appraisal of the piece. It is not considered lawful or ethical for museum curators or staff to appraise contributions to their collection. In some instances, museums hire outside appraisers to appraise all donations and gifts to the museum at one time, usually in early December. These appraisals are then sent to the donors for tax purposes. Other museums require that the donor himself acquire an independent appraisal of the contribution for his own tax purposes. In this case the financial burden of the appraisal rests with the donor; however, this is a professional expense and is tax deductible. Be sure to check the museum and find out which procedure they use.

6. *Q. My plate has "22-Karat gold" written on the back of it. Is it valuable?*

A. The value of the plate lies in its quality, manufacturer, design, and age. The use of gold on a plate may make it more expensive to purchase; however, gold in itself does not make the plate more valuable. This particular notation was used on a lot of china made in the United States in the twentieth century. Most of the china that bears this marking is not considered valuable by today's standards.

7. *Q. My mother has just died. We've got to divide her property three ways. Can an appraiser help us?*

A. When the family does not know the value of the property or has sentimental attachment to some items and not to others, and the children cannot agree on how to divide the pieces, an appraiser can be of great benefit. The appraiser is objective and looks at the property from an unbiased standpoint. Seldom can an estate be divided within a penny's equal share, but once monetary values are determined, the heirs have specific information that will guide them in their decisions.

8. *Q. We're getting ready to go on vacation and our neighborhood has had several break-ins. What should we do to protect ourselves?*

A. The answer to this question seems so obvious, but it is often overlooked. First, do not "broadcast" your vacation. Gossip columns in newspapers and idle talk at country clubs and hairdressers can fall into the wrong hands. Then, take the precautions listed in the Burglary Prevention Checklist in Appendix A. Consider using a timer on lights so there appears to be some movement in the house. If you are leaving a car at home, park it in the driveway so a van or strange car cannot pull all the way into the driveway close to the house, where it would be unnoticed from the street. Tell a trusted neighbor that you are leaving and have him or her check the house for packages or other deliveries, which make it obvious that the house is unoccupied.

Also, ask a neighbor to check the doors in the front and back on occasion to make sure that they are locked and that there has been no attempted or successful forced entry. In some instances, glass has been knocked out and homes have been broken into by burglars who intend to return to take more out of the house. In such cases, an alert neighbor's call to the police or the owners has prevented further theft.

Of course you may wish to consider storing or hiding particular items. Thieves know where to look, but you can certainly make the job of robbing your house more difficult if you use ingenuity in selecting your hiding places. In other words, the thief who can walk in and open up a single drawer and empty all of your silver has a much better chance of getting in and out in a hurry than one who has to look in ten or fifteen different places to find the items you have hidden. However, *you* also have to remember where you have put these pieces when you wish to take them out of storage or hiding. There is always danger of vandalism if everything is put away. For this reason, it is often suggested that if you're going to store a lot of personal property you leave out enough to make a burglar satisfied with what he is getting. This means you should leave out items that are easily replaceable, but hide or store your more prized and antique pieces.

9. *Q. Where can I find an appraiser?*

A. Numerous appraisal associations print membership rosters which are available to the public. The names and addresses of appraisal associations are given at the end of Chapter 22. You can write to them. The Yellow Pages have appraisal headings, but often the listing is simply a name without a listing of the appraiser's specialty. Ask your insurance agent for his or her recommendations. Museums and historical restorations often know of appraisers. Antiques shops that do not make appraisals themselves will usually supply names.

10. *Q. I have some fine antiques, but the time has come to sell them. I don't want a lot of dealers coming in and picking the good things first. Can I have a house or tag sale to sell my antiques?*

A. Most people don't feel confident buying expensive items out of homes or at tag sales. They will buy the same item at an auction or at an antiques shop and pay two or three times more for it than the price asked at a private sale. Most people need the authority of a dealer or auctioneer when spending serious money. Also, many people who buy expensive things simply do not go to house sales. You might wish to offer your collection privately to friends and interested individuals rather than opening your collection to a public house sale.

11. *Q. What sort of mark-ups do antiques dealers put on items in their shops?*

A. It depends entirely on what the piece is and how much the dealer had to pay for it. I even have seen dealers literally sell a piece for what they paid for it. Many times, an antiques dealer will pay a great deal for a piece just to have it in his stock, knowing that he has paid full retail value for the item when he bought it. Dealers will pay top dollar for one item in order to get a group of other pieces at very low prices. This happens especially when the dealer is buying from a private individual who tells him exactly what he wants for each piece. On the other hand, if the dealer buys a real sleeper, he can then put it into his shop at a several hundred percent mark-up.

You must remember that dealers are running a business. They have to pay overhead and employees, inventory and income taxes the way any business does. The dealer is entitled to make a profit on his merchandise.

12. Q. *I found out my antique is not an antique after all. What can I do? Do I return it to the dealer?*

A. The best way to face this problem is to avoid it before it happens. If you can't be more knowledgeable than the antiques dealer (and few people can be without spending a lifetime studying antiques), you need to protect yourself by getting a full description of the item on the bill of sale. Don't just settle for a bill of sale that says "Chair—$395" Request a written description that tells the kind of chair, its age and condition. Then ask the dealer if this item is returnable should you find it to be other than stated on the bill of sale. If the dealer says "No," be wary. On the other hand, if the dealer is reputable, he *should be* willing to take back any item that is other than what he has stated. While some antiques dealers violently oppose this practice, I do not see it as being any different from a retail store accepting the return of merchandise found to be faulty.

13. Q. *Will it hurt the value of my silver to have it replated?*

A. If your silver is true Sheffield silver from the eighteenth or very earliest part of the nineteenth century then it should *not* be replated, regardless of its condition. However, the silverplate of the later nineteenth century and that of the twentieth century may be replated without damaging its value. Copper showing through the silverplate is called "bleeding." Many people consider the contrast between the copper and the silver attractive and desirable, even on only semi-antique pieces. Others want their silver to be in pristine silver condition. Before replating a piece, consider whether or not the piece is worth the expense of replating. To find out, check with an appraiser or jeweler and learn the price of a comparable piece in perfect condition and compare that to the price of having the piece replated.

14. Q. *I need a low appraisal for tax purposes. Will you do that?*

A. Good appraisers understand the different types of appraisals that are needed at different times—the insurance appraisal, the private sale appraisal, and the estate appraisal being examples. There is a difference between an estate and tax appraisal and a replacement or insurance appraisal. However, the appraiser is the professional who determines the value of the pieces. Any attempt to tell the appraiser how low to value an item is an insult to the appraiser's professional integrity.

15. *Q. I've just had a fire. Can an appraiser help me?*

A. Because the appraiser begins each job with a fresh perspective she can be helpful. The appraiser who has had a lot of experience in fire claims can help the owner remember items that he may even have forgotten. My experience has shown that insurance companies will more carefully evaluate the merits of an appraisal when it has been prepared by an outside objective expert rather than by the owner, who may not even know what he has lost, much less the value of the pieces.

16. *Q. Why will some dealers make appraisals and others not?*

A. Some dealers believe that a conflict of interest exists when the dealer makes an appraisal and then offers to buy the piece for that amount of money. These dealers prefer to leave appraising to appraisers, and then, if offered items which have been previously appraised, they can either accept or reject the appraised value. If the dealer rejects the appraiser's value, which he is free to do, the dealer can then make an *offer to buy*. This is not an appraisal, but simply his offer of how much money he will pay for the item. Another reason why some dealers will not make an appraisal is because they are not equipped to handle the work involved in making it.

17. *Q. Where do I find the best buys?*

A. Generally speaking there are two places. One is from the dealer who specializes in a category and has pieces of the very finest quality. These are considered "best buys" because they will continue to increase in value, are often rare, and are highly desirable as investments. Such pieces are also found in auction houses where such objects are authenticated and sold. (Remember, the elite dealer or auction house "provenance" adds glamour and eventual monetary worth to the piece.)

The other place where you can find the best buys is any place where *you* know more about an object than the person who is selling it. This seldom happens if the seller is an expert on an item. However, it can happen if you are able to buy silver from the Oriental rug specialist who had to buy silver items in an estate sale in order to get the rugs, or if you are lucky in a shop or flea market stall where the dealer specializes, but has an odd piece or two with which you are more familiar than he or she.

18. *Q. I want to invest in some personal property for my portfolio. What should I do?*

A. The objects most commonly suggested for investment holdings today are Oriental rugs, diamonds, and fine-quality silver from the nineteenth and early twentieth century. In addition, some investment houses are recommending the stocks of the two major international auction houses— Sotheby's and Christie's—as good investments. However, before investing be aware that there are fakes and overpriced pieces in every category of personal property from gems to paintings to stamps to autographs to furniture. My first recommendation is that you protect what you have already by knowing what you own and what its value is. Then consider adding to your personal property portfolio.

19. *Q. I don't know if I need an appraisal. Is it possible to find out whether or not I really need one before I invest in having an appraisal made?*

A. Before you engage an appraiser's services you should have a thorough discussion with the appraiser either by telephone or in person. The appraiser spends all of his time dealing with personal property and knowing what is in people's homes. The appraiser can usually get a feeling for your property by discussing it with you. After the discussion, the appraiser may say "Yes, you definitely need an appraisal," or "No, an appraisal is not needed at this time." Remember, appraisers are selling their time and their services, and most appraisers are so heavily overbooked that they do not want to become involved in an unprofitable or unnecessary job. However, most appraisers are willing to go to your home or apartment for a minimum fee, take a look at your property, and at that point determine whether or not an appraisal is genuinely needed. If there is a long distance between the appraiser's office and your property, you can send photographs of the pieces to the appraiser so she or he can make a judgment as to whether or not they justify spending time and money for an appraisal. The appraiser will *not* be able to make the appraisal from the photographs, but the photographs will show what you have.

20. *Q. I had an appraisal made two years ago. Now I've been robbed. Should I contact the appraiser and will she be able to help me? And what about the values given two years ago? I know some things are more valuable now than then.*

A. Always contact the appraiser when you have a loss. If the appraiser has also worked for the insurance company, she can probably save both you, the victim, and the insurance company time and problems. Whether or not you will receive *full* compensation for your items two years or more after the appraisal was made depends upon the kind of insurance policy you have. Some have escalating clauses. Others lock you into a specific amount. Ask your agent about this *when the policy is first written.* If you do *not* receive sufficient compensation from your insurance, you may be able to deduct your loss from your income taxes. Check with a CPA or tax expert for guidance. But even an out-of-date appraisal is much better than *no* appraisal.

21. *Q. This last question is one I am often asked. It's a simple one: "How do you know?"*

A. There are three steps to the appraiser's thought processes. (1) She has first of all to know what the piece is, know whether it is a period piece, a reproduction, a forgery, a fake. Once she has determined what the piece is, then she must consider the quality of the piece as compared to the finest and the worst of its type. Next, she must note the condition of the piece. (2) Once she has properly identified the item, determined its quality, and noted its condition, she then must know the market value of the piece. (3) Finally, she must understand the different levels of appraisal evaluation. She must be familiar with the differences between estate values, fair market values, retail values, insurance or replacement values, and projected growth values when looking at personal property as investment potential.

Appendices

APPENDIX A

Burglary Prevention Checklist for Homes

Survey your home with this checklist. Every "no" check mark shows a weak point that may help a burglar. As you eliminate the "no" checks, you improve your protection.

Go through this list carefully and systematically. You may want to look over this situation in daytime, when most house burglars work, as well as at night.

Doors

	Yes	No
1. Are the locks on your most-used outside doors of the cylinder type?	☐	☐
2. Are they of either the deadlocking or jimmy-proof type?	☐	☐
3. Do your door locks prevent the opening of your doors even if a glass pane or panel of light wood is broken?	☐	☐
4. Do you use chain locks or other auxiliary locks on the most-used doors?	☐	☐
5. Do the doors without cylinder locks have a heavy bolt or some similar secure device that can be operated only from the inside?	☐	☐
6. Can all of your doors (basement, porch, french, balcony) be securely locked?	☐	☐
7. Do your basement doors have locks that allow you to isolate that part of your house?	☐	☐
8. Are your locks all in good repair?	☐	☐
9. Do you know everyone who has a key to your house? (Or are there some still in possession of previous owners and their servants and friends?)	☐	☐

Windows

		Yes	No
10.	Are your window locks properly and securely mounted?	☐	☐
11.	Do you keep your windows locked when they are shut?	☐	☐
12.	Do you use locks that allow you to lock a window that is partly open?	☐	☐
13.	In high-hazard locations, do you use bars and an ornamental grille?	☐	☐
14.	Are you as careful of basement and second-floor windows as you are of those on the first floor?	☐	☐
15.	Have you made it more difficult for the burglar by locking up your ladder, avoiding trellises that can be used as a ladder or similar aids to climbing?	☐	☐

Garage

16.	Do you lock your garage door at night?	☐	☐
17.	Do you lock your garage when you are away from home?	☐	☐
18.	Do you have good secure locks on the garage doors and windows?	☐	☐
19.	Do you lock your car and take the keys out even when it is parked in your garage?	☐	☐

When You Go on a Trip

20.	Do you stop all deliveries or arrange for neighbors to pick up papers, milk, mail, packages?	☐	☐
21.	Do you notify a neighbor?	☐	☐
22.	Do you notify your sheriff? His office provides extra protection for vacant homes.	☐	☐
23.	Do you leave some shades up so the house doesn't look deserted?	☐	☐
24.	Do you arrange to keep your lawn and garden in shape?	☐	☐

Safe Practices

		Yes	No
25.	Do you plan so that you do not need to "hide" a key under the door mat?	☐	☐
26.	Do you keep as much cash as possible and other valuables in a bank?	☐	☐
27.	Do you keep a list of all valuable property?	☐	☐
28.	Do you have a list of the serial numbers of your watches, cameras, typewriters, and similar items?	☐	☐
29.	Do you have a description of other valuable property that does not have a number?	☐	☐
30.	Do you avoid unnecessary displays or publicity of your valuables?	☐	☐
31.	Have you told your family what to do if they discover a burglar breaking in or already in the house?	☐	☐
32.	Have you told your family to leave the house undisturbed and call the sheriff or police if they discover a burglary has been committed?	☐	☐

APPENDIX B
Two Samples of Appraisers' Contracts

TERMS AND CONDITIONS OF APPRAISALS

Emyl Jenkins, ASA, will make an appraisal of personal property belonging to

_____ , _____ , _____
(name)   (address)   (phone no.)

on _____ , _____ .
   (day)   (month, date and year)   (time)

Explanation and Hints:

The appraisal is made by tape-recording verbal descriptions of the property. The tapes are transcribed in rough-draft form. After revisions are made, and the final values determined, three final copies of the appraisal are prepared. You receive two of these. I keep the third for future reference. (If, later, an updating of the appraisal is needed, one can be made from the copy in my files. Charges for an appraisal update are based on retyping, and the time required to change the prices. Generally, it is not necessary to return to the home at this time.)

Research time at the initial appraisal varies with each appraisal. Research time is that time spent in authenticating pieces, consulting other experts, and determining accurate values for the client's benefit.

To assist the appraiser, it helps when silver items are made visible and, if possible, grouped together. If you wish to arrange the silver further, please place sterling flatware patterns together, and separate sterling and plated hollow ware. If china and crystal are stored in boxes or closets, you may prepare a list of the number of pieces, but I will need to identify the maker and pattern to establish quality and value.

I do not appraise jewelry, Oriental collections of jade, ivory, netsukes, etc., or works of art—oil paintings, sculpture, wood carvings, etc.

The charges for the appraisal service are as follows:

Time on the premises figured at _____ per hour.
Transcription of tapes and typing figured at the specific cost per job.
Research time figured at _____ per hour.
Transportation and expenses estimated at _____

Please sign and return in the enclosed SASE.

_____
Emyl Jenkins

_____
(Client's signature and date.)

Two Samples of Appraisers' Contracts (Continued)

Sample of an Appraiser's Disinterest Statement

The following appraisal is made for insurance purposes, and the prices quoted for personalty, in my judgment, are based on the prices for pieces of comparable age and quality found for sale at shops and at auctions at this time. I have no interest in purchasing any item here listed, and there is no compensation contingent upon any value stated herein.

Emyl Jenkins, ASA
2215 Whitman Road
Raleigh, N. C. 27607

Subscribed and sworn to me, a Notary Public in and for the State of North Carolina, County of Wake, this _____ day of

_____, by the above-named appraiser, who acknowledged the same to be her free and voluntary act and deed.

_____
Notary Public

Personalty belonging to:

APPENDIX C

List of Leading Auction Houses Arranged by State

California
Butterfield and Butterfield, 1244 Sutter Street, San Francisco, Calif. 94109
Connecticut
Clearing House Auction Galleries, Inc., 207 Church Street, Wethersfield, Conn. 06109
District of Columbia
C. G. Sloan and Company, Inc., 715 Thirteenth Street, N.W., Washington, D.C. 20005
Florida
Schrader Galleries, 221 Third Street South, St. Petersburg, Fla. 33707
Louisiana
Morton's, 643 Magazine Street, P.O. Box 30380, New Orleans, La. 70190
Maine
Julia's Auction Barn, Route 201, Skowhegan Road, Fairfield, Maine 04937
Massachusetts
Robert W. Skinner, Inc., Route 117, Bolton, Mass. 01740
Robert Eldred, Box 796, AQ, East Dennis, Mass. 02641
Michigan
DuMochelle's, 409 East Jefferson Avenue, Detroit, Mich. 48226
New York
Christie's, 502 Park Avenue, New York, N.Y. 10022
William Doyle Galleries, 175 East 87th Street, New York, N.Y. 10028
Phillip's, 867 Madison Avenue, New York, N.Y. 10021
Plaza, 406 East 79th Street, New York, N.Y. 10021
Sotheby Parke Bernet, 980 Madison Avenue, New York, N.Y. 10021
North Carolina
Robert D. Bunn Auction Service, 16 Biltmore Avenue, Asheville, N.C. 28801

Ohio
Garth's Auction's Inc., 2690 Stratford Road, P.O. Box 315, Delaware, Ohio 43105
Pennsylvania
Samuel T. Freeman & Co., 1808-1810 Chestnut Street, Philadelphia, Pa. 19103
John H. Frisk, 1611 Walnut Street, Philadelphia, Pa.
Tennessee
Miller's Auction Gallery, Route 7, Box 208, Knoxville Highway, Newport, Tenn. 37821
Virginia
The Wilson Galleries, P.O. Box 102, Fort Defiance, Va. 24437
Wisconsin
Milwaukee Auction Galleries, 4747 West Bradley Street, Milwaukee, Wis. 53223

APPENDIX D

Example of a Professionally Prepared Appraisal

EMYL JENKINS
Appraisals

Antiques • Residentials Contents

ARTICLE	DESCRIPTION	APPRAISED VALUE
Sugar caster or muffineer.	By John Deacon, London, 1764. Height, 6⅞". On a round pedestal base with gadrooned motif. Crested and surmounted with an urn finial.	$2,200.00
Seal spoon.	Dating from London, 1593. With the maker's mark registered in Jackson but not identified. The seal is crested at the top, and the spoon is in excellent condition, with rare gilt bowl.	$1,500.00
Two skewers.	Skewer by William Eley and William Fearn, London, 1801. Measuring 11" long. Crested. With reeded finial at the top.	$ 300.00
	Rare smaller skewer, measuring only 6¾" long. In simple, plain styling. By Thomas Wallis, London, 1802.	$ 425.00
Berry spoon.	By William Eley, William Fearn and William Chawner, London, 1807. Measuring 8½". Crested. With bright cut grape leaf motif and with the scalloped bowl having the repoussé fruit and berry decoration.	$ 175.00
Mustard ladle.	By Benjamin Laver, London, 1823. Crested.	$ 65.00
Mustard pot.	Birmingham, 1913–14. With cobalt blue liner. After the earlier eighteenth-century style, with bright cut garland swag and urn motif, delicate beading, and classical finial at the top.	$ 250.00
Dish cross.	By William Plummer, London, 1786. With the four feet having a teardrop and delicate beaded motif. The beaded decoration is repeated at the movable guards, and the spirit lamp is in a bulbous form. Fully hallmarked.	$2,500.00

This appraiser has no present or future interest in the above property.

Appraisal purpose Silver appraisal-Insurance
Signed _____

Date _____ 19 _____

Appraiser

2215 Whitman Road • Raleigh
North Carolina 27607
919•782•6025

Bibliography

CHAPTER 3
General Books on Antiques & Terminology

Bragin, Joan. *The Weekend Connoisseur. The Antique Collector's Guide to the Best in Antiqueing, Dining, Regional Museums, and Just Plain Lovely Things to Do When Touring.* Garden City, NY: Doubleday and Company, 1979.

Brogan, Louise Ade. *House and Garden's Antiques, Questions and Answers.* New York: Simon & Schuster, 1973

Complete Color Encyclopedia of Antiques. New York: Hawthorne Books, Inc. 1975

Davidson, Marshall B. *The American Heritage History of Colonial Antiques.* New York: Bonanza Books, 1979.

Doane, Ethyl. *Antiques Dictionary.* Portland, ME: The Anthoensen Press, 1949.

Dreppard, Carl W. *A Dictionary of American Antiques.* Boston: Charles T. Branford Company, 1952.

Edwards, Ralph and L. G. G. Ramsey. *The Connoisseur's Complete Period Guides.* New York: Bonanza Books, 1968.

Kovel, Ralph and Terry H. Kovel. *Know Your Antiques.* New York: Crown Publishers, Inc., 1967.

Macdonald-Taylor, Margaret. *A Dictionary of Marks: Ceramics, Metalwork Furniture.* New York: Hawthorne Books, Inc., 1968.

Mills, John FitzMaurice. *The Guinness Book of Antiques.* Enfield, Middlesex, England: Guinness Superlatives, Ltd., 1979.

The Random House Collector's Encyclopedia, Victoriana to Art Deco. New York: Random House, 1974.

The Random House Encyclopedia of Antiques. New York: Random House, 1973

Revi, Albert C. *The Spinning Wheel's Complete Book of Antiques.* New York: Grosset and Dunlap, 1977.

A Short Guide to Some of the Mass-Market
General Price Guides

George Grotz. *The Current Antique Furniture Style and Price Guide,* Doubleday, 1979. $9.95

A realistic price guide which illustrates each piece it values. Many semi-antiques and reproductions are included.

Dorothy Hammond. *Pictorial Price Guide To American Antiques,* E. P. Dutton, 1981. $9.95
The full use of photographs and the geographic diversity of Mrs. Hammond's sources for prices make this a useful price guide.

Charles C. Colt, Jr. *The Official Sotheby Parke Bernet Price Guide to Antiques and Decorative Arts,* Simon and Schuster, 1980. $9.95
The name will sell the book, but the information won't be of much use to the layman.

P. S. Warman. *Warman's Fifteenth Antiques and Their Prices,* E. G. Warman, 1980, $10.95
A consistently good price guide. The editorial selections are generally relevant to most households.

Terry and Ralph Kovel. *The Kovel's Antiques Price Guide,* Crown, 1980, $9.95
Prepared by the deans of the layman's antique world, this price guide is painstakingly prepared by compiling current prices with the help of modern computer technology. The most comprehensive of the price guides.

William C. Ketchum. *The Catalogue of American Collectibles,* Mayflower Books, 1979. $25.00
If you want to know what has just come into vogue and is on its way up—probably temporarily—you'll enjoy this book.

Robert W. Miller, *Wallace Homestead Price Guide to Antiques and Pattern Glass,* Wallace Homestead, 1979. $10.95.
This price guide emphasizes 19th century and early 20th century collectibles. Price ranges rather than one price given. The repair services, auction houses and collectors listings should be noted. Some serious textual errors.

CHAPTER 10
Books On American Marks, Makers, Patterns, and Values

Hagan, Tere. *Silverplated Flatware, An Identification and Value Guide.* Paducah, Kentucky: Collectors' Books, 1981.

Green, Robert Allen. *Marks of American Silversmiths.* Harrison, New York: Robert Allen Green, Publisher, 1977.

Jewelers' Circular Keystone Sterling Flatware Pattern Index, Second Edition. Radnor, Pa.: Chilton Company, 1978.

Kovel, Ralph and Kovel, Terry H. *A Dictionary of American Silver, Pewter and Silver Plate.* New York: Crown Publishers, Inc., 1961.

Rainwater, Dorothy T. and Felger, Donna H. *American Spoons, Souvenir and Historical.* Nashville, Tennessee: Thomas Nelson, Inc. and Hanover, Pa.: Everybody's Press, 1968.

Rainwater, Dorothy. *Encyclopedia of American Silver Manufacturers.* New York: Crown Publishers Inc., 1975.

Robinson, Dorothy Nolan. *The Official 1981 Price Guide To American Silver and Silver Plate.* Orlando, Florida: House of Collectibles.

Turner, Noel D. *American Silver Flatware, 1837–1910.* Cranbury, New Jersey: A. S. Barnes and Company, Inc., 1972.

Publication

The Magazine Silver, P.O. Box 2217, Milwaukee, Oregon 97222.

Books on English and Continental Marks and Values

Bradbury, Frederick. *Bradbury's Book of Hallmarks.* Sheffield, England: J. W. Northend Ltd., 1980.

De LaPerriere, C. & S. *Silver Auction Records, 4th Edition.* Wiltshire, England: Hilmarton Manor Press, 1980.

Ensko, Steven G. C. and Wenham, Edward. *English Silver, 1625–1825.* New York: Arcadia Press, 1980.

Heal, Sir Ambrose. *The London Goldsmiths, 1200–1800.* Devon, England: David & Charles Reprints, 1972.

Jackson, C. J. *English Goldsmiths and Their Marks,* London, 1921.

Les Poinçons de Garantie Internationaux pour l'Argent, Tardy, 21, Rue des Boulangers, Paris, France, 1980.

Wyler, Seymour B. *The Book of Old Silver.* New York: Crown Publishers, Inc., 1937.

CHAPTER 11
Books on Crystal and China

Jacobson, Gertrude Tatnall. *Haviland China, Volume I and II.* Des Moines, Iowa: Wallace-Homestead Book Company, 1979.

Kovel, Ralph and Kovel, Terry H. *The Kovels' Illustrated Price Guide to Depression Glass and American Dinnerware.* New York: Crown Publishers, Inc., 1980.

Lehner, Lois. *Complete Book of American Kitchen and Dinnerware.* Des Moines, Iowa: Wallace-Homestead Book Company, 1980.

McKearin, Helen and George. *Two Hundred Years of American Blown Glass, Revised Edition.* New York: Crown Publishers, Inc., 1966.

Newman, Harold. *An Illustrated Dictionary of Glass.* London: Thames and Hudson, 1977.

Revi, Albert C. *19th Century Glass, Its Genesis and Development, Revised Edition.* New York: Galahad Books, 1967.

CHAPTER 12
Books on Furniture

Bjerkoe, Ethyl Hall. *The Cabinetmakers of America.* Exton, Pennsylvania: Schiffer Ltd., 1978.

Chinnery, Victor. *Oak Furniture, The British Tradition.* Woodbridge, Suffolk, England: The Antique Collectors' Club, 1979.

Grotz, George. *The New Antiques: Knowing and Buying Victorian Furniture.* Garden City, New York: Doubleday and Company, 1970.

Hill, Conover. *The Value Guide to Antique Oak Furniture.* Paducah, Kentucky: Collectors' Books, 1978.

Kirk, John T. *The Impecunious Collector's Guide to American Antiques.* New York: Alfred A. Knopf, 1977.

Kovel, Ralph and Kovel, Terry H. *American Country Furniture, 1780–1875.* New York: Crown Publishers, Inc., 1965

McNerney, Kathryn. *Victorian Furniture ... Our American Heritage.* Paducah, Kentucky: Collectors' Books, 1981.

Marsh, Moreton. *The Easy Expert in Collecting and Restoring American Antiques.* Philadelphia and New York: J. P. Lippincott, 1959.

Miller, Edgar G. *American Antique Furniture, Volume I and II.* New York: Dover Publications, 1966.

Nutting, Wallace. *Furniture Treasury.* New York: MacMillan Publishing Co., 1973.

Ormsbee, Thomas H. *Field Guide to American Victorian Furniture.* New York: Bonanza Books, 1962.

Riley, Noel. *World Furniture.* New York: Mayflower Books, Inc., 1980.

Sack, Albert. *Fine Points of Furniture: Early American.* New York: Crown Publishers, Inc., 1950.

Smith, Nancy A. *Old Furniture, Understanding the Craftsman's Art.* Boston: Little, Brown and Company,

Yates, Raymond F. and Yates, Marguerite W. *A Guide to Victorian Antiques.* New York: Gramercy Publishing Co., 1969.

Watson, Sir Francis. *The History of Furniture.* New York: William Morrow and Co., Inc., 1976.

Publication

The Antique Furniture Newsletter, Box 524, 59 Adams Street, Bedford Hills, New York 10507.

CHAPTER 13

Books on Accessories and Bric-a-Brac

Buten, David. *18th Century Wedgwood.* New York: Methuen, Inc., 1980.

Catley, Bryan. *Art Deco and Other Figures.* Woodbridge, Suffolk, England: The Antique Collectors' Club, 1978.

Evers, Jo. *The Standard Cut Glass Value Guide.* Paducah, Kentucky: Collectors' Books, 1975.

Eyles, Desmond and Richard Dennis. *Royal Doulton Figurines.* Stoke-on-Trent, England: Royal Doulton Tableware, Ltd., 1978.

Farrar, Estelle Sinclair and Jane Shadel Spillman. *The Complete Cut and Engraved Glass of Corning.* New York: Crown Publishers, Inc., 1979.

Franklin, Linda Campbell. *Three Hundred Years of Kitchen Collectibles.* Florence, Alabama: Books Americana, 1981.

Gardiner, Gordon and Alistair Morris. *The Price Guide to Metal Toys.* Woodbridge, Suffolk, England, 1980.

Godden, Geoffrey A. *British Pottery and Illustrated Guide.* New York: Clarkson N. Potter, Inc., 1975.

Godden, Geoffrey A. *British Pottery and Porcelain.* New York: Bonanza Books, 1965.

Gordon, Elinor. *Collecting Chinese Export Porcelain.* New York: Universe Books, 1977.

Hamilton, Charles F. *Roycroft Collectibles.* San Diego, California: A. S. Barnes and Company, Inc., 1980.

Hotchkiss, John. *Hummel Art and Hummel Art Price Guide.* Des Moines, Iowa: Wallace-Homestead Book Company, 1980.

Kaduck, John M. *Rare and Expensive Postcards.* Des Moines, Iowa: Wallace-Homestead Book Company, 1979.

King, Constance E. *Antique Toys and Dolls.* New York: Rizzoli, 1980.

Kovel, Ralph and Kovel, Terry H. *Dictionary of Marks/Pottery and Porcelain.* New York: Crown Publishers, Inc., 1953.

Kovel, Ralph and Kovel, Terry H. *Know Your Collectibles.* New York: Crown Publishers, Inc., 1981.

Kovel, Ralph and Kovel, Terry H. *The Kovels' Collector's Guide to American Pottery.* New York: Crown Publishers, Inc., 1974.

Krause, Chester L. *Guidebook of Franklin Mint Issues.* Iola, Wisconsin: Krause Publications, 1980.

Luckey, Carl F. *Hummel Figurines and Plates.* Florence, Alabama: Books Americana, 1980.

McClinton, Katharine Morrison. *Introduction to Lalique Glass.* Des Moines, Iowa: Wallace-Homestead Book Company, 1978.

Padgett, Leonard E. *Pairpoint Glass.* Des Moines, Iowa: Wallace-Homestead Book Company, 1979.

Ray, Marcia. *Collectible Ceramics and Encyclopedia of Pottery and Porcelain for the American Collector.* New York: Crown Publishers, Inc., 1974.

Revi, Albert C. *American Cut and Engraved Glass.* New York: Thomas Nelson and Sons, 1965.

Revi, Albert Christian, ed. *The Spinning Wheel's Complete Book of Antiques.* New York: Grosset and Dunlap, 1977.

Schlegelmilch, Clifford J. *Handbook of Erdmann and Reinhold Schlegelmilch Prussia-Germany and Oscar Schlegelmilch Germany Porcelain Marks.* Whittmore, Minnesota, privately published. 1973.

Scroggins, Clara Johnson. *Silver Christmas Ornaments.* San Diego, California: A. S. Barnes and Company, Inc., 1980.

Shiffer, Herbert, Peter and Nancy. *The Brass Book*. Exton, Pennsylvania: Shiffer Publishing, Ltd., 1978.

Shiffer, Herbert, Peter and Nancy. *Chinese Export Porcelain*. Exton, Pennsylvania: Shiffer Publishing, Ltd., 1975.

Sullivan, Edmund B. *Collecting Political Americana*. New York: Crown Publishers, Inc., 1980.

Van Patten, Joan F. *The Collector's Encyclopedia of Nippon Porcelain*. Paducah, Kentucky: Collector's Books, 1979.

CHAPTER 23
Price Guides

Andrews, John. *The Price Guide to Antique Furniture*. Woodbridge, Suffolk, England: The Antique Collectors' Club, 1978

Andrews, John. *The Price Guide to Victorian, Edwardian and 1920's Furniture*. Woodbridge, Suffolk, England: The Antique Collectors' Club, 1980.

Colt, Charles C., Jr. *The Official Sotheby Parke Bernet Price Guide to Antiques and Decorative Arts*. New York: Simon and Schuster, 1980.

Grotz, George. *The Current Antique Furniture Style and Price Guide*. Garden City, NY: Doubleday and Company, Inc., 1979.

Hammond, Dorothy. *Pictorial Price Guide to American Antiques*. New York: E. P. Dutton, 1981.

Hudson, Norman. *Antiques Priced and Illustrated*. South Brunswick, NY: A. S. Barnes and Company, 1978.

Ketchum, William C. *The Catalogue of American Collectibles*. New York: Mayflower Books, Inc., 1979.

Kovel, Ralph and Kovel, Terry H. *The 13th Edition The Kovels' Antiques Price Guide*. New York: Crown Publishers, Inc., 1980.

Miller, Robert W. *Fleamarket Price Guide*. Des Moines, IA: Wallace-Homestead Book Company, 1979.

Pennington, Samuel, *et al. Americana at Auction*. New York: E. P. Dutton, 1979.

Warman, P. S. *Warman's Fifteenth Antiques and Their Prices*. Uniontown, PA: E. G. Warman Publishing, Inc., 1980.

CHAPTER 25
Publications on Investing in Antiques and Collectibles

Newsletters and Publications

The Art/Antiques Investment Report, 120 Wall Street, New York, NY 10005.

The Gray Letter, P.O. Drawer 2, Tuscaloosa, AL 34502.

The Wall Street Transcript, "Connoisseur's Corner," by Richard Rush, 120 Wall Street, New York, NY 10005.

Books

Gilbert, Anne. *Investing in the Antiques Market*. New York: Grosset and Dunlap, 1980.

Rush, Richard H. *Antiques As An Investment.* New York: Bonanza Books, 1968.

Wagenvoord, James. *Cashing in on the Auction Boom.* New York: Rawson, Wade Publishers, 1980.

Wilson, Jose and Arthur Leaman. *The Collector's Catalogue.* New York: Holt, Reinhart and Winston, 1979.

To make you a more astute buyer, here is a listing of books on detecting fakes, frauds and reproductions.

Cescinsky, Herbert. *The Gentle Art of Faking Furniture.* New York: Dover Publications, 1968.

Hammond, Dorothy. *Confusing Collectibles, A Guide to Identification of Contemporary Objects.* Des Moines, IA: Wallace-Homestead Book Company, 1979.

Mills, John FitzMaurice. *How To Detect Fake Antiques.* New York: Desmond Elliott Publisher, Ltd.,

Peterson, Harold L. *How Do You Know It's Old?* New York: Charles Scribner, 1975.

Savage, George. *Forgeries, Fakes, and Reproductions:* A Handbook for the Art Dealer and Collector. New York: Praeger, 1963.

Yates, Raymond F. *Antique Fakes and Their Detection.* New York: Harper and Brothers, Publishers, 1950.

Magazines on Antiques and Collectibles

American Art and Antiques, Billboard Publications, 1515 Broadway, NY 10036.

American Collector, 13920 Mt. McClellan Boulevard, Reno, NV 89506.

American Collector's Journal, P.O. Box 1431, Porterville, CA 93257.

Antique and Collectors' Mart, P.O. Box 17063, Wichita, KS 67217

Antique Gazette, 929 Davidson Drive, Nashville, TN 37205.

Antique Monthly, P.O. Drawer 2, Tuscaloosa, AL 35401.

Antique Trader Weekly, Babka Publishing Company, Inc., Box 1050, Dubuque IA 52001.

Antiques and The Arts Weekly, Bee Publishing Company, Newtown, CT 06470.

Antiques World, 122 E. 42nd Street, New York, NY 10017.

Art/Antiques Investment Report, Wall Street Reports, 1230 Wall Street, New York, NY 10005.

Collector, Drawer C, Kermit, TX 79745.

Collector Editions Quarterly, 170 5th Avenue, New York, NY 10010.

Collector's Journal, Box 601, Vinton, IA 52349.

Collectors News, 606 8th Avenue, Gruny Center, IA 50638.

Early American Life, P.O. Box 1831, Harrisburg, PA 17105.

Fleamart Quarterly, Box 243, Bend, OR 97701.

Fleamarket USA, Route 1, Number 470, Cantonment, FL 32533.

Gray Letter, P.O. Drawer 2, Tuscaloosa, AL 35401.

Hobbies, 10006 S. Michigan Avenue, Chicago, IL 60605.

International Art Magazine, 150 E. 58th Street, New York, NY 10022.

Kovels On Antiques and Collectibles, Box 222000, N. Beachwood, OH 44122.

Magazine Antiques, Straight Enterprises, 551 5th Avenue, New York, NY 10017.

Magazine Silver, P.O. Box 22217, Milwaukee, OR 97222.

Maine Antiques Digest, Box 358, Waldoboro, ME 04572.
Ohio Antique Review, P.O. Box 538, Worthington, OH 43085.
Spinning Wheel, American Antiques and Craft Society, Fame Avenue, Hanover, PA 17331.

Index